WINIFRED GREY

A Gentlewoman's Remembrances of Life in England

and the Gulf Islands of

British Columbia

1871—1910

Edited by MARIE ELLIOTT

Gulf Islands Press

Copyright © by Marie Elliott

Cover photograph of Winifred at age nine years by The London Stereoscopic &
Photographic Company, from Winifred Grey's collection.

Back cover photograph of Winifred and her sister Mabel, South Pender Island, 1896,
from Winifred Grey's album, courtesy of Geraldine Goldsmith.

Layout and graphics prepared by G. Bennett, Victoria, B.C.

Printed in Canada by Friesen Printers

Published by Gulf Islands Press, 1745 Taylor Street, Victoria, B.C. V8R 3E8

ISBN 0-9691674-1-5

Canadian Cataloguing in Publication Data

Grey, Winifred, 1871-1951
Winifred Grey

Includes bibliographical references and index.
ISBN 0-9691674-1-5

1. Grey, Winifred, 1871-1951. 2. Immigrants—British Columbia—Gulf Islands—
Biography. 3. Women immigrants—British Columbia—Gulf Islands—Biography.
4. Frontier and pioneer life—British Columbia—Gulf Islands—Biography.
5. Gulf Islands (B.C.)—Biography. I. Elliott, Marie Anne, 1938—
II Title.
FC3845.G8Z49 1994 971.l'28 C94-910851-0
F1089.G8G74 1994

Elliott, Marie, 1938
Winifred Grey, A Gentlewoman's Remembrances of Life in England and the Gulf Islands
of British Columbia, 1871 - 1910

Bibliography
Includes Index

Contents

For

Eve Grey Smith

ACKNOWLEDGMENTS

A visit with Eve Smith at her home on South Pender Island was always a rare treat. Her living room window overlooked the island fields and beaches that first captivated her mother and aunt on their summer visit in 1896. Intriguing piles of books and treasures from nature swirled around the room and across the window sill, making a colourful setting for good conversation and laughter. Eve's keen interest in preserving her mother's story and her willingness to share anything that might be of some use was irresistible. She had carefully saved not only Winifred's handwritten manscript, but countless other family documents and photographs. How could I turn down the challenge to present Winifred's story to a larger audience? Although Eve's health was failing, she constantly gave me her support, and I am thankful that she approved the final version of the Introduction before her death.

Although Eve Smith's role was most vital, this book would not have been completed without the added encouragement and generosity of many friends in British Columbia, and the numerous contacts in Great Britain who willingly supplied information to verify Winifred's story.

John Smith of South Pender Island unfailingly supported me over the years, and I thank him for his generosity and great patience. Dora Payne, Vera Greene, Gordon Robson and Fred Robson, descendants of the Gulf Island pioneers who were Winifred's friends, corrected and approved parts of the manuscript. Winifred Spalding of South Pender Island welcomed me into her home on numerous occcasions and permitted me to copy the painting of Ore Place and the photographs of Thomas and Elizabeth Spalding. Dorothy Sweet carried out important genealogical research. The staff at the British Columbia Archives and Records Service, especially Frances Gundry, assisted with further research problems.

In England, Gwen Hayball, Poole, Dorset, provided encouragement and valuable background information about Warburton Pike. Mr. H.J. Griffiths and Mrs. Leslie McQuhae of Great Cornard, and Michael R. Hills, Town Archivist, Sudbury, Suffolk, supplied historical material on Samuel Higgs. Photographs and documentation on Ore Place came from Rev. W.J. Walsh, SMA Fathers, St. Theresa's Abbey House, Perthshire, Scotland; M.E. Berkeley, and Pamela Haines, Local Studies Librarian, Hastings; Lt.Col. H. Brown, Ministry of Defence, and D. Dine, Hastings Borough Council.

For the Spalding family, valuable assistance came from Lyne Arlotte, Local Studies Librarian, London Borough of Waltham Forest; Charles A. Rivington, Hon. Librarian, The Worshipful Company of Stationers & Newspaper Makers, London; Mrs. K.M. Stanley, Parish Council of Horton Kirby and South Darenth; A.L. Hawker, Administrative Assistant, G-P Inveresk Corporation; George Musgrave, Heathfield, Sussex; Rev. B.G. Thorogood, General Secretary, Congregational Church Federation, London; Sheila Pratt, St. Helen's Park Preservation Society Ltd., Hastings; E. McNeill, Librarian, The Honourable Society of the Middle Temple, London; Glenn Dymond, The Honourable Society of Gray's Inn; Bryan Mathews, Uppingham School, Rutland; and Fred Keay.

Information on Winifred and Mabel's boarding school days came from B.C. Harte, Assistant Divisional Librarian, Central Library, Kent; and on the Ryle family from E.G.W.

Bill, Librarian, Lambeth Palace Library, London. Various other information was provided by John Stewart, Assistant Archivist, Kamloops Museum Association; Margaret Tong, Municipal Reference and Records Center, City and County of Honolulu and Janet Pitchford, Victoria. Trevor Davis skillfully prepared the maps.

Last, but not least, Geraldine Goldsmith, granddaughter of Em and Leonard Higgs, generously shared photographs and memorabilia that Winifred obviously referred to while writing a large portion of her memoirs.

NOTES ON EDITING

As far as possible I have retained Winifred's original manuscript. The only changes made were to pull together widely separated paragraphs on the same topic, correct punctuation, and eliminate repetitive sentences. Winifred's "love of language" included recording the first phrases spoken by her daughters. These are always delightful remembrances for the people involved, but hold little interest for most readers.

Unless otherwise indicated, all photographs are copied from Winifred Grey's collection.

INTRODUCTION

In the late 1860's at St. Leonards, Hastings, a brother and sister, Howard and Amelia Spalding, married a sister and brother, Maria and Thomas Higgs. In due course Amelia gave birth to a son and two daughters: Leonard, Mabel and Winifred; and Maria gave birth to a son and seven daughters: Thomas, May, Ethel, Lilian, Margaret, Hilda, Dorothy and Muriel.

The Higgs and Spalding families were members of the elite upper middle class of Victorian England.[1] In the 1860's, Thomas Higgs worked with his father Samuel, mayor of Sudbury, Suffolk, in a complex business that included weaving, malt and brewing companies,[2] and Howard Spalding inherited a large wholesale stationery firm on Drury Lane, London, from his father Thomas.[3]

While the Spalding and Higgs children accepted the curtsies of the gardener's children as a matter of course, they would soon learn that social status and a sound financial position were no bars to misfortune. Before Winifred Higgs was twelve years old, she experienced the breakup of her parents' marriage, and the premature deaths of her cousin Thomas at age ten, her Aunt Maria at thirty-seven, and her mother Amelia at forty. Later, as young adults, Winifred and her sister Mabel found their boarding school education had ill-prepared them for employment. To escape the humdrum existence as governess and children's nurse in London, the two sisters emigrated in 1897, to the Gulf Islands of British Columbia, Canada, to join their brother Leonard and his family.

As emigrants, Winifred and Mabel were once again part of an elite group, for of the 4300 Irish and English women who came to Canada that year, only twenty-two gave their occupations as governess or gentlewoman.[4]

Numerous memoirs published in the last few decades have contributed greatly to our understanding of late Victorian women.[5] But very few of the genre contrast an upbringing in England with the emigrant's experience, thereby allowing us to understand how women endured the dramatic changes in their lives. Winifred's account gives us this opportunity and much more. We meet a fascinating variety of people—from John Charles Ryle, First Bishop of Liverpool, to Johnny, a Japanese handiman, living half way around the world on South Pender Island. At a time when the death rate for women was declining in Great Britain, we learn how the Higgs and Spalding families coped with the premature deaths of Amelia and Maria. Unique personalities and experiences are woven into the tumultous background of social and economic changes occurring in Great Britain and the colonies between 1850 and 1910.

These chronicles were never meant to be published. Winifred wrote them for her family's enjoyment only, and, as such, they are all the more candid regarding family relationships and her innermost feelings. For the general reader and for the academic, her memoirs make a rich contribution to social history in three areas: late Victorian women's history, emigration history, and the settlement history of southwestern British Columbia.

* * * * * * * *

By the 1850s the main thrust of the Industrial Revolution was over in England; manufacturing, mining, shipping, and railway concerns were perfecting the new technology.[6] Between 1850 and 1870, the mileage of railway track doubled, bringing quaint village hamlets such as St. Mary Bourne, and sleepy coastal towns such as Felixstowe, into daily contact with rapidly growing industrial cities, especially London. By the end of the century, dependable steamships would replace the sleek clipper ships trading to China and Australia, on which Winifred's future husband, Ralph Grey, trained as a young midshipman, and her brother, Leonard, suffered misadventure.

The Crystal Palace, erected in 1851 in Hyde Park, London, for the Great Exhibition, showcased all that was new in technology and visual pleasures. It was moved three years later to a new site in the suburb of Sydenham [Anerley], where from 1878 to 1882 Winifred and her family resided. Winifred's memoirs record the multitude of fantastic displays, and the introduction or the perfection of new technology: the sewing machine, electricity, the telephone, indoor plumbing, phonographs, automobiles, xrays, bicycles, cameras and motion pictures.

Discoveries in the natural sciences were also advancing, dominated by Darwin's *Origin of Species*. As both adult and children's books became more available to the masses, the volumes on butterflies and seashells sent late Victorians to the countryside and seashore with nets and collecting jars. Some of Winifred's happiest hours as a child were spent reading children's classics, or searching for wildflowers and other natural specimens out-of-doors.

Many of the upper middle class businessmen of this period had risen on the solid foundations laid down by their fathers and grandfathers during the early stages of the Industrial Revolution. They were also Nonconformists. In the late 1830's and 1840's they fought for the abolition of the church rates, and the right to hold marriages and funerals in their own churches. After 1850, they became involved in the resurgence of evangalism, and in philanthropy.

Samuel Higgs listed his occupation as a Dissenting minister at the time of his marriage to Maria Hibble in 1838.[7] Before retiring from his stationery business, Thomas Spalding had given generously to the building of Congregational churches at Hendon and The Hyde near London. When he moved his family to Ore Place, he supplied the building stone from the quarry on his estate for St. Leonards Congregational Church.[8] His father-in-law, Andrew Reed, was a well-known Congregationalist minister and philanthropist, responsible for establishing five orphanages and asylums in England before his death in 1862.

In the early years of Victoria's reign, the wives of these businessmen were expected to play a supporting role only. Their days were proscribed by supervising servants and children, and visiting with friends and relatives. At respectable ladies' academies their daughters learned music, French, German and good deportment.

After 1850, however, courageous women from the upper middle class began to speak out. They fought for admission to medical school, to Cambridge and to Oxford; for the repeal of the Contagious Diseases Act; and for equal property rights after marriage. They also promoted emigration as a proper pursuit for gentlewomen.

Although Ralph Grey's aunt, Josephine Butler, led the crusade against the Contagious Diseases Act, and is considered one of the most outstanding Victorian feminists, the women in Winifred's family were true to the conservative social demands of the times. Elizabeth Spalding, Amelia's stepmother, devoted her days to caring for her husband and family, and supervising the servants. Most of her spare time was occupied by philanthropic work, and because she was the daughter of a minister, she made certain that her family were raised devoutly.

Winifred's mother Amelia rebelled against her stepmother's religious values, but she had attended Mrs. Pechey's boarding school for girls in Walthamstow from 1857 to 1859 with her future sister-in-law Maria Higgs, and she reflected the "woman as ornamentation" role that society expected. In chiding her sister-in-law Margaret (Marnie) Higgs in 1867, she wrote:

> I am glad you are not going up for the Cambridge exam-
> inations. It's all very well for girls who will have to
> support themselves as governesses to have some proof
> of efficiency in the various branches, but young ladies who
> adorn the domestic hearth need hardly desire any
> distinction of that sort. I think we should have you in
> Parliament next! I'd come to listen to your maiden speech.[9]

Amelia departed from the norm when she terminated an unhappy marriage. She separated from her husband Thomas Higgs at a time when marriage breakdown was a social stigma. Her father Thomas Spalding provided an allowance for his daughter, having sold his wedding gift of a home in Ballingdon, Sudbury, Suffolk. Thus, Amelia continued to live in the manner to which she was accustomed, employing a cook and a maid, and a nursemaid when the children were young. A bachelor brother, Thomas Alfred Spalding ("Unc"), boarded with her to provide a male presence. When they reached adulthood, Amelia's children, Winifred, Mabel and Leonard, reacted negatively to the social demands of late Victorian England by escaping from them completely.

Up until her untimely death, Amelia had indulged her children with good books, music lessons, visits to the theatre and season's passes to the Crystal Palace, in addition to a private school education. She also took a relaxed attitude towards her daughters' tomboyish playing habits.—Historian George M. Trevelyan stated that the Victorian's "enlarged sympathetic attitude towards children" was one of their major contributions to civilization.[10]

And so when Winifred, Mabel and Leonard were taken in by their grandparents at Ore Place, following Amelia's death in 1881, they had acquired a love of music and nature, and, most importantly, the strength of character to endure their step-grandmother's strictness, the spartan conditions at boarding school, the class distinctions as working men and women and the challenge of emigration.

Public education was introduced in Great Britain in the 1870's, but it affected only gradually the upper middle class, who could afford governesses for their children in the younger years, and private boarding school for advanced education. Winifred and Mabel's boarding school experiences run parallel to a number of other published sources.[11] Although both women were capable of further education, their reduced financial circumstances following the deaths of their grandparents prevented Winifred from realizing her dream of attending the Royal College of Art, South Kensington, London. Instead, she found work in the only occupation available for a woman with her education, that of governess. And Mabel found unpaid work as a nurse's aid in a children's hospital. Winifred's memories of her working years as a governess in London reveal the sensitive nature of young adulthood. Through delightful vignettes we are made aware of her great love for children, her lively curiosity, her high spirits, and her unsettling experiences with a class conscious society. While her freethinking employers, Dr. and Mrs. Reginald Ryle, may have treated her as an equal, in the eyes of strangers Winifred was not a member of the upper middle class. A member of her family, Aunt Marnie, broke off contact with her because she was now involved in "degrading duties".

The monthly income from their grandfather Spalding's estate was small, but it gave Mabel and Winifred a certain measure of independence, permitting them to indulge in philanthropic work. They paid for summer holidays for a slum family, and on days off Winifred willingly helped Mabel care for disabled children at the nursing home where the latter worked. This inheritance was an influential factor when the time came to emigrate to British Columbia in 1897.

Emigration to the colonies was promoted as early as the 1850's as a way for gentlewomen to advance themselves. In the 1860's, two bride ships, the *Tynemouth* and the *Robert Lowe*, brought single women to British Columbia. Later in the century, Winifred and Mabel would have been aware of the growing amount of advertising through visits to colonial displays at the Crystal Palace, and at Earl's Court, London, and they may have read some of the numerous books and articles promoting emigration. Jesse Saxby's book on emigration to Canada, *West Nor'West* (1890), for example, advocated that the educated middle class woman was better off living abroad:

> If the mother, sister, daughter, sweetheart, wife cannot go with the men they should certainly follow at an early date, should never contemplate retaining the old home when its best element is withdrawn; their first duty should be to follow the men!
>
> The secret of 'getting on' in a new country lies in casting off the trammels of old-world habits, and in learning quickly to be 'in touch' with novel surroundings. [12]

Frequently, articles written for English periodicals claimed that the departure of young men for the colonies had led to a surplus of women in England. But marriage statistics for 1850-1900 indicate that roughly the same percentage of women married by the time they reached fifty years of age during all five decades. Certainly, Winifred does not seem to be aware of herself as "surplus" before she left England for British Columbia. [13]

The British immigrants who arrived in British Columbia during the 1880's and 1890's found that much of the province's fertile land was still available for pre-emption. They poured into the Okanagan Valley and planted the fruit orchards that would make the region famous. In smaller groups, they established themselves in the farming regions on Vancouver Island, and on some of the semi-isolated Gulf Islands that lie between Vancouver Island and the mainland. [14] The Gulf Islands had particular appeal to those young men who had some training at sea or in agriculture, and wanted a life free from

Victorian restrictions. As Arthur Spalding on South Pender Island wrote in 1888:

> I'm a recluse, as certain people term it,
> In other words, a sort of budding hermit.
> In a lone island, 'midst Pacific waters,
> I shun the sons of men, still more their daughters.
> ...No starchy cuffs, no stick-up collars I,
> No studs to fasten, no confounded tie.
> ...No calls to pay, no parties to attend,
> No money in my purse, so none to lend.
> No church to go to, no confounded tribe,
> Of parsons with their watchword, "Please subscribe."
> ...Pals of my youth, it's possible that ye,
> When stuck for what to think of, think of me.
> And in your pleasing manner wonder how
> The deuce old Spalding likes his life there now.
> Spare me your pity, and believe it true,
> You wretched beggers, that I pity you.[15]

Arthur and his step-nephew Leonard Higgs arrived on South Pender in 1886. Because the most of the prime agricultural land on the more accessible southern Gulf Islands had been pre-empted a decade earlier, they, and a small group of English bachelors, settled on Samuel, South Pender and Saturna between 1886 and 1900.

Back in England, Winifred and Mabel witnessed Leonard's and Arthur's departures. Then in 1892 their sister-in-law Em left with young Thomas to join Leonard. During the next few years, while the two sisters worked in the London suburb of Barnet, they knew of two neighbourhood women who left to homestead on the Canadian Prairies. Thus, when Winifred and Mabel accepted Leonard's invitation for a summer visit to South Pender in 1896, they followed a well-blazed route to Western Canada.

On their arrival on South Pender Island in June 1896, Leonard's rude cabin and fields of stumps scarcely fazed them, but the freedom and relaxed social codes of a western frontier were overwhelming. Moreover, they had been made aware of the harsh living conditions on the Canadian Prairies when they paid stopover visits to the George family in Saskatchewan, and to the Church family near Calgary, Alberta. The beautiful marine environment, and the verdant fields and forests of the Gulf Islands in early summer, presented a stunning contrast.

The summer of 1896 passed all too quickly, filled with picnics, camping and fishing expeditions to nearby islands. Toward the end of their holiday, Winifred and Mabel realized that life in England would be "very tame" in comparison. They easily arrived at the decision to purchase property from Leonard at the most southerly tip of South Pender Island, and they arranged to have a small house built there while they returned to London for the winter of 1896-97, to prepare for emigration.

If Winifred needed any further encouragement to leave England, she received it at Bournemouth in the spring of 1897, while caring for three children at a resort hotel. The snobbish clientele and the restricted life of her charges provided an uncomfortable reminder of what her future would be like should she remain as a governess in Barnet.

Reflecting the philanthropic example set by their step-grandmother Elizabeth Spalding, Winifred and Mabel adopted Janet Wilde, a physically disabled daughter of a poor widow, and brought the young girl with them when they returned to the Gulf Islands. Upon their arrival on South Pender in June 1897, they immediately settled in to meet all the challenges of a new life in a new country. Winifred describes the next few years as the happiest since childhood, with no cares or thoughts of tomorrow. Their adjustment would have been easier than those of their sister-in-law Em, or Lilias Spalding, who were the first white women on South Pender. Not only did Winifred and Mabel have a modern little house (not a rustic log cabin) to move into, but their summer visit in 1896 greatly eased the transition to pioneer life.

The two young women continued to show their childhood spunk by purchasing a sixteen-foot, double oared rowboat in order to visit with friends, or to fetch groceries and mail from nearby islands.—Most of the wives of the other settlers were not that adventurous.—And their genteel upbringing stood them well on long winter evenings when they passed the time sewing, playing the piano and reading aloud to one another.

Perhaps more romantic than Mabel, Winifred delighted in anything that was new and challenging to her imagination. In England she studied electricity, photography and astronomy. In the Gulf Islands, the relaxed social customs and the puzzle of new languages—Chinook Jargon, which was rapidly dying out, and Japanese pidgin English—were intriguing. She writes, "I always loved the sound of new words." The many photographs that she took in England and in the Gulf Islands provide us with a valuable historical record of her two social worlds.

On July 7, 1900, Winifred married Ralph Grey, who owned Samuel Island. Her experiences living on an isolated farm, and her new role as wife and mother add to the study of rural women in British Columbia at the turn of the century, and can be contrasted with the lives of other farm women on the Islands. While most of the latter group preferred (or could only afford) to have their children with the help of a midwife on Mayne Island, Winifred chose to travel to Victoria for the services of a doctor at a private nursing home. She employed a series of young English "home helps" to care for the children, and when she needed to recover from a bout of ill health in 1908, she travelled to Hawaii. Home helps, urban maternity care and tropical vacations were extravagant luxuries for most island families.

Winifred generously gives Mabel a great deal of credit for helping her through the difficulties of childhood, boarding school, emigration and motherhood.—Following the Grey's marriage, Mabel moved from "Blue" on South Pender to a new little house, "the Loggia" on Samuel.—In June 1908 Mabel initiated the exodus from the Islands when she married Martin Allerdale Grainger (who became the second Chief Forester for the province in 1917), and took up residence in Esquimalt, a suburb of Victoria. It was not long before Winifred and Ralph followed suit.

Major events presaged each move that Winifred made in her life. Queen Victoria's Diamond Jubilee marked her departure from England in June 1897, and Halley's comet marked the end of her country life on Samuel Island in 1910. The Greys returned to Samuel during the summertime for a number of years, but their future would be spent in Victoria and Vancouver, the two largest cities in British Columbia.

When a debilitating illness in 1938 forced Winifred to rest for a long period of time, she began to set down these memories on paper at the urging of her well-known physician, Dr. G.F. Strong of Vancouver.[16] Writing was part of her heritage, for there were many published authors in the Spalding and Higgs families. Thomas Alfred Spalding had been especially prolific, writing on subjects as diverse as Shakespearean demonology and the reform of the House of Lords. Howard Spalding had been a music critic for a London periodical, and had published seven books on the Swedenborg religion. His daughter Ethel wrote a series or social studies textbooks for high school students while she was principal of the Bingley College for Teachers in Yorkshire.[17]

Forty years had passed since Winifred, Mabel and Janet joined Leonard and Em on South Pender Island. Winifred's health was now fragile, and the threat of World War II hung in the air, yet her writing conveys the anticipation and wonderment that many young immigrants experienced when they arrived in their new homeland. Although we are rarely allowed to forget Amelia's maternal influence, the binding elements of the story are Winifred's spirited zest for life and her love for children and for her family. Her personal choice of a title for her memoirs was, "Remembrances of a Happy Childhood and Life Thereafter."

Eliza Amelia Spalding Higgs

CHAPTER ONE

Eliza Amelia Spalding Higgs

Long years ago, away back in 1857, 1858, and 1859, two girls were having a good time at boarding school: my mother Amelia Spalding, and her friend Maria Higgs. Another girl, Annie Scrutton, joined them there and, being younger and a shy, mousy girl [her cause was immediately championed by Amelia.] The three girls became life-long friends, and they gave each other Mizpah rings as a token. It was a select boarding school, or academy for young ladies, kept by Mrs. Pechey at Walthamstow, near London. The girls loved Mrs. Pechey dearly, and she [remained] in touch with them long after they had left school.[1]

Amelia's home was Shire Hall, Hendon, then a country village with no street lights, by now swallowed up in Greater London.[2] Maria came further, from The Moat, Sudbury, Suffolk. Annie Scrutton's father was a large importer, and had a fleet of ships trading from the East India Docks, London. When we were children we knew Annie Scrutton well, but somehow [her background] always remained remote and obscure. I never thought of her as having had a home, with mother and father. To me, she was just "Auntie Annie," and no questions asked.[3]

Amelia was petite in figure, with fair hair and expressive gray eyes, but she was anything but petite in character. Vivacious, charming, strong-willed—even head-strong at times—always sympathetic and kind to the downtrodden, and with a likeable spice of mischief, she was well-read, was no mean amateur artist, as her pictures will testify, a wonderful needlewoman, and had a small but clear singing voice. Years later we children loved to hear her sing such dear old favourites as, "O, Mary, Go and Call the Cattle Home" (but it was sad), "Gloria Tibi Domini" and "Nancy Lee." Her brother Howard had a good tenor voice. When he came to spend an evening, Mabel and I fell asleep to the singing of "Twickenham Ferry," "The Vicar of Bray," "The Leather Bottell," or "Sally in Our Alley."

Maria Higgs was the opposite in many ways. She was a tall, handsome brunette, with classical features, a Roman nose—the real thing. She was a thoughtful, religious girl, and even at that age (sixteen and seventeen), she and Amelia had great discussions about God and a possible life hereafter, upon which they did not agree. Amelia was already skeptical of some of the accepted doctrines of the church.[4]

Young Mr. [Adolph] Sonnenschein was the visiting mathematical master at the school, and was evidently a great favourite with the girls of that generation. He had a most engaging smile, disclosing a row of perfect teeth, a mop of curly, coal-black hair, and his rather sallow face was framed within bushy, black whiskers. One day when his class was assembled, Amelia was nowhere to be found. A combined search located her on the roof, bursting with merriment. She was always up to pranks.

Mr. Sonnenschein was the originator of that wonderful system of teaching and learning arithmetic by means of cubes and staves, and the author of the accompanying books for the purpose. Years later Mabel an I went to Mr. Sonnenschein's school in Anerley, where he taught his system. I was a complete dunce at figures, but to my surprise found myself away ahead when I went on to another school. Unfortunately, I have never grasped the subject again.

After the three friends had left school, Mrs. Pechey arranged an old girls' reunion. They talked over old times, and Mr. Sonnenschein came and promised to give *cartes* to a favoured few, among them being Maria, Amelia and Annie, of course. *Cartes* was an abbreviation of *cartes de visite*, a term which was still in use when we were children.

[The girls] exchanged holiday visits, Amelia going to The Moat, and Maria to Shire Hall, and Annie Scrutton to each in turn. Maria had an older brother Tom, an amusing fellow and good company, and two younger brothers: Horace, who died at the age of six, and Arthur, a dark, brooding, very clever boy, who later took his M.A. degree and became a coach at Oxford. And lastly, [two sisters] little Marnie (Margaret) and Elizabeth.[5]

Maria and Amelia had great times together on these visits. Maria notes in her diary their discussions on books, religion, etc. One time, when she and Amelia went for a walk, they had to keep to the back streets as they had not got their bonnets. It was evidently quite an escapade[6] .[Amelia], too, had an older brother Sam, a jocular fellow who first joined his father's business, and later became interested in one of the southern English railways, I think. Then came Henry, a budding young Army officer; Howard, a quiet, studious boy; and little Alfred (Unc) who later in life developed such a sardonic humour. They all adored their sister. Years later Henry went through the Zulu War, South Africa, and became a Colonel, also a bit of a gourmand: "The liver wing of spring chicken, my dear fellow!" "Gout! *Did* you see that twinge?"

Now, to make the background of the past a little clearer. Thomas Spalding the elder, 1762–1819, Amelia's grandfather, lived at Kentish Town, in those days "a country place, rural and delightful." He started the Drury Lane business of wholesale stationers. When he died in 1819 his eldest son Thomas was only thirteen. He [later] was my grandfather of Ore Place, Hastings. He was already working in some capacity at Drury Lane.[7]

In due time Thomas married Eliza Halton. They raised the usual large family, Amelia, my mother, being the only girl. Time passed. Amelia's mother died, and her father married again: Elizabeth Reed, daughter of the Reverend Andrew Reed, a [Congregationalist] minister and well-known philanthropist of his time. He founded Reedham Asylum, Surrey, for orphan children, and other institutions. Elizabeth's brother, Sir Charles Reed, was an M.P. Her brother Andrew was a [Congregationalist] minister in St. Leonard's, adjoining Hastings, and her brother Martin had a boys' school just outside the gates of Ore Place. Elizabeth became our step-grandmother, or "Grannie" as she appears in this story.[8]

The family left Shire Hall [for] Ore Place, Hastings, Sussex. Thomas Spalding bought a forty-seven acre estate, with the old house which had once belonged to John of Gaunt, Duke of Lancaster. The house was falling to pieces, so he demolished `the remainder, leaving a few ruins, making the immense old kitchen fireplace into summer house. Then he built a long, low house on a magnificent site overlooking Hastings, the surrounding country, and the English Channel. It was very substantially furnished in mid-Victorian style. This was in 1864; MDCCCLXIV was carved over the front door. A vinery, orchards, two large, walled gardens and a farm were in the making, employing quite a large staff of gardeners, etc.[9]

Amelia was not happy at home under the new regime. She resented the religious atmosphere which brooded over the household. A young family was springing up: Herbert, Ellie, and Arthur. [She] took a mischievous delight in shocking some of the family and visitors, especially those who came with oily platitudes to browse on her father's kindly generosity. She rarely went to church, and then only if she considered there was someone whose sermon was worth hearing—like Mr. [Hugh R.] Haweis, a broad-minded churchman and later a Canon. He was the author of *Music and Morals*, and other books which mother had.[10]

And so when Cupid, in the deceptive form of Tom Higgs, offered marriage and freedom from this growing irksomeness, she accepted him. It was a most unsuitable match. Tom was still attractive, but dissolute. The family did all in their power to dissuade Amelia, her stepmother even offering up to the last minute to cancel all the wedding arrangements. But, no, her present dissatisfaction with home life, and her headstrong will caused her to make this fatal mistake, which wrecked her life.[11]

Amelia's father built a fine, red brick house in Ballingdon, a suburb of Sudbury, Suffolk, as a wedding gift for her, and there the young couple started married life. Things probably went pretty well for a time, but tragedy was lurking around the corner.

* * * * * * * * *

Maria's mother (nee Maria Hibble) had also died, leaving her to look after her father Samuel Higgs, our paternal grandfather, and her brothers and sisters. Samuel Higgs was a wool stapler, a dealer in wholesale wool (sounds like *John Gilpin*, or Mr. Glegg in *The Mill on the Floss*), and for several years mayor of Sudbury. He supplied the British Navy with handmade bunting for flags. He also invented a number of things, among them the original luminous paint. We were taken as girls to an exhibition of its various uses at the Crystal Palace, and were thrilled to see watch and clock faces, match boxes, and other things glow with this weird light in the dark room.[12]

And now Maria married Amelia's brother Howard, and they settled at Bromley, Kent. They were married from Ore Place as there was no mother at her home, The Moat. They were very happy. The babies came thick and fast—almost one a year. Maria (May) was born in February 1869; then Thomas, always known as "little Tommy," in 1870. He was born with a weak heart and could not live at home on account of the growing family. He spent his short life at Ore Place, with every care, dying at the age of eleven—a little angel boy, if ever there was one. Ethel and Lilian followed in quick succession, 1871 and 1873, and Margaret in 1874. Hilda, Dorothy, and Muriel came in due course.

Meantime, the babies had been arriving in the brick house at Ballingdon, and the sunny nursery was occupied by Lewis Leonard Spalding Higgs, born August 23, 1867; Mabel Florence Halton Higgs, March 5, 1869; and Winifred Grace Spalding Higgs, December 20, 1871. But happiness had fled. Tragedy had come from its ill-concealed hiding place and was making havoc of the home. It was a case of "wine, women and song," and the wreck of Amelia's young life was complete. No good would be served by going into what details we know. What she suffered will not bear thinking about, even now.

As a respite, mother took us children to stay at Ore Place, the refuge of so many orphans and those stranded by the way. Mabel and I were to be among them, not many years hence. While there, her father and others persuaded her not to go back to Ballingdon. Marriage ties were very strong, and divorce was unthinkable. For our sakes, she consented to a judical separation, and we were made wards in Chancery until we

Maria Higgs Spalding

Opposite: Top - Mabel, age ten
Winifred, age three
Bottom: Amelia with Winifred,
Maria with Hilda

should come of age. Leonard was now seven, Mabel five and myself about two. The year was 1874. Mother was thirty, with but nine more years to live.

I only saw my father once that I can remember. I was about seventeen or eighteen, living at Ealing with the Howard Spalding cousins, where Auntie Lizzie Higgs kept house most efficiently for her widowed brother-in-law. She had taken a bunch of us girls to a furnished house at Walton-on-the-Naze for a summer holiday. By pre-arrangement, my father met us on the Esplanade for which I had very short warning. As a stoutish, middle-aged man came towards us, Auntie Lizzie said to me, "This is your father." I suppose I must have given him a dirty look, because he grumbled, "My daughter doesn't like me," and in a gruff aside to Auntie, "Huh! Like her mother!" Then he asked me to go along the Parade with him. He began making disparaging remarks about Leonard, who was a young man of about twenty or twenty-one, and occasionally saw his father. I hated it, and made it quite plain that I did. So we turned, and before parting he pulled out a sovereign. Seeing me hesitate, he said that it was to spend on a treat for us girls. I thanked him and said good-bye. I gave the sovereign to Auntie, telling her I did not want to share in his blood and hush money, or words to that effect. (I see now it may have been kindly meant.) So she took the others for some outing. She understood my feelings; no reproof, though he was her brother. She was like that. Tom Higgs want on his own way, dying in 1894 at the age of fifty-two.

After staying some little time at Ore Place, mother took us to Boulogne for about six months. I used to think I could remember being wheeled in my pram over a bridge, while we nibbled potato chips, hot from a brazier at the roadside (a custom there), but as I was only two, I expect it was what I had heard spoken of afterwards.[13]

When we left Boulogne, I went with a nursemaid to stay with my godmother Emma Edwards, mother's first cousin. The [Edwards] family lived in a substantial red brick house, covered with ivy, with the historically suggestive name of Danesfield, in Honor Oak. The oak, a gnarled old tree, rather the worse for wear, was perched on a little hill just opposite the house. Queen Elizabeth had honoured this hoary relic of centuries by sitting beneath its shade, which gave the district its name. The hill had probably been a lookout station for a Danish encampment, as it commanded a fine view of the surrounding country.

John Scarr Edwards, Emma's father, was a very prosperous, wholesale commercial ink manufacturer, with offices and works at Red Lion Court, London. He was a dandy of the old school; wore dapper clothes of immaculate style, also corsets, and always carried a smart, gold-headed riding crop. But beneath this exterior he was a man of impeachable honour, dignified and courteous. He maintained a good stable, with thoroughbred hunting dogs. Guns of every description hung on the walls of his den, and he had a library of horsey and doggie books, being quite an authority on those subjects. Mabel and I were fortunate to come in contact with these fine characters: great uncle John Edwards and our grandfather, Thomas Spalding.

My very first recollection is going out, with my nurse, to the hill at Honor Oak and making daisy chains; at least she made them and hung them round my neck, or crowned my head. I think my love of flowers dated from that early delight, when I was two and a half.

I don't know where Leonard and Mabel were at this time. These weeks at Danesfield came to an end because, in the meantime, mother had taken a house in Bromley, Kent, where the Howard Spalding family were already living, and it was arranged that Unc should come and live with us.

"The Moat" Photo courtesy
Leslie McQuhae
Samuel Higgs Photo courtesy
Michael R. Hills

7

CHAPTER TWO

Bromley 1875 – 1878

Five Fairlawn Villas, a semi-detached little house on a country road with fields opposite, was to be our home. I have only to close my eyes to see it all so plainly: the low fence, with wicket gate, and a gravel path leading up to the front door; a small lawn to give point to the name; a flower bed, the pride of Unc's heart, but also the burying place of Lorne's bones; a May tree hanging over the fence in one corner, and a tall tree of some sort in the other, facing the Holmesdale Road. The back garden was larger, with an apple tree and a chicken run, where lived our pet mummahen and her companions. There was a little country lane beyond, where we used to go and hunt cheesecakes—the seeds of the pink mallow. We had no bathroom, and no hot water laid on, and I think we used candles and kerosene lamps for light. There was no means of warming the bedrooms (unless perhaps a small grate in one room), but we did not miss any of the modern comforts and conveniences because we had never heard of them. They had yet to be invented. All water was heated on the kitchen range and carried upstairs in cans.

Dear old Lorne, a beautiful tan and white collie, was our constant and almost human companion. He was one of the family, and treated as such. I heard mother telling friends that she got him from *The Queen*. Not knowing anything about the periodical of that name, and never having heard of the Marquis of Lorne, who married Princess Beatrice, a daughter of Queen Victoria, I fondly imagined he had belonged to Queen Victoria.

Unc loved Lorne just as much as we did. He looked on him as a steadfast, human companion, while we made him a playfellow. He called mother "the Mit," or plain "Mit" (being the diminutive of Missus), and spoke of Lorne as "the durg." At breakfast Unc would say, "Mit, Unc and durg," pointing a finger at each, with his sardonic smile. When it came to "durg," Lorne would thump his tail on the floor and smile in a tolerant way, as much to say, "I see your little joke."

When mother took us for a walk, Lorne would prance about with delight as he saw me being buttoned into the pram. He knew that meant a walk, with a chance to talk to other dogs. The town of Bromley was quite a distance for us to walk there and back, and there were no buses or public conveyances of any kind. An antiquated growler could be hired for special occasions, but there were no telephones to ring for one.

On our way to town we passed a little cottage sweet shop, with a few jars of sticky sweets in the window. It was always a thrill when we climbed the four or five rickety steps and pushed open the door, which rang a bell attached to a spring. We were very rarely allowed sweets, just the occasional penny stick of plain chocolate, which was considered "wholesome." I don't think anyone would eat such rank stuff now, it was so gritty; but it was sweet, and we liked it.

8

We had two maids, or servants, as they were called then: a cook, Emma, a queer sort of hunch-back woman of rather uncertain temper, and a house-parlourmaid (if that was the title). I knew where mother kept the raisins for cake making, and on more than one occasion climbed on a chair and helped myself from the kitchen cupboard. If she had found me she would have said, "Ask me if you want some, don't take them." But Emma would say, "You's better hide, yer ma's coming!", or, "You'd better not let yer ma catch you at it!"

Very occasionally, mother and Unc would go out in the evening, or to dinner, as we grew older, leaving the maids to put us to bed. We had a romp first, and I daresay it was a case of "when the cat's away, the mice will play," for them. Once we had an uproarious game of blindman's bluff. Emma, who was "blind man," and clumsy on account of her deformity, fell, bumped her head, and fainted. The game came to an abrupt end. We were very awed, and instructed "not to tell yer ma."[1]

Mother would have been horrified had she known we were being taught small deceits, fear of detection and punishment. She was very strict with all of us, regardless of age, when it was a matter of right and wrong, and taught us to do right for right's sake, not for fear of punishment in the life hereafter—an idea that was very prevalent in the religious teachings of the day. We had to learn to stand on our own legs, without any excuses for wrong-doing. She did not teach us to say prayers to the Almighty, not having very much faith in Him herself, which probably shocked some more orthodox members of the family badly.

Church going was quite optional for us children. Consequently, we enjoyed going with mother sometimes. When we lived at Bromley, my mother and Unc would say on a Sunday, "Let us go and hear Mr. Greenfields." Of course, it was their jocular way of saying they would go to the green fields, instead of to church. And then again, when we were at Anerley, our Sunday outing would often be to "the green hill far away without a city wall." There certainly was no wall, but grownups were often puzzling when you were only five or six.

Unc did not figure much in our lives at this age. He was studying to be a barrister, went off to London every morning, and probably came home after I, at any rate, had gone to bed, which would be 5:30 or 6:00. He was a bachelor, devoted to his sister, but not very keen on children. He looked on us as a bit of a nuisance, and we probably were.[2]

He and mother had great larks together. We could hear them joking and laughing after we were in bed. We got to know Mr. [Arnold] Kennedy about this time. He came to give Unc music lessons, perhaps on Saturday afternoons. We thought it was a great joke for a grown man to be having lessons. We were told that if we listened at the keyhole of the drawing room door we should hear Mr. Kennedy rapping Unc's knuckles with a ruler. Perhaps we were not unacquainted with that ourselves.

* * * * * * * * *

The Spalding cousins lived about one-half to three quarters of a mile away, in a semi-detached, but much larger house than ours. They had the usual rooms, with a sewing room tacked on, and upstairs a day and night nursery, but no bathrooms. As there were already four [children], not counting Tommy, who did not live at home, they had a nurse and nursemaid for this growing swarm of babies.

Martha Puttick, or Barpsh—the little ones' attempt at her name—was an autocrat in the nursery, even as a young woman. A tall, angular, sharp-featured despot, who knew her job, kept her place, bossed the maid, and adored each new baby as it came along: "There had never been another like it!" She raised the whole family, and then went on to the second generation, having taken a course in maternity in the meantime. I don't know what mothers with large families would have done in those days without the Martha Putticks. They were invaluable. Rough diamonds, but jewels, nonetheless. We were a little in awe of her when we went to spend an afternoon. She had such piercing eyes, and we were not accustomed to being ordered around in a peremptory way.

In the kitchen was Ann Foreman (Spanny), another treasure, who was already in her third generation serving the family, having been kitchen maid in her early teens to old Samuel Higgs of The Moat, Sudbury, and now here she was cooking for his grandchildren. Ann came from Suffolk, and had the sing-song speech of the country, was quite illiterate, but with a heart of gold. She and Barpsh made a solid foundation on which to build a family.

Miss Cornish reigned in the sewing room. It was always a strew of half-made garments and mending. She had a sewing machine, which was quite an innovation. It was loked upon rather contemptuously as something used either by lazy people, or those who were too rushed to sew by hand. Of course, it was the latter in this case, because all the children's clothes were made at home. Auntie was too busy having the babies and keeping house to do all the sewing, too. Sometimes, we all fell in on the top of Miss Cornish and fussed her about for fun, making hay of her and her work, while she, between vexation and reluctant laughter, tried to shoo us out.

We loved to go and play with the cousins, May, Ethel, and Lilian. Margaret was still a baby, a little cherub, with large, dark brown eyes, and light brown ringlets. Ethel was only four months older than I was, but far more advanced. She could read well at five, and completely put me to shame, but she never taunted me with it. Of course we scrapped at times, but it did not amount to anything.

[May Spalding] was just two weeks older than Mabel, very fair, and, curiously enough, far more like our mother than her own in appearance. Her early attempts to say Aunt Amelia produced "Auntie Mimi," and "Mimi" my mother became to almost everyone. Many years later I should like to have perpetuated that endearing name in one of our little girls, as it meant so much to me. She would have been my own little Mimi, a constant reminder of the mother I loved so much. But plain Jane or Sally had not completed their cycle, so the family would not stand for Amelia. The name Maria was equally difficult for children to negotiate. It became "Aunti Var" (spelled Wahr, German fashion).

Leonard was a school boy now. He went to a small day school for little boys, in a private house. Mabel was galloping ahead with the 3R's, mother teaching her, while I was struggling, with little interest, over "pot hooks and hangers," and pecking at ABC. But I could easily learn little verses and recite. When Mabel was about eight or nine, Unc offered to give her a cloth-bound, gilt-edged copy of Shakespeare if she would learn and recite to him the tragic scene between Hubert and little Arthur. This she accomplished, and won the coveted volume, which is still in the family. Unc was a great Shakespeare enthusiast.[3]

Children had very few books in the old, old days. The illustrations were crude and lurid in colouring. The three-color process was used in printing, and these had to be stamped, with more or less success—generally less—over one another to get somewhere near the colour required. We had the tale of the fox who "looked out one still clear night" in verse. He was a fox of brilliant scarlet. Then there was Henny-Penny, very highly coloured. The third book (and I only remember these three) distressed me terribly. It was about two girls. When they spoke, out of the mouth of one came jewels and pearls, but out of the other—frogs, snakes, and toads. It made me so unhappy for her that I can remember rolling on the floor and sobbing with pity. The pictures were so realistic, and I took it all as gospel truth. (I expect that the maids had enhanced the horrors to me, as mother would never frighten me. I was quite a nervous child.) These stories seem to illustrate the simplicity and credulity of the people of an earlier date, a "hangover" from the days of witchcraft.

On my fifth or sixth birthday, Auntie Emma brought me a lovely book of nursery rhymes with music, illustrated by a new artist named Kate Greenaway. It was called *The Baby's Bouquet*, and we were entranced with delight. It was the beginning of a new era in children's books. Kate Greenaway was followed by Randolph Caldecott, with his inimitable *John Gilpin*,and others. These books opened a whole new world for children.

* * * * * * * * * * *

And now we come to that bad, bad bird Grip, the raven, as black in character as he was in shiny plumage, and with a crafty eye that would have done credit to Old Nick himself. I don't remember his arrival, but he had not been with us long before Mabel and I tasted a sample of what he could do with his sharp beak on our bare legs. [We] found comparative safety in the garden by making sorties, armed with old brooms. If Grip saw us, we dashed for the apple tree. Leonard and Mabel could scramble up quickly, but I was left screeching below, vainly trying to beat Grip off with the broom, till someone came and rescued us. If it was Unc, he would call me a "little ass" for tempting Grip. But there was a sort of dare-devil fascination about tempting him. Woe betide us, though, if he chanced to catch us without our brooms!

Lorne was disgusted at this invasion of his home. Grip was inquisitive and made dabs at him. Lorne got up patiently and lay down in another spot. The same thing happened again. Lorne looked appealingly at mother, as much as to say, "What does this mean?"

Unc took a great pride in the garden, and every autumn meticulously planted bulbs at the correct depth and equally spaced, to ensure a good showing in the spring. Grip watched this process with deep interest, and when it was finished, hopped innocently away. The next morning, every one of those bulbs was lying neatly on the surface again. They were planted once more, but the result was not quite so neat this time. In fact, the bulbs were pecked and strewn about all over the place, and the few that survived being dug up entirely came up just anywhere. This was only the beginning.

Milk in small cans was delivered and left on the back steps of each house in the small hours of the morning. One day when Emma went to take in our can she found it was upset, and came to tell us there would be no milk for breakfast. Then a neighbour came round to know if she could borrow a little milk as her can had been upset mysteriously.

But more trouble was in store. Every house down the road reported their milk cans overturned the next day, and pointed the accusing finger at Grip. Next morning, he was caught redhanded. Something had to be done. "Old Grumpy" was called in to make an enclosure, as it was evident that mother and Unc would soon find themselves in the law courts if Grip continued at large. When the cage was finished, we all shooed him in with brooms and sticks. [4]

Like Hookey-Beak the Raven, "so mild he did appear" that mother thought she would raise some little ducklings in his pen, where they could not spoil Unc's gardening

11

operations. [5] A pan of water was set level in the earth to make them feel at home, and we all went out for a walk with a clear conscience. When we came back, Grip was just drowning the last of the ducklings by holding it under the water. We tried a brood of half-grown ducks, but these he ran off their legs till they died of exhaustion.

One day we were looking out of the dining room window, and seeing a rose in Grip's enclosure, mother, with us running behind, went round to pick it just in case. Too late! When we got there he was slowly pulling it to pieces, petal by petal. The way he forestalled us at every turn was quite uncanny. Then he escaped from his enclosure. His fame had spread abroad, fortunately for us in this case. Two men appeared and said they had located him down the Hayes Lane. They took a large meat dish and cover, and presently came back with Mr. Grip neatly dished up. We were so pleased to have him back, but mother was set back half a crown in her accounts.

I think we had [Grip] for more than a year, and then when we moved he was sent, temporarily, to uncle John Edward's Ink Works in London. While there, the workmen taught him such shocking swear words and bad language generally that we could not have him back again, to our great grief.

Years later Unc wrote a book about Grip, calling him Sancho, for a children's series. It was not strictly true to facts, or intended to be, but it made a good story. The end was entirely fictitious, and the illustrations vile. To keep the book within the cheap limit he had to employ a cheap artist, if such he could be called. It was a travesty to see mother, Unc and Lorne, not to mention Grip, in such guise. *Sancho* is still among my books.[6]

* * * * * * * * * *

Mother had not many intimate friends. Those who were not worthy of her shied off, drawing in their skirts, because she had separated from her husband, and was leading an unconventional life, without the aid of the church. But she got along quite well without them.

One of her great friends, Eva Asquith, was to be married, and Mabel and I were to be her bridesmaids. I think I must have been about four and a half and Mabel about seven. The wedding was to be quite an event. Mabel and I were instructed beforehand that we were to stand very quietly behind Miss Asquith, and mother would sit close by so that I could see her. I think we must have looked rather sweet in our short-waisted, frilled muslin frocks, with puffed sleeves; Mabel in pink and I in pale blue. We each carried a long-handled basket of flowers, which we were to strew in front of the bride.[7]

At last [the ceremony] was over. Miss Asquith kissed us and called us "darlings," but we were so entirely unselfconscious that I did not realize the import of all these caresses. Eva's brother Herbert, the future prime minister of England, was best man. He was very dapper, with white kid gloves, and white buttonhole in his black frock coat. I noticed these things even then, probably because I was accustomed to Unce's free and easy way of dressing at home, with old clothes for the garden. I think Unc was there, but I hardly recognized him in his wedding garb.

[Miss Asquith] had married a Nonconformist minister, the Reverend Wooding. Some years later Mabel remembers him coming to preach in a church meeting house in Anerley. We were taken to hear him. He made a good play on words which amused mother very much: "Instead of bearing their cross, people became unbearably cross." Uncle Howard once or twice preached in the same hall.[8]

* * * * * * * * * *

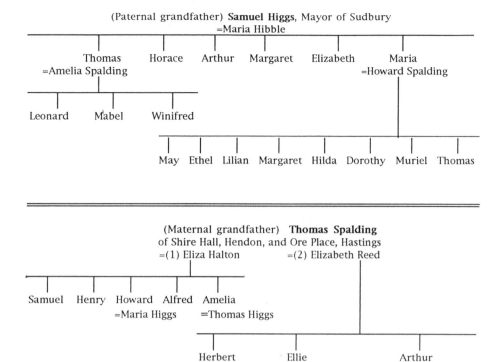

(Paternal grandfather) **Samuel Higgs**, Mayor of Sudbury
=Maria Hibble

Thomas — Horace — Arthur — Margaret — Elizabeth — Maria
=Amelia Spalding — — — — — — =Howard Spalding

Leonard — Mabel — Winifred

May — Ethel — Lilian — Margaret — Hilda — Dorothy — Muriel — Thomas

(Maternal grandfather) **Thomas Spalding**
of Shire Hall, Hendon, and Ore Place, Hastings
=(1) Eliza Halton   =(2) Elizabeth Reed

Samuel — Henry — Howard — Alfred — Amelia
=Maria Higgs — =Thomas Higgs

Herbert — Ellie — Arthur
=Charles Knox Shaw — =Lilias MacKay

Pat — Harold — Thomas — Helen — Helen — Elizabeth — Beatrice — Herbert

Winifred's Family Tree

Elizabeth Spalding, "Grannie"
Photo courtesy Winifred Spalding

Thomas Spalding
Photo courtesy Winifred Spalding

NEW CONGREGATIONAL CHURCH AT ST. LEONARDS-ON-SEA.

St. Leonard's Congregational Church, Hastings Library Collection

15

Ore Place Photo courtesy Winifred Spalding

Opposite: Top - Main entrance,
Ore Place
Bottom - The clock stand,
main staircase

Page 18: Top - The Adams
mantlepiece, Ore Place
Bottom - "The Ruins"
All photographs courtesy D.Dine,
Hastings Borough Council

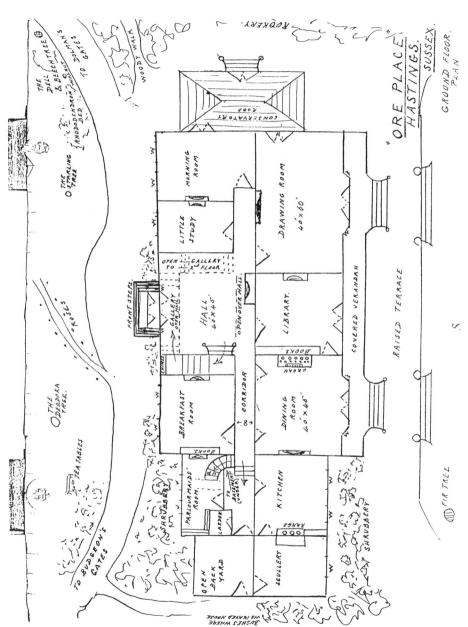

Floor Plan of Ore Place, sketched by Winifred

19

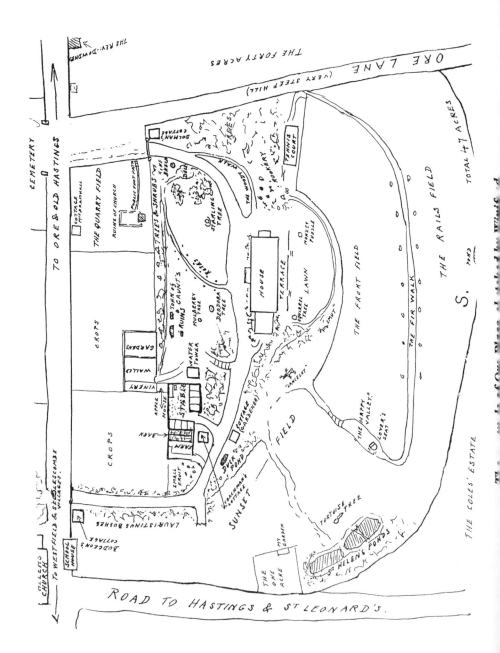

A rough Plan of Our Place, sketched by Winifred

But the real event of the whole year was when the time came to pack up and go to Ore Place for the summer. Mabel and I hardly knew how to contain ourselves. Poor Lorne went around with his tail drooping, pathetic eyes, and in a state of utter dejection when he saw the old wooden trunks being got out. He knew what that meant! But Mabel and I were all excitement. We skipped about, got in the way, and hindered mother by asking innumerable questions. The last evening we had a final tub in the oval, enamelled iron bath, which always went with us. All the last things went into that, and the iron lid was strapped on. Mother was a most careful packer; nothing was ever "stuffed in" at the last moment.

We tossed about, whispering in bed instead of going to sleep. Being summer time, daylight came early, and we woke, calling to mother to know if it was time to get up. "Four o'clock! Go to sleep again, chinnoes." (My word for children.) We woke again. "Is it time to go now?" "Six o'clock. My lambs, you'll be worn out before the day is over!" No more sleep after that.

We choked down some breakfast, and at last the old growler arrived. The trunks and bath were strapped on the top, we gave Lorne a last hug, and rumbled off.

The train journey was quite a thrill, about one and a half hours, I think. After a time, I generally had a nap, having waked up so early. As we neared the coast we popped through the occasional tunnel. The last one was long, right through a chalk cliff. We were all coughing with smoke as the train emerged into daylight at last, and slowed down for Hastings station.

One of the carriages would be there to meet us, and we drove the two miles up to Ore Place, wide-eyed for remembered landmarks. We climbed the stone steps, a maid opened the double glass doors, and we were kissed by Grannie and other members of the family, feeling just a wee bit shy at the spaciousness of everything. Maids bustled about, trunks were taken round to the back premises by Budgeon, the family factotum and handyman, and we children finally went to the nursery for tea.

We little ones were not allowed to scamper all over the house. In fact, it was rather a treat, and I was a little awed, to go up the front stairs, wide and soft-carpeted, holding the hands of a grownup. The chimes clock was on a broad ledge, half way up, and if you were in luck it might chime the quarter or half hour, or even the hour, as you went past.

These visits covered a period of four or five years, with not much change, except in our ages. Mabel, being nearly three years older than me, had stepped up from the nursery to the school room, so I write chiefly of my own memories at this time.

The family at Ore Place was an odd conglomeration of individuals, thrown together by circumstances. When our mother was still living at [Shire Hall] as a girl, one of Grannie's sisters died, leaving her young daughter Florence to Grannie's care. She and mother were about the same age, and became great and lasting friends. (She was Mabel's godmother, hence her name Mabel Florence.) There were two brothers, Basil and Clement, but I expect they stayed with their father. Auntie Florrie Holmes was a dear, but we, or I, did not see much of her, unfortunately. She moved on a higher plane when we were at Ore Place.

Then Grannie's brother Howard lost his wife, leaving three little girls: Bessie,____, and baby Carina, all of whom came under Grannie's wing and Grandpapa's provision. Howard Reed emigrated to Australia, and when the two older girls grew up they joined him. Carina had never known another home, and called Grannie "mother," though she was really her aunt.

So, when we went for these summer visits, there would always be Grandpapa, Grannie, Herbert, Ellie and Arthur; Florrie Holmes, Carina Reed and little Tommy

Spalding as a starter. Among the extra grownups would be our mother, and perhaps one or two of her own brothers—Henry, Howard or Alfred—not to mention the odd relations and visitors. And in the nursery or school room: Mabel, May, Ethel and myself, or some of the younger Howard Spaldings.

Grandpapa's younger brother Henry came with his second wife, great aunt Nellie, as a young bride. He already had a large family or grown-up sons and daughters, among them Dick, Mary, who married George Fleetwood, and Nell, wife of John Capper (later called Espie to save confusion with her stepmother's name.)

There were many other relations on both sides of the family circling round in their orbits, which generally included a stop-over at the family headquarters at least once a year. These reunions at a central home were a great help in binding the various members together. But I notice now that none of Grandpapa's first wife's relations ever came. Our darling Auntie Emma was his niece and her mother was his sister-in-law, but Ore Place never had the honour of showing them hospitality.

I always looked forward with the greatest joy to seeing little Tommy. Some of his sisters were generally there at the same time as we were.—Perhaps May and Ethel, and later some of the younger ones, as they arrived at the visiting age. Tommy was as plucky as a little game cock, a regular boy in spirit and sharp as a needle. His legs were like sticks, and he was so frail that it looked as if a breath would blow him away. But no one ever heard him complain. Sarah, or "Say" as she was called, had been with him since he was a baby, and was absolutely devoted to her "darling boy." Ethel and I adored him, too, and we three got on finely, with the occasional hitch on account of there being two girls to one boy.

The family dined at the unearthly hour of 4:30 or 5:00 p.m., having had a good lunch at 1:00 p.m. We had nursery tea about the same time, and when we had finished, like the oysters in *Alice*, "Our hair was brushed, Our faces washed, Our shoes were clean and neat," ready to go down to the dining room for dessert. Each ran to a favourite grownup, getting a taste of jelly, or sharing a peach or nectarine, strawberries or raspberries, according to the time of year. One of the things I liked best was a horseman of cheese—a minute piece of cheese sitting on a cube of bread. This was rather frowned upon, as cheese was supposed to be unwholesome for children which, of course, enhanced its value to us.

After dessert, we went to the drawing room for a short while. It was so vast, about forty by sixty feet, that to me there were whole regions entirely unexplored. The immense chandelier, with its cut-glass pendants tinkling merrily if there was a slight breeze, was the chief attraction. Near the door was a glass chiffonier filled with silver trowels in plush-lined cases, the ghastly relics of the laying of innumerable corner stones. Also, an odd assortment of gifts from missionaries: moccasins, native bead work, and so on, greatly prized by Grannie, but for us, "You may look but do not touch." A whatnot stood in the corner close by, loaded with knick-knacks, the dusting of which must have been a "weariness of the flesh." A three-way settee intrigued us very much. We should like to have romped all over it, but had to content ourselves with each kneeling in a seat, laughing face to face, or rubbing noses, which was a huge joke.

The conservatory was lovely. It smelt of warm, damp moss and ferns, primulas and eucharist lilies. Tall palms grew in the centre in immense tubs, and passion flowers intermingled with festoons of smylax, drooped from the roof. (The flowers and ferns for house decoration, or to give away, were grown in the greenhouses near the vinery.) The fun was, you could go in through the glass doors from the drawing room, go round the conservatory, smelling all the flowers, and out through the other glass doors, to find yourself in the morning room. And then it was time to kiss goodnight, and be off to bed.

The basement was as large as the main part of the house. The dairy, with its huge, brown earthen pans of set milk, and the churn were there, the apple room, with storage shelves, a trunk room, and a large, stone-flagged place where Budgeon cleaned the family's innumerable boots, shoes and knives (no stainless steel then). Two hedgehogs, named Moses and Aaron (but not by Grannie!) lived there, to feast on the black beetles that threatened to overrun everything. Then there was a servant's hall, where they could sit in the evening, but didn't, and, lastly, a most lovely large play room which, of course, had been built for an earlier generation of children. There was an immense rocking horse, with real hair mane, and a thing called a rocking boat, but it did not much resemble a boat. It held four, one at each end, and two tinies, strapped in, back to back, in the centre. That caused a little dissention as it was ignominious to be strapped in. The fun was that if you rocked it, it travelled about the room, and with little skill could be made to go where you wanted. The rocking horse would do that, too. As we grew older, we played games of "travel," rocking to visit places we had heard of such as America, Ventnor, or Scotland. Say would come down sometimes just to see we hadn't broken any bones. [9]

Arthur was very fond of Tommy, called him "Toe," and let him into his mischievous plans. At one time he kept guinea pigs, very secretly, in the big old doll's house, which stood in the passage just outside the nursery door. We were threatened with all kinds of devilment if we told tales. Say protested, "Oh, Mast'r Arthur!" to no avail. Arthur and Leonard teased and cheeked her most unmercifully. The guinea pigs were living in almost total darkness, no fresh air, no drainage. So after a short time they began to smell to heaven.

Grannie happened to come to the nursery one day. Sniff. Sniffed again. Something smells unpleasant here. Sniff. *In the doll's house!* What is it? *Guinea pigs!* The secret was out, and out went the guinea pigs. If the culprit had been anyone but Arthur, there would have been all kinds of trouble, but Grannie could never give her precious boy more than a mild reproof.

Ellie had arrived at the age of helping her mother in household duties. She arranged all the flowers, no small undertaking where there were so many rooms, even if the gardener brought a truck basket of flowers from the greenhouse. But she liked to go and pick them herself, if allowed. She also put out the stores: tea, coffee, biscuits and other things which were bought in large quantities and doled out to the head parlour maid. There was a large cupboard, kept locked, under the main stairway where all these things were [stored].

Young people in those days rarely went to day school. There were board schools for the poor children, but no private schools in scattered communities for those who could have afforded to send their children. Nearly every home had its resident governess who taught the 3 R's, recitation of verses, already hackneyed, a few "accomplishments," and the use of the globes. I used to wonder what that meant, but have come to the conclusion that it was actually the terrestial globe. There was a large one, which revolved on a mounted frame, in the school room at Ore Place.[10]

If we stayed for several months, Mabel had lessons with those who were still in the school room: Carina, Arthur and, I daresay, Tommy did a little. Miss Edna Jackson, the governess, was very dark, sallow-faced and plain, and of unquestionable rectitude towards her young charges.—The type that is known as "worthy," a dusky violet "born to blush unseen." Perhaps these were the chief requirements of a resident governess.

Dear old Grandpapa was so nice to all the children, and we loved him. He was already getting on in years, about sixty-eight to seventy, with iron gray hair, and wearing a stock collar, when I first remember him. He was a great one for exercise. He used to take his stick and stride briskly along for his daily constitutional, as he called it; sometimes with

Grannie, but more often alone. He had always walked to his office at Drury Lane, London, in the old days, and attributed his good health largely to this habit of walking regularly.

When we were little and went for walks in the grounds with an aunt or nurse, we might meet Grandpapa anywhere: down the Woody Walk; in the dell, where the lovely double white cherry grew by a cosy little seat, and the big old beech tree just beyond; or peeping at robins who always built a nest in a certain hole in the old ruins. The hole was in an archway, and must have held some clumsy old door catch or hinge. We might find him admiring the view from the Fir Walk, bordering the Rails Field, which eventually led round by the Happy Valley, with its lover's seat, back into the garden again. He loved to poke about with his pet roses on the lawn, but whatever he was doing he always stopped and gave us a friendly dig with his stick, made some kindly little joke, and smilingly passed on.

I had almost forgotten Lancelot, Lightfoot and old Smut. Smut had been the family donkey, once black, but now a motheaten brown, growing gray around the muzzle. He strongly resented the intrusion of another generation of children, and showed it by showing his heels, so we left him to his own old age devices. Lancelot and Lightfoot were a beautiful stag and doe, who wandered around in one of the large enclosures, and came to the fence for carrots or pieces of bread, which delighted us children. A trail ran through the place, and as the deer grew older, Lancelot was known to have chased intruders. When he grew altogether too fresh with those big antlers of his, Grandpapa reluctantly presented the pair to a park.

And so these happy summer holidays, year after year, came to an end. The trunks were packed and we ran round saying goodbye to everyone. But there was always the fun of looking forward to getting home again. Lorne knew the signs. Furniture was uncovered, dust sheeets put away, and there was a general "washup and brushup" of everything. He wandered down the road for several days, all expectant, and when he saw the familiar old cab, went wild with joy, leaping and barking a glad welcome. We jumped out and nearly hugged him to death.

Southern England

Views of the Crystal Palace, from postcards in Winifred's collection

CHAPTER THREE

Anerley 1878 - 1882

It was the spring of 1878, and we had arrived at the close of another period in our lives. I was about six and a half. The Howard Spaldings had left Bromley, and had taken a large, furnished house, named "Largs," in Weybridge, Surrey, for a year. I am not sure why, but perhaps the old house had grown too small, as two more babies had arrived on the scene: Hilda and Dorothy (Do). There was not much point in being the baby in [this family] because there was always another one close on your heels. You hadn't even the advantage of being a boy baby in this case, because each succeeding one was a girl, until there were seven. And yet every one was welcome, and few families are as united and affectionate as they.[1]

Anyway, it was very dull without them, and, somehow, after a time it was arranged that we should leave Bromley, too, and take furnished rooms opposite them at Weybridge. I expect that the four year lease was up, and mother did not want to renew it for various reasons. Unc was now a full-fledged barrister, with chambers at the Inns of Court, London, hoping for clients, probably.[2]

Then there was the question of our education, which had some bearing on the Howard Spaldings' move, also, I expect. Mabel was nine and a school had to be found somewhere. Mother still had a great admiration for Mr. Sonnenschein, which had evidently increased with the passing of years, and he admired her. By some magic cajolery she managed to persuade him to start a girl's day school so that Mabel and I might go to it. Bromley was only a very small provincial town, and would probably remain so, with no opening for a girl's private school. So Mr. Sonnenschein chose Anerley, an already populated and growing off-shoot of Norwood, Syndenham, Chiselhurst, Bexley and Penge, adjoining them on the outskirts of London.

In the interval between leaving Bromley and finding a house in Anerley, we spent these few months in Weybridge. Leonard was between ten and eleven, and he went to a boarding school at Rickmansworth, Middlesex, where Mr. Hurndall was headmaster. A few years later he went to Uppingham, Rutlandshire, which was one of the smaller public schools, but had a very good reputation. I expect the fees were less than at Eton, Harrow and Winchester which would be a consideration.[3]

[Mabel and I] had a gorgeous time with the cousins. Auntie Wahr's younger sisters, Marnie and Lizzie, had been living with a family in Germany for about a year to learn the language (and possibly in France, too), and while we were all at Weybridge they came home to Largs. It was great fun. They were quite young, about twenty and twenty-one, full of glowing stories of Raoul and Hedda (the children of the house), and spouting German at every pore. We were all *liebeskind*, and were quick to pick up a few words. The aunts often spoke it at meals, which was very tantalizing because sometimes we knew they were speaking about us.

Laurie and Frank Shaw, the two younger sons of Dr. Shaw of St. Leonards, and medical students at Guy's Hospital, London, came to spend a day. Maria's two very attractive and accomplished young sisters may have had something to do with it, but that is purely guesswork. Laurie was very quiet, fair, and with a nervous blink of the eyelids. Frank, dark, with merry brown eyes, [had] plenty to say. Of course, we younger ones did not count, but May and Mabel were growing up and developing "character." I have heard that Laurie made up his mind, when May was only ten, that she was to be his wife some day.

[Finally] we went to Anerley, where mother had succeeded in finding a small house. Number 8 Thicket Terrace was within walking distance of Mr. Sonnenschein's school, which was to open after Christmas. It must have cost mother many a pang to give up our dear little country villa at Bromley and come to this land of shops and chimney pots. I think it must have been her faith in, and devotion to Mr. Sonnenschein, and his ability to make a good school, which influenced her decision. But what was more attractive from our point of view, and probably influenced mother in the choice of a house, was the fact that we should only be a stone's throw from one of the entrances to the grounds of the Crystal Palace.

We arrived at Anerley in the afternoon, and while Mabel and I ran about, investigating the empty rooms, mother had a watchful eye for the moving van. A charwoman was supposed to be in the house, giving it a good sweeping, but no char had arrived. Also, one of the uncles was coming to help mother to get the furniture in place. Something seemed to have gone wrong with the arrangements, and for the first time I knew mother was worried.

What delighted us children was a row of tiny milk cans on the drawing room mantle shelf. Even in those days there was an overlapping of milk deliveries, and each dairy sent a sample, highly salted with cream, to all newcomers. At last the van arrrived. Out came the well-known chairs, beds, and other things. By the time the men had gone it was just beginning to get dusk. By some mistake the gas meter had not been turned on, so that in half an hour we should be in darkness.

Mother called us to her and explained how we must "go to the corner, turn to the right," and we should find a little chandler's shop where we could buy candles and matches. This was a real adventure to me. To go out alone with Mabel, in a strange place, and to buy something in a strange shop we had never even seen. Mabel took my hand and, holding the purse in the other, we walked sedately to the corner. There was no skipping this time; it was too solemn an occasion. Of course, Mabel had her head screwed on and was quite equal to the occasion at nine and a half.

At last the char arrived, a sour woman, not at all anxious to help, and with some feeble excuse for not having come earlier. But the uncle never turned up at all. The beds were set up by the light of one candle, and the place straightened up as well as could be under the circumstances. Mabel and I were soon asleep. The next day we had the fun of arranging the furniture—the bow-backed dining room chairs and sideboard—and laying the carpets, etc. I think the grand piano must have come in a van by itself, and someone brought dear old Lorne.

Just at the time we moved into No. 8 on the Terrace, a young man of nearly seventeen was living with his father and stepmother at No. 8 Thicket Road. His name was—Ralph Geoffrey Grey, my future husband. Life is full of coincidences, but I certainly should have been surprised and so would he, had we known we should meet twenty years later on the islands in the Gulf of Georgia, British Columbia. The family left Anerley about 1879 or 1880.[4]

Our house was the eighth in a row of ten. The Terrace was built on a hill, which curved round into Thicket Road. There were a few remnants, about half an acre, of the original thicket after which the terrace and road were named. Later, some small villas were built on this land, and the bushes disappeared forever. The Terrace, though built on a hill, was level, with steps leading down into the road again. This gave the last five or six houses a large basement under the terrace, with a tradesman's entrance into the street.

Mabel and I had great times bowling our wooden hoops, or skipping up and down the concrete walk in front of the houses, which must have been fifteen or twenty feet wide. Each house had what was known as an area to give light to the basement. (In London houses, where there was no approach at the back, steps led down into these areas to give access to the kitchen.) We had a nice, large drawing room with a bow window and open grate. All the rooms had open grates [because] there was no furnace. Behind was a dining room, with a French window and steps leading down into the garden. (The word "drawing room" was originally "withdrawing room." After a meal in the dining room you withdrew to another room. I remember the older people saying, "Shall we withdraw?," or "Let us withdraw," leaving the servants to clear the remains of the meal.)

Half way up the stairs was a small room which we used as a bathroom, and beside it a pin-sized toilet. Upstairs were two bedrooms and a dressing room and, in the attic, a servant's bedroom. We were never allowed up there.

Every house had a scullery where the washing-up was done. No water was laid on upstairs, except in the toilet tank, which was high up, near the ceiling, and released by pulling a chain or cord. All the bath and washing water for the bedrooms had to be carried up from the basement in a large can. It was the custom to have hot baths only once a week in those days, and I don't think a bath had any part in a servant's life. Our cook would have scorned the idea that she needed one. We used our faithful travelling bath, and china jugs and basins on a washstand in the bedrooms, with a slop pail for waste water.

The bedrooms were each lighted by a single gas jet. Mother and I slept in the front bedroom, I on what was known as a truckle bed, a sort of collapsible iron affair, all in one. Mabel had the unlighted dressing room. (The room behind was for Leonard, when home for the holidays, or for an occasional visitor.) We slept in starched, white calico nightdresses all the year round, and the bedding was covered with a white cotton counterpane. A can of cold water was put in the bath in Mabel's room overnight, and first thing in the morning we had to jump into it, winter or summer. I can remember how we took turns to break the thin coating of ice during an exceptionally hard winter, 1880-81, I think, when the whole country was frozen stiff.

There was a small grate in the bedroom, but it was only considered necessary to light a little fire when we had colds. I don't think anyone had ever heard of hot water bottles. A few large houses, such as Ore Place, still used the old-fashioned copper warming pan on a long handle, which was taken round from room to room, and put in the large double beds for a time to take off the chill.

Anerley was a recent off-shoot or extension of Norwood, concentrated round a central High Street—a long, long hill, with the Crystal Palace at the top, and what would now be called a small shopping district at the bottom. A bridge spanned Anerley Station just beyond. There were a few shops near us, and nondescript villas and other things between. A brewery for one. The smell of malt, for some reason, made Mabel and me think they were killing pigs. The districts of Syndenham, Penge, Beckenham, Bexley, Battersea Park, Peckham Rye, Clapham, Dulwich and Chiselhurst were in the vicinity. Bromley and Honour Oak were within reasonable walking distance. These are all fascinating names to me.

There were practically no ready-made clothing sold in the local shops. People made their own clothes, generally by hand, except perhaps the odd coat which might be bought in London. A linen draper sold stuff by the yard: calico, hooks and eyes, buttons, a few varieties of ribbon, and quite coarse, black cotton stockings (no silk or even lisle stockings, or rayon, which were not invented for many a long year). The shop was small and dark, with only one counter. There was no rush of shoppers, or things "on sale." It was the only one that sported two show windows. Into one was crammed as many samples of goods as possible, and the other might have a few really tasty ladies' bonnets, and straw sailors for children.

I hardly remember what was sold in the small grocer's shop. There were so few things to sell. I remember a delicious smell of cheese, treacle and currants. There were Bryant and May's matches, Crosse and Blackwell's jam, put up in earthenware galley-pots, and covered with parchment. Peek Freans, and Huntley and Palmer were old, established biscuit makers, but their biscuits had to be bought from Mr. William Whitely in Westbourne Grove, London. He started the first department store, and advertised that he was the "universal provider," or "the great U.P.," and would supply anything from a baby to an elephant. There were no canned goods at all. No fruit or vegetables were put up for the winter.

Tea and coffee were expensive. It paid to import a fifty pound chest, lined with tinfoil, direct from China. Mother did this through her friend's father, Mr. Scrutton. In the chest would be one or two quaint china figures as a gift. Once we got a goat and a horse. We also imported barrels of apples from Canada.

The chandler's shop near us sold rope, kerosine oil for lamps, beeswax for polishing floors, nails, matches, tallow candles, soap and little bundles of sticks to light your fire. There was a fascinating smell of tar, turpentine and unknown things. Next door was a tiny sweet shop, at which Mabel and I cast longing glances. Once, when Leonard came home for the holidays, he took me along there and spent tuppence, two whole pennies, on sweets! One doesn't forget an event like that. I was as proud as Lucifer to hold the hand of my big brother.

There was a baker's, where you could buy penny buns and scones. They had fruit in them, too. You didn't have to whistle for each currant as you do now. An iced cake could be ordered for a birthday, but were not for sale otherwise. You could make a meat pie or cake, and have it baked in the baker's large oven if your own was not suitable, for a small sum. We bought Neville's bread, a most delicious product, made in London and shipped to outlying depots for delivery.[5]

Then, of course, there was the chemist, a very modest place where legitimate drugs and medicine were sold. He made up doctor's prescriptions at about 1/ or 1/6 (25 cents or 30 cents) a bottle. Mother was a homeopath, and the large bottles of physic prescribed by allopaths were looked on with disgust. When we had colds or other ailments, mother got out her little medicine chest and Dr. Phillips prescribed minute doses of belladonna, aconite, mercurus sol, camomilla, phosphorus or camphor. A few drops were carefully measured into a glass of water, which was then covered with a piece of paper, and a teaspoon with which to take the dose.[6]

Camphor was a different matter. It was very strong, and blinkish. Two or three drops on a lump of sugar—cubes of sparkling crystals, not the dull, unform pieces cut by machine today. The sugar was nice, but plus the camphor the result was about 50-50. Another remedy was to sit in front of the tiny bedroom fire, bundled up in a blanket, with your feet in a little bath of mustard and hot water. The doctor's stethoscope was just a wooden tube flattened at one end, and the other he put in his ear.

30

Hastings and vicinity

Soon after we got settled down mother had to make a trip to London to choose light fixtures. A group of Venetian glass blowers had set up works at Whitefriars, London, and the firm was known by that name. It was not a regular shop, but they showed us samples of their work. Mother chose a very pretty amber colour, with blue handles.

Then the floors had to be done over. There was a carpet in the middle, but round the edge mother painted a sort of tile pattern in two shades of brown. It was an age of plenty of ornamentation. Brackets of various shapes and sizes hung on the walls, and she embroidered strange and wonderful draperies, or sort of petticoats for these and the mantlepieces. The latter was a gigantic labour and took months. Vases of peacock's feathers adorned dull corners. It looked like heavy Indian embroidery when finished, and was much admired. Now, we should call such unnecessary things dust traps, but the ideas were clever and ingenious, nevertheless. All the work was so original.[7]

The next thing she did was to paint some underwater scenes on the drawing room door panels; copied, I think, from Chinese pictures: fish swimming among reeds. They were very pretty. I had an idea I would like to add another fish, so I got a pencil and began, but there was only room for half a fish, and I hoped mother would paint it, and not notice that I had drawn it. Then I got frightened and tried to rub it out, but it would not rub. So when mother asked me about it, I said I had not drawn it. She just looked at me. That was enough. I don't think I ever told another lie.

Mother made all our clothes. We were beautifully dressed, always, and in good taste. I never wore Mabel's outgrown things, and we were always dressed alike, except perhapd Mabel might have something pink, and I blue. Black silk for children had given way to aesthetic colours. Velveteen was much favoured, with a contrasting sash, tie, or hat trimming. One winter we had *vert de mer* (sea green) velveteen dresses, with high waists, broad-brimmed Kate Greenaway felt hats, trimmed with terra cotta silk, tippets (or capes) and scarves to match, for outdoor wear. All hats had elastic under the chin to keep them on.

Another time it was Venetian blue velveteen, with wide silk sashes. I think now that our good clothes must have made us rather conspicuous in those drab surroundings. Mabel can remember people turning and staring at us, but I did not notice it. I was accustomed to being well dressed, and never thought about it till some years later, when we had to wear shabby and dowdy clothes. Other colours of the day were old gold and old rose, and crushed strawberry. Gilbert and Sullivan satirized this craze for aesthetic colours in their play "Patience." One of the characters, with a shock of hair and wearing a velveteen jacket, posed, with sinuous knees, in ecstasy before a sunflower. It was a great joke at the time, and touched the spot.

Our undergarments were: first, a calico chemise and a cotton bodice, with two sets of large linen buttons. To one set were buttoned loose-legged cotton drawers, and to the other, in winter, a flannel petticoat. Over these, a cotton petticoat, and then a dress and embroidered white pinafore. Mother made them all, scalloping the hems, necks and armholes. She invented a combination garment for Mabel—drawers and chemise in one, which was a great innovation.

In summer we had print dresses for everyday wear. For "best" mother made "all-over embroidery" (as we should call it now), and then cut it out into dresses, with hand-made swiss embroidered collars and cuffs to wear separately. I simply marvel at the amount of work she put into our clothes. It *was* a labour of love!

One winter we went to London and mother ordered sealskin (not rabbit made over) muffs, caps, gloves and collars to be made for us. I kept my little cap for many years—even bringing it out here, I loved it so.

My seventh birthday came and went. Auntie Emma spent the day with us, and christened me her "little woman," which remained till long after I was grown up. I should like to write a lot about Auntie Emma, my godmother. She was such a darling, and I know now such a really good woman. She often spent the day with us, bringing her little be-ribboned lace cap, which she wore in the house, in a round, covered basket, made for the purpose. Occasionally, she would need new ribbons or even a new cap, and then it was our joy to be given the old ones for our dolls. One birthday Auntie gave me *Alice in Wonderland* and *Through the Looking Glass* in the original calf-bound editions. And another time Mabel and I were each given the choice of a framed picture. Mabel chose Frank Dicksee's "Harmony," and I chose Landseer's "Dignity and Impudence."

There were compensations in our new home. The afternoons closed in early, and that brought the lamplighter. We could see him from our window, with lantern and ladder, as he came posting up the street, taper in hand. He propped the ladder against the post, dexterously opened the little glass door, lighted the gas jet, and was off to the next lamp in no time. They were few and far between.

Then there was the muffin man, who came several times a week. He carried the muffins and crumpets wrapped in a clean, white cloth, on a wooden tray, balanced on his head. He tinkled a bell on a spring as he strode down the road. Another man brought steaming hot rolls, crusty and brown on the top. He came quite early in the morning, and hurried along, so that people could have the rolls for breakfast. His attraction was a cry instead of a bell.

The Crystal Palace and grounds were a perfect paradise for children. We had season tickets, and went almost every day, till we knew every inch of it, inside and out. The turnstile where we went in opened on the Big Lake, on the shores of which were the prehistoric monsters made of concrete: a giant sloth, grasping a large oak tree, long-necked dragons wading in real water, flying lizards, and a huge sort of frog [iguanodon], whose mouth was so big we could get inside it easily.[8]

We saw the wold-famous African Blondin, who had crossed the Niagara Falls and Victoria Falls on a tight rope in 1859. With a very long balancing pole [he] walked a tight rope stretched between two towers, about one hundred feet in the air, with no net beneath.[9]

There were immense conservatories full of camellias and tropical ferns and palms, a monkey house, bird house, camera obscura, panorama and an endless variety of interesting things in the main building. We loved the [Ploquet] Collection of wild animals, stuffed, housed in a long hall upstairs. Some of them were a bit moth-eaten. There was a scene depicting some rabbits sitting round a table, eating off plates. The door had just opened and sly Mr. Reynard was peeping in.[10]

The troups of life-sized natives—Zulus, South Sea Islanders—among natural surroundings were most interesting. There was a replica, in gold and rich colours, of the Alhambra Palace, with its wonderful fountain of lions. At the Egyptian Temple, with the walls covered with pictures of Egyptian art, we stood gazing at them, trying to find a full-faced figure, but there was only one tiny one. The ivory stall, where you could see tusks of ivory made into ornaments (or buy them at an exorbitant price, if you liked), was always our meeting place when Auntie Emma joined us.

Brock's famous firework plant was hidden away in the grounds. We came across it one day, quite by accident, and were hustled out. There was a firework display every Thursday night, and as we got older sometimes we were allowed to watch the rockets from the spare room window. Once we went to the grounds and saw the "golden rain," Roman candles, etc. Finally, the set piece was called "The Bombardment of Alexandria," an historical fact at the time. It was too thrilling. There was a fort, with guns firing at battleships, which were bombarding the fort. I shall never forget that. I was ten and a half.[11]

Then there were new contraptions called tricycles, things with three thick wooden wheels, and a sort of saddle. You paid three' (about 5 cents) for a short ride, with a man walking beside you to see you did not fall off. We never went on one, though we would have liked to try, but they did not look very safe.[12]

Every four years the Handel Festival was held at the Crystal Palace, and we were fortunate enough to be there for one. The gigantic pipe organ, with the organist hardly visible at that distance, boomed forth the music of the Messiah, while two thousand singers, tier upon tier, sang the choruses. The conductor was the distinguished German, August Manns, with his flowing white hair, and among the soloists were Madam Adeline Pattie, Santley, Watkin Mills and other world-renowned celebrities—the Carusoes of their day. How lucky we were! The Crystal Palace was an education in itself. These wonderful experiences sank into your bones and became a part of you forever.[13]

* * * * * * * * * *

About that time mother took us to London to hear Madam Schumann play. I think it was at the Queen's Hall. Of course, I was hardly old enough to appreciate what it meant, though I had heard plenty of good music from Mr. Arnold Kennedy and at the Palace. Mother impressed me with the fact that I was to listen to someone I should feel honoured to have heard when I was grown up. Madam was a little old lady, dressed in black, but with the gift of the gods. I do feel honoured.

We were raised on Beethoven, Schumann, Mendelssohn, Chopin and Mozart, but we heard Wagner spoken of with rather shocked disapproval—so noisy! Anything that was not classical was termed drawing room music and scorned, but that did not apply to Wagner, of course. Somehow, I got the idea that there was something suspiciously wicked about opera.

Mr. Kennedy lived just down the road, and gave us music lessons. He was a funny-looking little man, like "Tom Noddy, all head and no body." Plenty of brains, as well as a fine musician. He came nearly every evening and played to us. If Mabel and I had gone to bed, we often crept to the top of the stairs in our nighties and listened to Schumann's Aufschwung, Etudes Symphonesques, the Moonlight [Sonata], and many another treasure of memory. Mabel was learning to play quite well, "Scenes from Childhood," and so on, but I was slow. The capacity for work was dormant in me, and I didn't want to be bothered to learn anything. Mother was quite strict with us, I am thankful to say, when it came to a matter of duty. She sat beside me at the piano, with a brush in her hand, and if I was careless she rapped my knuckles with the back of it.

Mother read to us a great deal. A lot of it was over my head, such as Kingley's *Westward Ho*, when Leonard was home for the holidays. But I loved to listen, and absorbed, I am sure, a certain amount of good taste in books, for I never cared for fairy stories or rubbishy books, and the sentimental trash which girls used to read at boarding school later on. I was easily touched by sad stories. Tennyson's "Enoch Arden" always made me weep. George Eliot's poem "Two Lovers" contains this verse: "The two still sat together there/The red light shone about their knees,/But all the heads by slow degrees/Had gone and left that lonely pair." It made me so sorrowful, though I did not understand its full meaning. I wondered how children could be so cruel as to leave their mother alone. But George Eliot's "Brother and Sister" was much more simple (in our case

34

it was two sisters). It begins: "I cannot choose but think upon the time/When our two heads grew like twin buds..."

You never hear of people reading George Eliot's verses now. The thrills of modern life have largely taken the place of those quiet pleasures when people had time to think and read beautiful things, and absorb their meaning. "Those hours were seed to all my after good." (George Eliot)

We had a few more books now. Everyone was well worn and known from cover to cover. I have the original copy of Charles Kingley's *Water Babies*, given to Leonard as a little boy.[14] We also had *The World at Home*, a lovely book, with a picture on every page, *Chaucer for Children*, *Spenser for Children*, with the story of Una and the Lion and the Red Cross Knight. We were awed by the really fine picture of him going down into a dark cavern on his white charger. Macaulay's *Lays of Ancient Rome* [15] and Lamb's *Tales from Shakespeare* I did not understand very well. Mrs. Gatty's *Parables from Nature* were delightful. I was given *Aesop's Fables* in verse, many of which I got to know by heart.

We had *Helen's Babies; The Hunting of the Snark*, a clever satire on scientific research of the day by Lewis Carroll; and *Hookey-Beak The Raven*, translated from the German. I gave May a copy of *Hookey-Beak* for her ninth birthday, February 1878. Many years later she returned it to me thinking I would like to keep it.

* * * * * * * * *

[Mother] had a little coterie of faithful old friends who were not shocked at a married woman living alone, and having men as well as women friends to see her. It was "not done," but she did it and did not lose the respect of those who admired her. But no one called on her, as was customary. When mother had a special little dinner party of three or four friends, Mabel and I were allowed to stay up later than usual, perhaps till 7:30. It was a great treat to sit behind the dining room door, while the meal was in progress, but the rule "children must be seen and not heard" was in force. We were not allowed to speak and the visitors might not take any notice of us, but I realize now there were furtive glances in our direction, with an occasional veiled smile. We were entirely unselfconscious, and content to wait till we got the signal to run to the table, where kind arms and smiling faces were ready to welcome us, and we got our share of fruit and nuts.

It was on these and other occasions that we heard talk of Mr. Gladstone and Home Rule, or Mr. [Charles Stewart] Parnell and Mr. [Charles] Bradlaugh, the Sudan War, General Gordon, Arabi Pasha, The Mahdi, Sir Garnet Wolseley, and Tel-el-Kebir. Young Major Kitchener was being talked of at this time, too.

We heard of Mr. Ruskin and his book, *Sesame and Lilies*, George Eliot's *Middlemarch, Dorothea*, and *The Mill on the Floss*; [of] the Phoenix Park murders in Ireland; [of] that odd man Benjamin Disraeli; and of books by Charles Dickens. The Zulu War in which Uncle Henry Spalding took part was in progress. Mabel and I were fascinated by the names of the native chiefs: Lobengula and Cetewayo. All these things meant very little to me at the time. Often, they were merely an undercurrent of sound heard during our games, but they have since resolved themselves into the current history of those times, and will always have a magic significance.

One of mother's greatest friends was Clement Holmes, brother of Florrie and Basil. They used to have very skeptical discussions on the possibility of life hereafter. There was a great craze for spiritualism, "authentic" messages from the dead, sceances, consulting ouija boards, and what not. The names Annie Besant and Madame Blavatsky were frequently heard. Well, anyway, mother and Clem made a solemn pact that whichever of them died first would make every possible effort to communicate with the other. The lot fell to Clem, but, needless to say, mother never received any message.[16]

Some times May or Ethel came to spend a day or two with us, and occasionally we spent a day with them. How we all enjoyed it. I remember climbing the stone wall, pushing past the dirty branches of trees, and making my clothes in such a mess. The cousins asked, in awe, if I wouldn't get in a row for making myself so dirty.[17]

I must hurry over our lovely made-up games—putting the bow backed dining room chairs on their sides to form a maze, and then crawling through them, etc. Our games were much rougher when Leonard was at home, naturally. We slid down the stairs on an old tray, which cannot have improved the carpet, but I expect mother remembered her own childhood and wild pranks.

We kept white rats as pets in cages in the basement, and took them out in the garden to play with. Leonard named his Helen of Troy, Mabel's was Lars Porsena of Clusium, but mine was always just Winifred's rat. I remember, even now, how indignant I was at not being allowed to choose a name. After a time the rats got out, having increased in number, chewed their way into the trunks of winter clothing, and raised several families before they were discovered. One or two found their way down a drainpipe onto the road, and were seen being dragged along by street boys, strings tied to their tails. That gave the show away, and the rats had to be given away when the damage was discovered.

Mother bought Mabel and me each a wonderful doll of the latest Paris manufacture. They had kid bodies and legs, with bisque heads and hands, and real wigs. Such dolls had never been seen before. We were overjoyed. They cost one pound each ($5.00), and came directly from Paris by parcel post. Mabel named hers Gladys, a very popular name at the time, and mine was Rica [after Mr. Sonnenschein's wife, Frederica]. When mother made our clothes, she always made dresses for our dolls of the same material and pattern, and they always wore pinafores as we did.

Visits from the travelling Punch and Judy man, with his little dog Toby, were getting fewer. He came down the street, making those ridiculous squawking, Punch noises, so alluring to all children and grown-ups, too. Little Toby, once white, and the frill round his neck in the same condition, [trotted] behind his master. In no time children had sprung from every direction, as in the days of the Pied Piper of Hamelin, but I have not space to tell more. The fascination of a performance cannot be put into words if you have not seen one.

There were some dear old rhymes, which are being lost sight of, perhaps because they have no meaning for present day children. "Lucy Locket lost her pocket, Kitty Fisher found it. But all the money she had got was in the ribbon round it." Pockets were bags, tied round the waist. An under pocket [was tied] with tape, and you had to lift your skirt to get at it. If the pocket was outside your skirt, it would be tied with ribbon. Poor Lucy had spent the money she intended to put in her pocket on a fancy ribbon to tie it on with.

Mabel and I had pockets hanging from our waists, too. It was some years before pockets were let into the side seams of a dress, and they were very large, and would hold a multitude of odds and ends. People went without any pockets and lost their handkerchiefs in consequence. (And now it's patch pockets, which in our childish days were only for workmen.)

"Pat-a-cake, pat-a-cake, baker's man/Bake me a cake as fast as you can./Pat it, and prick it, and mark it with B/And put it in the oven for Baby and me." That would refer to the old custom of taking your cakes or pies to be cooked by the baker or his helper.

There were comparatively few toys in those days. No bicycles, cameras or flashlights. Boys had iron hoops, tin soldiers, pop guns, and marbles, and made slingshots. Girls had dolls, work boxes, battledore and shuttlecocks, hoops, and skipping ropes. Mabel and I each had a tiny cardboard box containing a family of crude china animals. Mine were spaniels with red ears.

At Ore Place there were two boxes of blocks, one large one with a fine assortment, made of oak, for week days, and the other was for Sundays—coloured pictures of Biblical scenes: Joseph and his coat, Daniel in the lion's den, etc. You turned over a whole row of blocks at one time to get a new picture.

* * * * * * * * * *

Sometimes we went to spend the day with Auntie Annie Scrutton. She was no relation, really, but children often called people Auntie in those days. She lived in just about the dingiest part of London you can possibly imagine, in a smoke-encrusted house. At the back was an apology for a garden, with a few sooty shrubs, struggling for existence, and a tiny piece of what might once have been grass. Some scrubby roots of "London Pride" were the only poor flowers which could battle against such awful conditions. The shrubs were laden with the most wonderful cobwebs and huge spiders I have ever seen. Everyone was a masterpiece.

Mabel and I liked to go up to Auntie Annie's room, where she turned out her ragbag for us, provided needles, cotton and scissors; and there we amused ourselves for hours, making doll's clothes. When teatime came we all went out to buy something at the baker's. Mabel and I always chose brioches, tiny loaves of French bread, and tea there would not have been complete without them.

Auntie Annie always spoke very correctly. I can remember mother and her talking about these new words which were coming into use: "can't" and "won't." they were considered very slovenly. And then came "shan't." Worse still. People held up their hands in horror.

Once or twice we went to see Unc in his Chambers at the Inns of Court, London. When we first got there he was just as we knew him. After a while, glancing at the clock, he would disappear for a moment or two, coming forth arrayed in wig and gown. He didn't seem to be quite the same person, somehow. He had married Maude Shaw, sister of Charlie, Laurie, Frank and Grace, of St. Leonards, and they had the prettiest home in the new suburb of Turnham Green, called Bedford Park, near London. All the houses were built in the Queen Anne style, with nice gardens and old fruit trees— remains of a former orchard. Unc had bought beautiful antique furniture, every piece hand picked, and lovely Oriental rugs. It was a charming place.

One summer mother took rooms in Pelham Crescent [Hastings], so that we could be near the sea. My great delight was to be allowed a goat carriage drive along the Parade, and I made up my mind I would own one when I was grown up. People in immense bath chairs were propelled up and down in the sunshine.

Another time we joined forces with some of the cousins on the Marina, and had a grand time. Air balls at a penny were the rage, not so much to play with as to see whose

Old Hastings

Ore Church, Hastings
Hastings Library Collection

would last the longest when hung from the doorknob. Those were the days when you had to hire a bathing machine on wheels. A big cart horse pulled the machine out into the waves, which were grand at Hastings.

We did not like the fat old bathing woman who spent the day in the water, dressed in draggled cotton garments, which showed her profuse figure to perfection. She enticed or pulled the reluctant children into the water and ducked them.[18]

* * * * * * * * * *

[When] Christmas came again we joined the crowd at Ore Place. Every room was full to overflowing. We children all hung up our stockings and, waking at some unearthly hour, joined forces in one of the immense double beds to look at them. Addison's in Old Hastings sold all sorts of fascinating things suitable for stockings. Chocolate animals, cigars, etc., were a great novelty and almost too precious to eat. There were tiny, round boxes of chocolate pills which looked real, [and] Chinese glazed cotton wool animals, which have come and gone again since then.

A thirty-foot Christmas tree was cut on the grounds, and stood in the hall, which was open to the second floor. The uncles and grown-ups decorated it on Christmas Eve. It was loaded with presents, which seemed to take hours to distribute from a tall step-ladder. As my birthday was December 20th, some people combined that and a Christmas present, which was rather a "chouse." There was a bust of Grannie's father high up over the hall fireplace, and the boys always decorated it with a top hat, at a rakish angle, which shocked Grannie, but she could not reach it to take it off.

Christmas dinner was a gigantic affair, with several leaves put in the already large table. The turkey was a monster, and when the holly-crowned, flaming pudding arrive, of course we all cried, "O-o-oh!" In the evening, there were snapdragons, raisins in a fiery dish of brandy, which was set in the middle of the table in the servants' hall. You had to grab raisins out of the flames. It was very exciting, and there was lots of squealing, but I don't think we children cared to eat them.

On Boxing Day, after the family Christmas tree and celebrations were over, the tree was re-laden with presents. All the children on the estate, with their mothers, were invited to come for a Christmas treat. Each one received a good present and a bag containing oranges, nuts and sweets. Then came the climax: Grandpapa presented a shiny, new silver sixpence to each beaming, rosy-cheeked child. It was the moment of the year for them, and looked like a million dollars. On being asked, one little girl said she was going to buy a carriage and pair with hers.

Mother and Unc took us to the Christmas pantomime at Drury Lane Theatre several times. That always gave us something to talk about for months. It was an evening performance, and meant getting home after midnight. I feel sure those pantomimes have never been equalled anywhere in the world, and those who have not seen one can have little idea of their splendour and magnitude. The boxes and stalls were filled to capacity with ladies in exceedingly low-necked dresses and pinched waists, and the gilded ceiling made us open our eyes in wonder.[19]

We loved to see the little golden slippers of the dancers tripping along, just below the painted curtain, before it was rung up. Once the story was "The Babes in the Wood," but it really had very little to do with the original tale. The hero's part was always taken by a girl. There were always a lot of extra characters and songs, which did not belong in the story. Mother and Unc chortled for days afterwards over a large man who came on the stage wearing an out-sized child's sailor suit, hat and socks, and carrying a tin pail and wooden spade. He announced in a droll voice, "I am the villain of the piece, and I have disguised myself with this spade and pail." There were roars of laughter. I thought he meant "villain of the peace," and that he was going to make a disturbance.

Another time the play was "Aladdin and His Lamp." There was always a Harlenquinade—Columbine, Harlequin and Clowns—doing the original slapstick from which the present meaning of the word is far removed.

The finale—the *piece de resistance*—was the transformation scene. This time there was an immense, domed Moorish Palace, high up and dimly lighted, built on crags in the background. In the foreground were caves, large ornamental vases standing around, and "flowers" with closed petals. As the music proceeded, the transformation took place. The sun gradually rose on the Palace, the petals of the flowers unfolded, and out of them, and from the caves and vases, stepped graceful little fairies, with gossamer wings, and dressed in spangles of gold and silver, pink and blue. Meantime, the illumination of the Palace had changed from one colour to another, making the scene, with dancing fairies, more and more gorgeous. The whole thing beggars description.

When it was all over, and the last curtain rung down, it was past eleven o'clock. We had a growler to take us to the station, and I fell asleep at once. Mother roused me to look at a funny, very bright light outside a building. "That is the new arc light," she said, "the first that people have ever seen. But some day the streets may be lighted like that instead of gas lamps." I blinked out of the window, but "The shard-born beetle with his drowsy hums/Hath run night's yawning peal," and so I fell asleep again, not knowing that, thanks to Mr. Thomas Edison and Mr. Swan, I had looked upon one of the greatest marvels of modern discovery and invention—the first electric lights. In 1882 the Crystal Palace had a room lighted by electricity on exhibition.[20]

* * * * * * * * * *

The year 1881 brought our first great sorrow. Auntie Wahr had her last little baby girl, Muriel, born in March, from which she did not recover. It may sound fantastic, but I had a very realistic dream in which Auntie appeared as an angel, with other angels grouped around. They said they had come for her. Of course, we saw pictures of angels, and servants talked of such things, but this dream was one of three distinct things of the same kind in my life. I did not know Auntie was ill, yet the next day mother told us she had had a letter to say Auntie had died. We were so sad, but our grief was nothing compared with that of all those little cousins left motherless. She was only thirty-seven.[21]

Little Tommy was never told because his short life was almost ended. He died a few months later. I was heartbroken and miserable for a long time, and I know Ethel was. The thought of Ore Place without him was terrible. But life went on.[22]

Unknown to Mabel and me, our happy childhood was now rushing to its tragic close. One day mother told us she must go to London and leave us behind with Mrs. Hart, a most unusual thing for her to do. She would be back about five. We spent the day happily enough and as the time drew near, we danced up and down the abbreviated hall, singing, "Five's the clock! Mother's to come! Five's the clock! Mother's to come!," over and over again.

At last we heard her step and rushed to open the front door with a shout of welcome. But—she put her arms round us and burst into tears, a thing entirely foreign to her nature. Of course, we cried, too. It was the beginning of the end. Probably she had been to the doctor who told her she had cancer of the throat, and there was nothing to be done.[23]

Old friends came to the house, looking sad and worried. There were long talks at which we were not allowed to be present. Finally, one of the Ealing aunties came one day and took me away to stay with the cousins; and later Mabel went to her friend Rose Miall, so that she would not miss school. It was the first time Mabel and I had been separated except the few weeks I was with my godmother as a baby.

My eleventh birthday and Christmas came, 1882. I spent all the money I had, 1/6 (35 cents) on a Chinese flower pot for mother, and someone took it to her. Not long afterwards I was sent to Ore Place, and was told that mother would soon be coming, but that she was very ill.

Ore Place without Mabel or Tommy! Say had gone, and Ellen Pankhurst, the head housemaid, now reigned in the old nursery. It was used as a sewing room. Arthur was somewhere in Norfolk, learning farming, so I was given his bedroom at the top of the stairs. Carina was at finishing boarding school in Brighton, and Herbert was in London. Auntie Ellie had the old school room as a bedroom, now, and Miss Jackson had left. Auntie Florrie Holmes had married. So altogether it was quite a changed household.

Auntie Ellie was very good to me. Every evening she came and sat on my bed and sang songs: "The Cruiskeen Laun," and "Cockles and Mussels," and others. I always knew when she was coming because of her little "corridor cough" as she came up the front stairs and round the open gallery above the hall, which led to the second floor. Everyone knew and joked about this little habit.

I think it was not long before someone told me mother was coming by ambulance on a certain day. I had hardly ever heard of an ambulance, and was quite vague as to what it was. They were very primitive in those days, and it was a long journey from Anerley to Hastings. I think, perhaps, they put the ambulance on the train.

The day arrived. I was shut alone in that vast drawing room, and told not to open the door till someone came for me. I was excited at first, and played about with one thing and another, thinking I should soon be able to run and see mother. And yet things didn't seem right. Time dragged on. No one came. I longed to know what was happening; what all the mystery could be. When would somebody come? At last I heard a sort of commotion in the hall. Men's voices. Orders being given. The temptation was irresistible. I opened the door a tiny crack and peeped out—just in time to see some men carrying a sort of bed and on it, I knew, was mother. I was in an agony of suspense, half crying, till at last Ellen came. She was a kind, sympathetic soul, and explained that mother was very tired after the long journey, but that I should see her later. How she had changed! She could hardly speak, and towards the end, not at all.

I must pass quickly over these last few months. I constantly asked Auntie Ellie when mother would be well. She always said she thought "when spring came." It was kindly meant, but was, in reality, a cruel deception. If only she had told me the truth, instead of buoying me up with hopes she knew were false, she could have prepared me to face the blow which was to fall. I have always felt that.

Mabel came later on, to my great joy and comfort, and we were given a room at the end of the corridor, up four flights of stairs. It was near mother's room. She had a species of trained nurse, rather primitive, but a cut above the old gamp.[24] Nurses were called Sisters then. Every day, and sometimes twice, we were allowed to go in and see mother. She wrote me little notes reminding me to practice my music carefully, just as if she were there. I tried, but I'm afraid I was often slack about it. Everything seemed to have gone wrong with life, though I did not put it like that. It was a "feeling."

One evening I was just going in to see mother; the room was dark, except for a wax night light burning on the dressing table, when I saw she was out of bed. I had grown accustomed to seeing her in bed, but could this little, shrunken, tottering figure, clinging to the foot of the bed possibly be the mother I knew so well? I crept away, too terrified to go in. Her independent nature resented to the last being waited on.

The end was near. One morning Mabel and I had just finished breakfast with Grannie, when Ellen came to the door, white-faced and shaking. "You are wanted upstairs if you please 'm." Without a word Grannie got up and went out of the room, and we were left alone, with an indescribable feeling of impending disaster. We collected the crumbs off the table, and fed the birds, as usual, on the verandah, but the joy had gone out of it.

After what seemed an interminable time, Grannie came back, and we followed her into the morning room, like sheep going to the slaughter. There she sat down, drew us to her, and told us mother had gone: April 3, 1883.

Leonard came the next day, and we three walked about the familiar grounds as in a dream. Leonard appeared quite nonchalant, but it was only assumed. Boys of sixteen don't show their feelings. He had been away a great deal, so he would naturally not feel the loss as much as we did.

Before she died, mother had expressed a wish to see her husband, but the message was not delivered. She was buried in Highgate Cemetery. We had lost our mother, but she will always remain my most precious memory of a happy childhood.

* * * * * * * * * *

When there was a death in the family, it was customary to go away for a time. So Grannie ordered trunks packed, and we all went off, with several of the maids, to a furnished house in a high Terrace, overlooking Tunbridge Wells. Carina was recalled from boarding school at Brighton, where she was having, literally, the time of life; free to think and act independently with girls of her own age. She, too, had a strong character, which had never had a chance to show itself, always being subordinated at home. (Independence seemed to run in the family, on all sides.) It was a terrible blow to her, but to her everlasting credit be it said that she never once let Mabel and me know it. She threw herself whole-heartedly into the job of keeping an eye on us two rapscallions.

This upheaval was a good idea. It turned one's thoughts and gave fresh interests. It helped me to forget, for a time, how Jane, a really good soul, had said to me as I ran laughing down the corridor of Ore Place, "Oh, Miss Winnie! How can you laugh, with yer poor mother not cold in her grave!"

Carina took us on lovely, long walks through country we had never seen. We trudged miles to see a beautiful old estate, Penshurst, and were shown through endless rooms with wonderful chandeliers and massive furniture, draped in dust sheets, as the family was away.[25] We spent long days plunging through the marshes of Eridge and Frant, hunting for birds' nests and mollyblobs (marsh marigolds), or wandering among the sweet-smelling pines and climbing the famous Toad Rock. Or we went down into the town, along the more famous Pantiles, gazing into shops at things made of Tunbridge Wells ware: work boxes and all sorts of things with intricate patterns of inlaid coloured wood.

The maid Emma had a pillbox-sized sitting room in the basement, with a minute fire grate. When Mabel and I came in, raging hungry, we went and made love to the not unwilling Emma, who got out a loaf of bread and butter, and we proceeded to make immense slabs of smokey, buttered toast over the few coals in the tiny grate. I think we stayed about a month at Tunbridge Wells, and then the time came to pack up, go back to Ore Place, and settle down to brass tacks.

CHAPTER FOUR

Grannie

Poor Grannie! Having raised her own and various other children, she had long rested on her laurels. And now here she was, in her declining years, called upon to take two unregenerate girls into her peaceful home and try to mold them according to her approved pattern.

She had always disapproved of mother and her lack of religion. She disapproved of the way she had brought us up, and, finally, she disapproved of us, the product of that bringing up. How could it be otherwise? She and mother were poles apart, and each was independent and strong-willed. Every day must have brought fresh evidence that it was going to be a super-human task.

We showed no gratitude. I had lost my guiding star, and did not realize that I *ought* to be grateful to my grandparents for giving me a home. At eleven, I was still a child, hopelessly at sea. Mother had laid the foundation, but I had yet to learn to stand on it alone. Mabel, older, and naturally of far stronger character than I, was in a firmer position. I don't know what I should have done without her.

We must have been a sore trial. I can see it now. When Grannie was five, she had "sat on her little stool and darned all her father's and brother's socks." And here were we, big girls of eleven and fourteen, and had never used a darning needle. On Sundays, Grannie had read the Bible at her mother's knee, but we wanted to run out and climb trees, or hunt for rats in the barn.[1]

As little children, we had *never* taken off *our* red flannel petticoats to give to the poor, which was one of her oft-told kind deeds. I once took off my cotton chemise, but that was a different story. One summer Ethel and I were sleeping in the "small spare room" (30 x 35 feet). We took off most of our clothes and then had the wildest pillow fights. One evening, I was balanced on the feather bed, pillow in hand, when the door opened and there was Grannie! I dropped the pillow and in a moment of daring abandon snatched off my chemise and waved it over my head. Grannie was shocked beyond words at the time, but the next morning I "caught it in the neck" as we should say now.

All this must be remedied as soon as possible. Having once put her hand to the plough again, there was no turning back. I had to sit at Grannie's right hand at table, so I hadn't a chance. Frequently I was sent away to wash my hands or brush my hair. (She was quite right there.) Sometimes I flounced out of the room. Grannie set her lips.

Miss Hughes, sewing instructress at the local board school for village children, was engaged to come and teach us darning, thread by thread; to put on a patch; the correct way to put in a gusset; to fell a seam; to make a buttonhole; to French seam; to measure a hem; to gather stroke; and put on a band. And each thing had to be properly done. No scamping as long as we were with her. We made aprons for our dolls, to

43

include as many of these stitches as possible, putting on a pocket and sewing on tapes in the correct way [in order] to tie a bow at the back. That is one thing for which Mabel and I have always been genuinely grateful to Grannie. Once learnt, never forgotten.

I often scamped my darning when alone, but woe betide me if Grannie asked to look at my stockings! She made me sit beside her in the library while she read to Grandpapa, unpick the whole thing, and do it all over again. We had been taught more by example than precept and, as mother's influence faded, constant shocked reproof made me rebellious. I had never been accustomed to being moralized at, and didn't care a hang what God thought of me, but outwardly we had to be submissive.

Religious instruction must begin at once. On Sunday morning the carriage and pair of stolid grays drove up to the front door and we all got in. Stolid was the word. They were so well-fed, and got so little exercise that they could not go at more than a snail's crawl without sweating. We drove about a mile to the Congregational Church in the Mount Pleasant district, where Mr. B___(Soapy B___, as he was called) preached sickly sermons, turning up the whites of his eyes. How we loathed it!²

And as if that were not enough for one day, our advent started a Bible class on Sunday afternoons, for which the three younger maids had to sacrifice an hour of their precious Sunday afternoon off. Mabel and I sat at Grannie's right, and the maids on the left of the huge dining room table. We were supposed to have learned a hymn and to take turns in repeating it, verse by verse. On a certain Sunday, Grannie turned to the kitchen maid, saying, "Will you begin, Annie?" Annie was a raw country girl, with a round turnip head and a flat, expressionless face, shining with soap and water. She swallowed, gulped, and then blurted out, "Olyolyoly!" all in one rush. There was a moment's awful pause, and then, to our utter shame, Mabel and I giggled. Grannie glared, and after class was over she called us into the Library and gave us a good dressing down, which we well deserved. I have never been able to hear that hymn "Holy, Holy, Holy, Lord God Almighty" without thinking of that disgraceful episode.

We had to attend daily morning prayers, at which almost the entire household assembled. It was quite a lengthy affair: Bible reading and prayers, followed by the Lord's Prayer, in which we were all supposed to join. A little interest was caused by the filing in of the domestics—from seven to ten of them. First the pompous cook; then Ellen, the head housemaid; the head parlour maid, Emily; followed by their satellites, all crisp and shining. Budgeon brought up the rear.³

The younger ones were a little shy at the ordeal of sitting for ten or fifteen minutes facing the entire family. One might get a little diversion by peeping through one's fingers while kneeling, to see the boys, Herbert and Arthur, if at home, making faces. And Unc, if there, would give the occasional sly wink. But one had to be very careful as Grannie, like God, had an all-seeing eye for delinquents. She was Congregationalist, but managed to overcome her dislike for the Church of England to the extent of sending Mabel and me to share a governess with the children of the local parson, Mr. David Dowdney, at the vicarage.

Mr. Dowdney had three sons, Cecil, Raymond and Herbert, and augmented his boys' class by taking three others: John and Harry Knocker, and a tall boy named Kenneth Streatfield. Miss Isley taught the three Dowdney girls, Edith, Irene and Kathleen, and Mabel and me. She was one of the old-fashioned type, a sort of hangover, before private schools came into existence, and thoroughly old-fashioned in all her methods of teaching.⁴

The Dowdney family was related to Miss Elizabeth Fry, the champion of prison reform, and two Miss Frys (aunts) lived down the road. The young Dowdneys were a rowdy, happy-go-lucky crew at that time. They made cheap jokes, which have always revolted me—such things as we had never heard. Mabel and I learned slang words which would have shocked poor mother, but some of them seemed to bring more life to speech, I must confess.

For punishment, Miss Isley gave us lines—hundreds of them. She did not know how to make learning interesting, so her small mind fell back on this most futile form of punishment, calculated to spoil the hand-writing of any child.

But we had fun, too. One day, when Miss Isley was out of the room the local fox hunt went by in full cry, right across the fields in front of the house—horses, hounds and all. Mrs. Dowdney was a bit of a sport. She popped in and said, excitedly, "When the cat's away, the mice will play!" We didn't need a second suggestion. Like a flash we were all out of the French windows, and across the "forty acres," tearing along with the rest of those on foot. It was a pretty sight—a bright, sunny day, with the huntsmen in their scarlet coats and white breeches, strung out across the fields, and the hounds baying and rushing into every bit of scrub, with their noses to the ground. We girls were lucky enough to see Mr. Reynard scurry into some bushes, while all the huntsmen and hounds went off in another direction. When Miss Isley came back, all her pupils had vanished. (Some years before a fox had bolted right across the lawn in front of Ore Place, with the huntsmen after him. And wasn't there a row about the spoilt grass and garden!)

* * * * * * * * * *

Grannie must have inherited her father's interest in practical philanthropic work, for there was a succession of school treats for poor children, mothers' meetings and visits to orphan homes or asylums, in which Mabel and I always took part. Large treats were held in the quarry field, with races and sports of various kinds. The children had a sumptious meal, sitting on benches at impromptu board tables. A certain quantity of food was doled out to each child and they ate what they could, putting the remainder in bags of various descriptions brought for the purpose. Meat, bread and jam, buns, apples and sweets all tumbled in together. They ate till they nearly burst. It was a case of "I can still eat, but I can't swaller." (*Punch*). The contents of the bags must have been a gorgeous mess by the time they got home, but who cared?

The local village children were treated in the front field, and we joined in their games. "I sent a letter to my love, and on the way I dropped it. One of you has picked it up and put it in your pocket. T'isn't you, t'isn't you—T'is you!," and away they ran, was always the favourite game.

Teas for mothers' meetings were held in the village school house. We helped serve tea from huge urns, and wait on them, which was very good training for us.[5]

Occasionally, we went for country drives in the carriage and pair, with Grandpapa and Grannie. It was very nice, as long as we didn't have to sit still too long. There was a fashion for having "plum pudding dogs" (Dalmatians) trotting behind your carriage, but Grandpapa did not keep dogs at Ore Place. Arthur's black retriever Rover was the only one, and he had to be chained to his kennel, poor fellow.

Grannie gave us religious tracts to drop along the road, or hand to village folk when we stopped to pay toll at the turnpike gates, which were still in existence, as in the days of John Gilpin. We were also initiated in the gentle art of distributing charity to the poor and needy.

Two blind women lived alone in a little cottage along the road to Ore, doing all their own work, lighting the fire, etc., and knitting odd and wondrous garments for sale.

They could tell some colours by touch. One day we were told to take them a baked custard in a china dish, in a basket. Having lately made the discovery that a pail of water could be swung round without spilling, if you did it fast enough, we thought we would experiment with the basket and custard. Over and over it went, several times, quite successfully, till we got a bit reckless. Something went wrong with the swing, and out flew the custard into the road. Now, the Miss Crumps, being blind, would not know that it had originally fitted neatly into the dish, so—well—we picked it up as best we could, and delivered it!

In the winter, sewing bees took the place of jam and galley-pot evenings of summer, though the latter did not last long. Hundreds of garments had to be made to distribute among the "por" and for workhouses and orphans. Grannie bought dozens of yards of red flannel, which Miss Hughes cut out into petticoats or bed jackets for old women. (There was a curious class distinction, which is hard to believe now. The poor were "women" and the others "ladies.") Flannel petticoats and dozens of bodices for children were made from unbleached calico, covered with strips of list and selvedge off the flannel, all sewn on by hand, and then the bodice was bound with tape.

Sham carpet slippers for the old men at the Infirmary were made in the same way. No slipshod work was allowed. If you had an eye for a little adornment, you worked feather stitch round the petticoat hems. The hemming, backstitching and herringboning that went on would make people's eyes pop now, when everything is done by machine, and often scamped. Miss Hughes was too busy cutting, snipping and piecing the goods to read aloud, so grownups took turns at this job, as it helped us all along.

* * * * * * * * *

Grandpapa was about eighty now, and his right hand was paralyzed, but he always made some little joke about his "velvet claw" as he tapped us with what little strength he had in his gloved hand. He had bought quite a large pipe organ, which was in the dining room, to be the joy of his old age, and now, of course, he could not play it. But he managed to chuckle and make some whimsical joke about that, too. Ellie learned to play the organ for him. We never heard him complain about anything and Grannie looked after him most devotedly.

He was such a kindly old man. I can't help thinking that sometimes he must have had a fellow-feeling for us when we got in bad with Grannie, but experience had taught him never to show it by so much as a look in our direction. He evidently remembered his own boyhood, and it made him very human.

On one occasion the gardeners caught half a dozen little boys red-handed, stealing apples. Grandpapa called a sort of "court martial" in the big hall. The family assembled to make the occasion impressive, and the culprits were hauled before the tribunal, knuckling their eyes—the picture of guilt. Grandpapa began in a serious voice, about the evil of stealing, and so on. The boys blubbered, foreseeing nothing less than the lockup as punishment. Then he changed to gentle good humour. He remembered being a boy, and stealing apples himself, and, in effect told them to "go and sin no more." The boys were incredulous! The expressions on their faces were worthy of a George Belcher illustration as they scuttled out.[6]

* * * * * * * * *

The grounds of Ore Place had been beautifully laid out: perfect green lawns, threaded by weedless paths, bordered with standard roses. The flower beds always had a succession of flowers in bloom, by some new magic of the head gardener, Brooker. They changed overnight from daffodils to forgetmenots and wallflowers, then on to snapdragons, pinks and other summer flowers. Brooker was a master hand at carpet bordering, too. Of course, there was nothing like the variety or quality there is now. Such lovely things as nemesia, salpiglossis and dozens of others had never been heard of. There was a magnificent deodora cedar on the lawn, also a mulberry, with it luscious, red-purple fruit dyeing the green grass beneath. And the old starling tree, with its circular seat, was the home of a pair of those impudent birds. There were convenient little summer houses and seats tucked away in shady, hidy-places, and every one had its individual name. High up in the old fir trees was the rookery where "over all the dark rooks cawing flew."

There was a large depression in the quarry field, behind the old church, and legend had it that a meteorite had plunged to its doom there, but it seems more probable that the stone for building John of Gaunt's house, the church and possibly, later, the stone for building Ore Place, was quarried there.

The greenhouses, fruit gardens, and vinery were surrounded by a high wall, and were the joy and pride of Grandpapa's heart. Every bunch of grapes (all grown in hothouses), and every peach, nectarine and plum on the walls was neatly tied up in muslin to keep off wasps. To go in there, when Grandpapa opened the heavy oak door with his magic key, was like entering a new world.

Brooker, who had a pretty little cottage on the drive, knew his job. He also knew how to grow all the very latest flowers and vegetables to perfection, having every facility. He exhibited them in *his* name, and took most of the prizes at the local flower shows, to the probable annoyance of the less fortunate gardeners. The boys used to hoist each other up over the high stone wall, and "steal" their father's fruit.

The apple house was just outside the oak door, and occasionally Mabel and I could get in, if one of the gardeners happened to be there. We filled every available corner of our clothing, including the legs of our drawers, with Ribston Pippens and Blenheim Oranges (apples). Just beyond the farm was an old orchard and small fruit bushes, second-rate strawberries and raspberries. There, with luck, we could discreetly feast on fat, red, hairy gooseberries, or smooth-skinned green ones that popped in our mouths like pricked balloons.

The stables were built round a cobbled yard. The yard was deep in manure, and the cows were milked by hands that may or may not have been under a cold tap for a moment. Somehow no one got typhoid. Beyond the stables was the farm, if such it could be called. Farms were in a very primitive state then.

Rowse, the coachman, had a cottage near the stables, with his wife and several small children. Many of the children on the estate were named for the family, so that there would be Bessie, Nellie, Herbert or Arthur in each cottage. Rowse, being afraid he might not get another boy, took two names at one stride—Herbert Arthur.

The hens all had "the gapes" and laid their eggs just anywhere. Guinea fowl roamed around, but I don't think they supplied either fowl or eggs, and ducks had a happy life in the duck pond, without serving any useful purpose. There was stabling for cart horses, and a shed for pig killing. Once Mabel and I came upon men just "in the act." It was an eye opener! The pump house was made into an ornamental tea house, with the water tank above, and the pumping (all done by hand) machinery below, over the well. It must have taken hours every day to supply all the water needed.

The drive, this end, was bordered with lauristenus and small May trees, in one of which a chaffinch built its nest every year. Budgeon lived in the cottage at this entrance, with his hard-working little wife and an ever-growing swarm of children. Annie and Nellie were about our ages.

Once, when Grannie said I could choose what I would like for a birthday treat (my twelfth), I asked if Annie and Nellie could come to tea and play. This was quite an unheard of innovation, but they came. We had tea in the servants' hall, as being more suited to their station in life than the breakfast room where we had some of our meals. We tried to play afterwards, but they were not quite at their ease. All these children on the estate made a bob curtsy to Mabel and me, and we accepted it, without the slightest feeling of superiority. It was an every-day occurrence, just as all the servants called us Miss Mabel and Miss Winnie. We thought nothing of it.

The Budgeons, being simple people, began to run out of girl's names as their family increased. Having exhausted their stock, including Rose, the next baby, being another girl, was christened Rosy Rose.

The other entrance gate was kept by old Dolman. His children were grown up and his son "Black" Dolman worked on the place. Then there was Polson, [and] old and young Selmes, who kept the drives and paths free from weeds. Young Selmes was well over sixty. They had both hoed weeds so long that they couldn't stand upright, but Grandpapa never discharged a man for old age. Old Selmes drew his pay regardless of the amount of work he did.

Facing southwest was the Sunset Field, and it certainly lived up to its name. From there we saw the astounding and unbelievable spectacle of flaming skies, lurid and sinister with dust particles from the eruption of Krakatoa, the volcanic mountain in Java, for several nights in succession. It was awe-inspiring. I think I am right in saying, on the word of Sir Robert Ball, the astronomer, that the volcanic dust circled the globe three times.[7]

Down below were two small lakes, called the St. Helen's Ponds. A fallen tree across one could be negotiated with care. Once, when Winnie Close (Charlie Shaw's second wife) was staying at Ore Place, Arthur dared us to scramble over it. Winnie fell in, and Arthur had to haul her out and make peace with her mother. He nicknamed us, "The Winkers, Brothers, Contractors of Family Nuisances," because we were always badgering him.

The Rails Field bordered on the next estate, where the Coles family lived.[8] There were twin brothers of Arthur's age, Ted and Taff, and a little boy about my age, Geoff. [One day] when I was down by the wire fence, he came and asked if I would go to his place and play. I knew I might not do that, as I did not know him. He had on a clean, white sailor suit, with trousers. We sat on either side of the fence, but said little. Presently, he was called away. I thought how nice it would be to have a boy to play with (little Tommy being the only one I had really ever known), and suddenly decided, then and there, that when I was grown up I would marry a man whose name was Geoff. Oddly enough, I did!

* * * * * * * * *

"The night is long that never finds the day," and Mabel and I settled down to accept the inevitable. Summer came, bringing the long holidays. Life was good in spite of irksome restrictions. We three, Carina, Mabel and I, used to get up at unearthly hours — often 3:30 or 4:00 a.m. Taking hunks of bread and butter from the larder, we went down the Westfield Lane, the hedgerows crowded with golden celandines, stitchwort and cuckoo flowers, glistening in the early morning sunlight, out across the fields, hunting "mushies" (mushrooms) and cowslips; or into the woods, carpeted with bluebells, wood anemones, or primroses, according to the season. We searched eagerly for birds' nests, but never disturbed the birds if we could help it, and only took one egg if there were four. Once we found a bullfinch's nest—a great prize—the only wild one I have ever seen. Occasionally, a weasle or a stoat would scurry across the road, or we would find a colony of charming little coralcups to take home and put in a bowl of damp moss. We made cowslip balls by dropping the branching blossoms over a piece of string, and then tying it up like a baby's wooly ball. It was so delicious to bury your nose in its sweet scent. We hung them up and an occasional sprinkle of water kept them fresh for days. And were we hungry when we got home to 8:30 breakfast!

Sometimes, we packed up some lunch and went along the Battle Road to old Battle Abbey, site of the Battle of Hastings. For a whole day's outing, we would pass through the pretty little village of Westfield to Brede and the marshes, about six miles. There were shorthorn bulls turned loose there, and sometimes they chased us. They were very wild. The marshes were divided by dykes, and once I had to jump right into one, as my legs were not as long as Carina's and Mabel's. We had to keep on running because the bull looked as though he were going to jump it, too, and he was a nasty-looking customer.

Carina had a wonderful memory for the stories of books she had read. On the way home, when we were a bit foot sore, hungry, and weary, she would tell us the complete story of a book, chapter by chapter, which helped us along wonderfully. We stopped at Sedlescombe [once] and divided two penny bottles of ginger beer, and then to our dismay found we had no money. The old woman was very sniffy, as well she might be. We promised to go back and pay her, but she was very skeptical about that. A few days later we kept our promise, walking the four miles there and four back. Each village had a little shop where an old woman sold ginger beer, also raspberry, pineapple and acid drops. You got a big, cone-shaped bag for a penny.

* * * * * * * * *

A detachment of cousins came every summer. Sometimes it would be May, Ethel and Lillian, and at others, Barpsh (with that eagle eye, still) would have the younger ones in tow. It was jam-making season, and we had huge "scum teas" at the tables on the lawn. We all liked the scum off the boiling fruit better than the jam itself. Whole loaves disappeared like winking!

Preserving time called for all hands to string immense quantities of red, black and white currants (or "strig" as the country people called it), to top and tail truck basketsfull of gooseberries, and to tie down, with squares of parchment, hundred of galleypots of jam—no Mason jars then. It was Carina's job, with her unique but plain hand writing, to label these galleypots with name and date. We all congregated in the breakfast room, some of the younger maids joining us to help. The boys generally looked in for a bit, but their job was sampling the fruit, "contracting for family nuisances," or cheeking the maids to their embarassment.

Miss Hughes, of sewing fame, came to read aloud to us, which was very nice, though we were such a mixed company it was impossible to cater to all tastes. One time it was Dicken's *Nicholas Nickelby*. What the maids made out of that, it would be hard to imagine. Miss Hughes was a conscientious and simple soul, with little or no knowledge of the world. She read stolidly, and sometimes stumblingly on, not knowing what to make of the less sober scenes, where Nicholas and his rowdy friends punctuate every sentence with "Demmit! Demmit!," while carousing. "What *do* they mean, 'Demmit! Demmit!'?" she asked in a puzzled way. The boys howled with laughter, which only added to her confusion. (I was not quite sure what it meant myself.)

We bigger ones had glorious times in the beech tree, which had kindly grown branches from six inches up so that a tiny child could climb it. Of course, there were other beech trees, but everyone knew *the* beech tree in the Dell. We played house in its accommodating branches, each choosing one as a home and visiting each other. Sometimes we were monkeys, and then the tree was free to all. For the game of bats we had to hang upside down. Some of the older generation were rather shocked at this, if they happened to pass along the drive, as we wore white drawers, and little girls were not supposed to exhibit their drawers.

Once, when I was alone, my skirt caught on a knot and, struggling vainly in the air, I slowly descended as the bottom eight inches tore away from the remainder. I *was* in a fix. How to get to the house without being seen? I fled along the drive, clutching the detached piece, praying not to meet Grannie. My prayer was answered. I scuttled up the back stairs to the nursery, where good old Ellen came to the rescue, as usual. She somehow managed to make the join look like a hem (we always had deep hems to allow for growing), and if anyone noticed it, they must have thought I had suddenly taken a spurt as the skirt was one and a half inches shorter. Ellen was an angel. She constantly saved "the young ladies" (!) from all sorts of trouble with the higher authorities.[9]

Arthur had a great friend, Charlie Long, from Saxmundham, Suffolk, who was lots of fun.[10] (He was one of the original old-timers, with Arthur and Leonard, on South Pender Island, and years later we met him there again). He astonished Mabel and me by presenting us *each* with a five-pound box of cream sweets—fondants, we called them then. A sort of stock box they might have in a shop from which to sell a few ounces at a time to customers. We were accustomed to the odd penny's worth of sweets, so you can imagine what five pounds looked like to us.

If there was a good crowd of young people—Arthur, Carina, Charlie Long, Leonard, Ted and Taff Coles, May, Mabel, Ethel and myself, and possibly others, we had the most gorgeous of all games called "Bears." There would be two bears who had to keep more or less together and try to catch any of the rest of us as we ran from one "home" (summer house) to another, hundreds of yards apart. Ethel and I couldn't begin to keep up with the boys' long legs, so two of them very kindly took one each of us in tow. If a "bear" caught sight of us, we had to run like the pictures of the Red Queen, streaking along, "Faster, faster!," dragging Alice by the hand, our feet hardly touching the ground. It was wildly exciting.

The tennis courts were in great demand, but if there was a tennis party during the early years, Mabel and I were not allowed to appear. We used to peep through the bushes at the men in white flannels, and the girls in nice, long, full skirts, so suited to tennis playing! Carina was a first-class player of her day, and won local tournaments. We learnt to be pretty good ourselves, for our ages. Ellie was not at all athletic, and did not take much part in these activities, except to dispense tea and so on. She was very gentle, dutiful and sweet-tempered.

There was a succession of visitors all through the summer: Dick, Walter and Percy Spalding (Espie's brothers), Agnes, Talbot and Andrew Baines Reed, nephews of Grannie. Mabel and I were always glad when visitors of our own ages came. Among the younger ones were Josclyn, Millicent and Worsley Perkins, cousins of the Close branch of the family, I think. Josclyn [became] Dean of Westminster Abbey, and Worsley, a dramatist. [There was also] Annie Challis and Louisa, aunts of Irene Aikman; Mary and George Fleetwood, and Cousin Lucy Close, Winnie's mother. We were not allowed to call any of these by their Christian names, though many were only a few years older than Mabel. They all had to be addressed as "Cousin so and so." Even Herbert, we were supposed to call Uncle.

We had quite an adventure, of a mild nature, with Cousin Lucy one summer. A bunch of the family took a notion to walk to the evening service at the little church at Westfield. I went along, because it meant a jolly walk and staying up later than usual. When the service was over there was a raging thunderstorm in progress, and thunderstorms *are* thunderstorms in England! Cousin Lucy was petrified with fear. She absolutely refused to go home. Carina hunted round and finally found a large farmhouse in the village which offered us shelter for the night in their sitting room. And there Lucy sat, with her head covered, rocking backwards and forwards, moaning at every thunderclap. When we did not return, Grannie sent the groom with one of the carriages, but Lucy refused to budge, and would not let us go, either. I thought it was a great lark. We bedded ourselves down as best we could, and let the storm work itself out. By 4:00 a.m. the sun was shining, so leaving a note of thanks on the table, we opened the leaded glass casement window, climbed quietly out, and walked home in the fresh morning air to an early breakfast.

There were some less welcome visitors from our point of view: pet Congregational ministers or students who needed a holiday and feeding up. They certainly "fed up" on the fat of the land, and Mabel and I were "fed up" only in a different way. Toadying is a loathsome quality, and should expect no mercy, and mercy should not be strained to condone it. One of them would be called on to say grace, or offer up a thanksgiving. He would rise, pompously, lift a supplicating, benedictine hand, and pour forth oily platitudes to God, with one eye on the main chance, while breakfast got cold. With all these people to serve, meals took an unconscionable time. They ate so heartily, and in such vast quantities. For breakfast, not only eggs, bacon, kidneys, marmalade, etc., but on the sideboard, cold beef, ham and flagons of beer would be available. A cup of cocoa, a boiled egg, with bread and butter, were my portion, which was a good thing. It the meal was too prolonged, sometimes we were excused from the table. It was a great relief to leave all those stuffing people.

Someone brought the story from London that Mr. Gladstone attributed his good health and old age to the fact that he masticated each mouthful of food fifty times. This was a huge joke. Everyone began doing the same, counting aloud, one, two, three, four, munch, munch, munch, amid bursts of laughter. I started to munch and count, too, but a disapproving glance from Grannie soon put a stop to that little game.

There was one man who stood out from the rest of the visitors. He electrified the company at the table by talking of something new and strange, "The Darwinian Theory" of men being descended from monkeys, of all things. What an idea! He spoke of germs, protoplasm, evolution and other unheard of things, which were received with skepticism, incredulity or tolerance, according to the intelligence or interest of the listener. I always loved the sound of new words and listened with all my ears, but could not make much of it all, though it seemed to be very interesting. Grannie made sounds of disapproval in her throat, and tried to change the subject, while her little fair ringlets wobbled in shocked disapproval.

All these visitors had to be stowed away somewhere, but Ore Place always seemed equal to almost any amount of expansion. As a last resort, bachelors could be dumped in an overflow cottage at the far end of the quarry field, where a Bible woman lived, Mrs. Bramhall. Married couples were given the large or small spare rooms, according to their "rank." There was a truly immense, old, four-poster double bed in the large spare room, and also in the grandparents' room at the end of the passage. Each had a canopy, with a chintz valance and voluminous curtains to draw right around, with another valance round the bottom. The stuffiest things you can imagine!

Each room had a gigantic mahogany wardrobe, a dressing table, and a wash stand, with marble top, and necessary china and glass. An adjoining dressing room could be used as an extra bedroom when necessary. There was a lovely white star clematis outside, which scented the whole of the large spare room.

The small spare room was much the same, but the bed was a size smaller. The rooms known as Herbert's and Arthur's were opposite our grandparents' room. I think I am right in saying that water was only laid on in the two bathrooms, one at either end of the long corridor, in the men's cloak room off the hall, and in the scullery. The supply of hot water was very meagre, much of it being heated in huge copper kettles on the kitchen range. The family, Mabel and I included, only took a hot bath once a week, but a can of hot water was delivered to each room in the morning. Visitors were provided with a hip bath, and a large can of water. No provision was made for the servants. I expect they had to be content with what is called a body wash, or basin bath.

Most of the rooms upstairs and down were provided with a bell cord and tassel, dependent from the wall, near the ceiling, which, when given a good pull, rang a bell in the kitchen. There was a row of ten or twelve of these bells, each on a spring, connected by a wire to the cord.

CHAPTER FIVE

Growing Up: 1883 - 1887

Mabel and I had travelled a long way since our quiet life at Anerley. It might appear that life was now just one long round of pleasures, and that we had forgotten mother and all she tried to teach us and wished us to be. But it was not so. Fortunately for us, we had a great capacity for enjoyment, we were keen about things and not easily crushed, or our lives might have been a misery. Sometimes I used to cry in bed and then pretend to be asleep, with my head under the bedclothes, when Mabel came later. Or I would go off alone and lie under some pet tree or hide in the bushes and long for mother to love and help me, but I never told anyone. Mabel, though she had loved her just as much, had never been of a demonstrative nature, but I was, and mine needed caresses. For many, many years I could hardly speak of mother, and even now the feeling of loss is still poignant at times.

"You are wanted in the Library, Miss Winnie," from Emma, the under parlour maid, would mean a reproof, or a good scolding about something.

"Do not run down the corridor." "It is not ladylike to shout." "Have I no name? You should say, 'Good night, Grannie', not just 'Goodnight'," and so on.

I tremble to think what would have happened if we had dared to greet any grownup with "Hullo", or to speak of a family as "the Reeds" or "the Shaws", omitting Mr. and Mrs. For many years to come that was considered quite cheeky. I have no doubt that Grannie had good cause for annoyance. She was just doing what she considered her duty by us, with never a spark of affection. A little of that quality would have done so much with me. I was starved for love. People were very kind to us, but that is not the same thing.

Mabel and I went through a stage of squabbling. She being the [eldest], wanted to boss me in everything, and yet she told me to "have ideas of my own" and not copy her. I am sure I was often very irritating. But the trouble had no roots; it was just a weedy growth, like our long legs. It did not affect our fundamental affection for each other in the least. Friends have told us since that they were quite alarmed at the time, and thought it such a pity that two sisters left as we were should quarrel so. We were incredulous, having no idea that anyone had ever noticed it. I daresay it may have been partly due to the fact that Mabel was growing up and wanted more outlet for her strong character and energy, while I was still a child.

She and Carina used to go off together sometimes, and I felt lonely. I tried to revive Arthur's old garden down in the "one acre" as I loved flowers, and wanted to grow them myself. The gardeners gave me some roots, and I worked away there for a time, but the weeds were terrible, as it was surrounded by grassland. So after a summer or two I had to give it up.

I was shockingly untidy. The contents of my chest of drawers looked as though some mischievous puppy had been turned loose among them. My hair, of which mother had taken such care, was often a mat. It was very thick and down to my waist, and I generally only brushed the top layer. Once a week, on bath night, Ellen untangled the whole mess and nearly tore my scalp off in the process. My nails were black, and my teeth unbrushed and unattended to.

Mabel had the most appalling headaches, which completely laid her out, and it was not long before we both were suffering agonies of toothache, as the family teeth were proverbially bad. At last we were taken to a dentist, when all our teeth were full of cavities, where we suffered more torments. There was no thought of anything to dull the pain of extraction in those days. Out came the teeth with a yank; a cruel twist and a wrench and you were left in a semi-fainting condition. Exposed nerves were drilled on without a qualm for the wretched victim. Once, on hearing Mabel's suppressed cries of pain in the next room, I fainted completely, and had to be taken home in the brougham and come again another day for my turn.

Our clothes were made by a little dressmaker in Ore, about a mile away. The materials were always drab in colouring, and had no style. We were fitted in a tiny room, the window of which did not open, and the stuffiness was indescribable. "It smells of dressmakers" became a synonym for that stuffy, unwashed body smell for us. Our dresses were often made of beige because it was hard-wearing "stuff". (There was poplin, linsey-woolsey, worsted, and old ladies often wore bombazine or watered silk. Jerseys were called guernseys.)

Mabel and I had our tea in the breakfast room. In fact, that room was pretty well given over to us. Arthur sometimes paid us a visit and, on mischief bent, would push Mabel aside, saying *he* would show us how to pour tea. This he proceeded to do—with his teeth! He bit hold of the handles of the teapot and milk jug, making the most frightful mess on the tray and tablecloth in his efforts. Continued shrieks of laughter and remonstrations finally penetrated to the library. Our door slowly opened—Arthur sprang up and shot out of the window, leaving us to face Grannie's wrath. *"What* are you doing? *Who* made all this mess?" Of course, she had seen Arthur's legs, so we were not telling tales in stating the truth. "But you should not *let* him, dear! You should not *let* him!" As if we could stop a great galumph like Arthur!

Once he came in when we were doing our lessons, seized a large bottle of gum, and emptied the contents over my long hair. And gum was gum in those days, not a little sticky, watery fluid as now. Again, it was, "But you should not *let* him, dear!" when Grannie heard of it.

I was awfully fond of him, in spite of the fact that he was sometimes the cause of our getting into a row. We had spunk, and I think he liked us for it. He'd say, with mock ferocity, "Now, remember, young Winker, it's a word and a blow with yer Uncle!" We wandered about the grounds, and he gave us tests of skill and courage, with small money prizes which were very welcome. Once we went to the farm and he told me to catch a calf by the tail, mount it, and ride round the yard for 3 pence. (Mabel was getting a bit old for some of these stunts.) I caught my calf, after a wild chase through the sludge, clawed up onto its bucking back, but the ride was short-lived, as it pitched me off, head first, into the mud. I got 2 pence for making a "good try", and we went to the duck pond to clean up.

Sometimes it was a fence or thorny hedge to jump clear, or scramble up the steep barn roof and walk along the ridge pole. One time when we were doing that we heard the carriage coming, and just had time to lie flat on the far side, holding on with our eyelashes.

Every possible and impossible tree must be climbed for a penny or tuppence, according to the difficulty. There was queer old beech in the Sunset Field, called the tortoise tree (why, I don't know). It had an immense girth and then one huge limb, which

Mabel and I could barely touch, and no foothold of any sort. The rash offer of a shilling each was to be the prize for getting up onto that limb, and Arthur thought his shillings were quite safe. We said nothing, but day after day we went at that tree, jumping, clutching, scrambling, or running at it with a leap. At last we succeeded and called Arthur to witness. Sure enough, up we went, and he shelled out the prize money. It was a triumph!

The coming of autumn brought a fresh menace to our freedom. Sunday services—morning and evening for Mabel, but only once for me—with the afternoon Bible class were evidently not fulfilling their requirements, so Grannie started what she called "the willing class" in the Congregational Church schoolhouse because we were all supposed to be so *willing* to join. I wonder if any of those young people who attended were more willing than we were to give up their precious Saturday afternoon holiday. If Grannie really wanted us to "get religion", she could hardly have chosen anything more likely to make us loathe it, which we did. It made us stamping mad—in private. Experience had taught us there was no answering back to Grannie. She had succeeded there.

The afternoons began to close in, bringing the need for artificial light. Emily appeared, carrying a lighted taper, and going from room to room, setting light to the candles in the chandeliers and cut glass candle holders. If we could suddenly go back to those days, we should be astonished to think we ever lived with dim lights. Everyone was accustomed to *feeling* their way around, either with or without the light of one candle. At Grannie's end of the long corridor upstairs there was a table, on which burned a night light, so that people could just see to help themselves to one of the silver candlesticks with extinguisher. You lighted it with a wax taper from the night light, and there were snuffers to snip off the burnt part of the candle wick. Visitors in those immense bedrooms generally had two candles, which was luxury. (Turn out the electric lights and street lights now and try to dress for late dinner by the light of one candle, or perhaps two in a room 40 feet by 40 feet. "Where's that stud?", etc.)

With all the summer visitors gone, dinner and our tea were over by 5:30 p.m., so when our prep was done Grannie was very good about reading aloud to us while we sewed. Sir Walter Scott's *Ivanhoe* and other good books we all enjoyed. Sometimes we played Letter Game, but I did not like that because I could not spell. I got caught out spelling robin with two "b's" and was covered in confusion. We also played Lotto. Grannie always held the bag of figures and if, when she pulled one out it did not suit her card, she popped it back again as if she had not seen it, and picked another. Consequently, she nearly always won, but I believe the default was only semi-conscious.

There was no hot dinner on Sunday, so the maids laid the table while the family was at church, and then retired to the kitchen regions. Nothing would have been simpler than for a burglar to walk in at the French window, put all that solid silver into a sack, and walk off with it. To teach those responsible a lesson, the boys played this very trick to show how easily it could be done. Imagine the consternation when the "theft" was discovered. And the kick the boys got out of it. It was a useful lesson, and may have prevented a genuine burglary.

Some of the maids stayed for years. I don't remember Ore Place without dear old Ellen. But the cook, who had charge of most of the food, was constantly being replaced. The graft was terrible. Everything possible was sold or given to the cook's friends and relations, as the Spalding family diminished in numbers: butter, eggs, jam, fruit and vegetables. I actually saw them being handed out of the scullery door to strangers, with a furtive look or a wink, which gave the show away.

It was quite hard for Mabel and me to get a little jam with our tea, though we knew the enormous quantities that had been made. Apple jelly was the unfailing rule for dining room Sunday tea. I have never liked it since. When the cousins came we all had tea in the breakfast room, as Mabel and I always did. We had a regular joke about the jam, or lack of it. Having rung the bell several times, and been told by the good-natured Emma that cook said there was no more butter or jam (we never had both together), we balanced a damson stone on the end of our first fingers, saying, "Well, we must eat a piece of dry bread and look at a stone, then." In that house of plenty we actually had to eat dry bread. It was useless to appeal to Grannie.[1]

One cook, Mrs. Coppinger, or "Copsey," pitched head-first down the stone steps into the basement, with a huge crock of milk. The mess at the bottom would be hard to describe: two gallons of milk, in which Copsey floated—her face gashed wide open from ear to mouth—amid blood and broken crockery. She was hauled up, in a fainting condition, and put to bed in her private room. There she had to wait while a maid ran to the stables, a groom saddled a horse, rode the two miles to St. Leonards, and asked Charlie Shaw to come and sew her up. He was a surgeon and specializing in eyes. That accident necessitated several visits, and I was surprised when he gave me a copy of Kingsley's *Heroes*, dated Christmas 1891, from "Dr. Progeyes," as we called him.

* * * * * * * * *

Before going further, I must go back some years—in fact before we were born. Old Dr. Shaw had been the Spalding family doctor, much loved and respected. He lived with his wife and family in Warrior Square, St. Leonards, adjoining Hastings. Dr. Shaw had six children: Archie, Charlie, Maude (Unc's future wife), Laurie (May Spalding's future husband), Frank and Grace (who married David Capper). He often took his two eldest boys, Archie and Charlie, in his gig when he went to visit his outlying patients, and so they got to know the Spalding family of Ore Place. Dr. Shaw retired, full of years, and with the love and regret of his patients. Charlie took on his practice, later specializing in eye work. He eventually became one of Harley Street's well-known surgeons and consultants.[2]

There was an irreconcilable feud between the second Mrs. Spalding (our Grannie) and Mrs. Shaw, which was still active, even in our day. Each was of strong personality, religious, and very self-willed. They may have seen eye to eye about religion, but when they saw each other they saw red. They were like a couple of hens, each with her brood of chicks, sparring for the combat.

And now, years later, comes Charlie Shaw, daring to court Ellie Spalding, Grannie's one ewe lamb. He was forbidden to see her. Ellie was sent to friends in Ireland to forget him, and forbidden to write or receive letters from him. She obeyed, but with her mind made up. She returned, the courtship was renewed, and they were married. Probably, her one and only parental disobedience. Fortunately, it did not end like *Romeo and Juliet*, as there certainly never was a happier couple than they. Charlie finally won Grannie's good will and gratitude by making Ellie so happy, providing four grandchildren, Harold, Tom, Helen and Pat, and by being so gentle, kind and attentive, first to Grandpapa in his last illness, and then to herself. Never a word of reproach for all her un-Christian treatment of him.

Private day schools were beginning to spring up in various places, with smaller fees than the expensive finishing schools, one of which Carina had attended in Brighton.

56

It seems as if those who first made the venture began calling them colleges to differentiate them from the board schools, run by the government, which would have given the word "school" a lower class value, and from the older words "seminary" and "academy." But there was very little of the present meaning of the word "college" about them. You went to learn; that's about all. Anyway, to Wellington College Mabel went.[3]

I stayed on with the Dowdneys for a while. Miss Isley left (or was fired for incompetence), and was replaced by a far nicer and better-educated woman, of middle age, Miss Coulton. The Dowdney family was in quarantine for a time, so Miss Coulton came to teach me alone in the breakfast room at Ore Place. I liked Miss Coulton, and wanted to please her, but somehow I was always getting into difficulties with my lessons. Sometimes my head seemed to go so solid, and try as I would I just couldn't think. I know now these were the symptoms of high blood pressure, which I have "enjoyed" from time to time ever since, but such a thing had never been heard of then. It must have appeared to Miss Coulton that I was being stupid on purpose, and she threatened time and time again to go and tell Grannie. I was scared stiff, and implored her not to, with tears. Sometimes we got so wrought up we both cried. One day, no Miss Coulton appeared. Later, a boy brought a message to say she was ill, and a few days later she died "from bursting a blood vessel in her head." I was very sorry.

After Miss Coulton's death it was decided that I should go to Wellington College with Mabel. I was a bit nervous at the thought but she encouraged me by saying she knew I should do well. We had a long, two mile walk, starting along the drive, past the rhododendron bed, the old walnut tree (where we filled our pockets in the autumn, and didn't they stain our clothes), the dear beech tree, and out through Dolman's gates, down the long, very steep Ore Lane, over a rickety little bridge, and up a hill; past the Morningside College for Ladies and Kindergarten (a private house), through the cheap, mushroom growth of the new Mount Pleasant district (with the spire of "Bolty's" church pointing a shocked exclamation mark at us), past the cricket ground, and, finally, into Wellington Square.

It was Monday, and I discovered to my horror that every Monday morning the class I was in had five minutes in which to write out one of three things: all the kings and queens of England, with the dates of accession; all the weights and measures; or the multiplication table up to twelve times twelve. Whew! There was not one second to spare for thought, so I knew I was sunk the first morning. Of course, I was excused the first time, but Miss de la Mare was a great disciplinarian. As each Monday came round the new girls had to know their dates, weights, or tables as the case might be. We each had a proper school desk, and I soon settled down to work. It was here that I discovered the value of Mr. Sonnenschein's arithmetic.

Grannie was now giving me 6 pence a week (10 cents) with which I was supposed to buy my gloves, writing paper, and stamps. With a little manoevering, this small sum was fairly easily diverted into other channels as well as supplying these needs. One pair of gloves could be made to do duty for quite a long time, and cotton gloves probably only cost nine and a half pence (20 cents). I hardly ever wrote a letter, so writing paper and stamps could really be counted out.

On our way back from school, which was over at 12:30, we were desperately hungry, with dinner two miles away, up that long Ore Lane that we had run down so gaily in the morning. Passing a few shops, some of my pennies went on a bag of cherries or other fruit, which we munched after leaving the houses behind. (Fantastic that we should have to *buy* fruit!) Occasionally, it was a penn'oth of sweets to stave off the pangs of hunger, as we did not get home till 1:30 or later.

This [arrangement] was unsatisfactory, so when autumn came we stayed to dinner at school, and had a few classes in the afternoon. Wednesday and Saturday were half holidays, but we had quite a lot of prep and 7:30 was my bedtime. We were really learning something at last, and thoroughly enjoyed having girls of our own ages to lark about with in recess.

I got a "leg up" when Fraulein was teaching us to sing "Die Lorelie." *"Ich weiz nicht was soll es bedeuten, das ich so traurig bin."* She turned sharply round, saying, "Who spake German? You, Vinnie? *Zer gut!"* (The influence of the aunts.) A little praise always helped me along.

Arthur and Charlie Long got us into hot water once by writing "Remarks" in a mock grandiose style in our exercise books, purporting to be by an examiner, and signed with a fictitious name. Miss de la Mare wrote to Grannie about it, and we got the blame, as usual, but I don't think the boys meant to get us into trouble. It was just another case of "You should not let them, dear!" (We did not have marks, which I think was a very good thing. It saved lots of heart burning.)

* * * * * * * * * *

Summer came again. There were picnics to Fairlight Glen, with its dripping well, a real beauty spot which was already spoilt by "trippers" and rowdy parties of 'Arrys and 'Arriets swilling ginger beer out of stone bottles; young men and women (or "gals") exchanging hats, which was a favourite joke, cracking cockney jokes with bursts of raucous laughter, or singing "Sweet dreamland fices, passin' to an' frow," or "In the gloamin', O me darlin'." They were just having a good time in their own way, but to us, with our bringing up, they only appeared vulgar.[4]

Then there was Pett Level, a long, low, sandy beach, beyond the reach or desire of trippers. Some of the picnics there were quite large when there were visitors at Ore Place. Huge hampers of lunch were packed up in the kitchen, and we all bundled into the wagonette, a four-wheeled, open sort of affair, with long seats, facing each other, and a door at the end. You climbed up into it by several steps, which were shut up when all were in. The ticklish point was, which one of us younger ones would have the joy of sitting on the box seat, between Rowse and a passenger, when the cousins were there. But, of course, we had got beyond the stage of squabbling for things. It was a case of give in, with as good a grace as possible.

Occasionally, we made a longer expedition in the wagonette to Winchelsea or Rye, both former seaport towns, but now left high and dry by the sea, which was five miles away in places, with cattle feeding on grassland that used to be under the sea. Both were delightful little, old-world places, sleeping peacefully. Rye was perched on a former sea cliff, with narrow, cobbled streets crawling up its side; a church and quaint old cottages propping each other up, probably not changed in a hundred years or more. Herstmonceaux Castle, built of beautifully mellowed red brick, is the best preserved of the old Norman remains. [It is] a charming place, with drawbridge and lilied moat.

Ellie was married to Charlie Shaw on September 2, 1884. After the service there was a gigantic picnic to Bodiam Castle, a splendid old Norman ruin on the Downs.[5] The wedding was held in the little village church, St. Helen's, just outside the grounds of Ore Place. Grannie went to the service, but history does not relate what her feelings can have been to have her only daughter married in a Church of England. Carina was bridesmaid, and Laurie, Charlie's brother, made a very blinking best man (blinking eyelids, not a "blinkin' best man"). He was probably thinking of the time when he hoped to be leading May Spalding to the altar.

The preparations [for the wedding picnic at Bodiam Castle] must have kept the maids busy for a week, though I daresay a lot of food came ready-cooked from Addison's and other shops in Hastings. Every available conveyance was pressed into service, and filled with happy, laughing, joking people. May and Mabel were going but, alas, there was no room for Ethel and me. As the last wagonette drove off, we two rushed down the drive after them, waving a half-excited, half-doleful farewell. But what's this? "Ho! Stop! Wait a moment. Can't we find room for these two kids?" The wagonette paused, willing hands grabbed us, just as we were, and wedged us in, though they were already packed like sardines. It was one of the thrills of a lifetime.

Charlie had built such a pretty Elizabethan house in St. Leonards, so different from the frousty old Victorian houses around it. It was suitably called "the Gables," and was prepared with large day and night nurseries. Charlie was always so dapper and smiling that some people looked on him as a bit of a fop, but one can't tell by exteriors. He had one of the kindest hearts, was equally kind and generous to poor and rich alike, and never bore anyone a grudge. He had a telephone installed in his house; the first I had ever seen. It was a large, clumsy contraption, with a receiver for each ear. It was almost a religious rite to call or receive a message, with clicks and bells ringing, and plenty of "Are you there?" I was fascinated to watch Ellie battle with it, when Charlie was out. She had a special voice and face for the ceremony.

Months passed. One evening I went into the old nursery at Ore Place and discovered dear old Ellen trimming a baby's cradle in blue and white. She was very pink and flustered at being caught red-handed. I asked who it was for, but she only murmered, "You must wait and see." I remembered having seen another being made, and later Auntie Florrie had had a baby.

One day the brougham fetched Mabel and me from Wellington College, and then we drove on and picked up Carina at "The Gables." She came out saying the enigmatic word, "boy" to Mabel, and they both seemed very excited. Aunt Ellie had a baby boy, Harold, now professor of Astronomy at Johannesburg, South Africa. The year was 1885.

I venture to say that Arthur was the first one in our family to call children "kids", and get away with it. It was an entirely new expression, and the older generation shrugged their shoulders at it, as much as to say, "What is the world coming to?" But you might call a little child a "lamb".

In 1886 Tom [Shaw] appeared, though it had still been kept a secret. I can see Harold toddling round the drawing room and Grandpapa patting him with his velvet glove, so lovingly, and saying, "So they call you a kid, do they?", chuckling at his own daring.

Carina was taking cookery classes in Hastings in preparation for being married. Sad to say, he jilted her (or perhaps was not worthy of her), but she bore this blow to her future freedom with her usual fortitude.

I must skim over the preparations for, and departure of Arthur for America. Grannie provided him with enough supplies to make several Arctic expeditions; also tools and dangerous-looking bowie knives to stand off the raids of hostile Indians. So little was known of the western continent then. We did not even differentiate between Canada and the United States. The whole thing was just called "America". Arthur went to Fresno and Denver, where he was not even "held up", and came home in about a year, probably a good deal wiser. He returned later to [British Columbia, Canada].

Mabel and I had been to an occasional entertainment in Hastings. The hand bell ringers gave a wonderful performance of the art. But what was far more interesting (though we did not realize it at the time) was a demonstration by a young man named Thomas Edison of a machine he had invented which played music. He stood on a little platform in a small entertainment hall, and showed us his box, with a sort of horn sticking out of it. He put a hard, black wax disc in the box, turned the handle, and lo and behold it played a tune. The disc (or records as we call them now) would only play once, so he broke it up and gave a few people in the audience a piece. My squirrel nature secured one of them, which I treasured for many years. Mr. Edison called the box a graph-o-phone (written sound) or phone-graph (sound writing). We know it as the gramophone.[6]

For Queen Victoria's Golden Jubilee Celebrations, May 24, 1887, we got a half holiday, and Miss de la Mare took the school along the Esplanade to see the decorations.

The family at Ore Place generally went abroad every year, but they never took Mabel and me. What a chance for education missed! Lausanne, Berne, Geneva, the Matterhorn, and Grindelwald were magic words and I, for one, longed to know what happened there. The family just disappeared into space, to these mysterious places, which always remained just names. We had never seen a mountain, much less a snow mountain, and there were no illustrated papers or picture postcards to give children an idea of unknown parts of the world.[7]

Someone generally brought us back a souvenir: a Berne bear carved in native wood, or a wee Swiss cottage in a box. One of my greatest treasures was a tiny tumbler in a screw-topped, polished maple case, from Grindelwald.

We were rarely allowed to visit from home. Aunts and friends, knowing how particular mother had always been, did what they could on our behalf, but interference would not have been tolerated. I feel sure there must have been invitations of which we heard nothing, but when the family migrated abroad we got our chance, and went to stay with Auntie Emma, Auntie Maude, or the Gladstone family.[8]

The Gladstone family lived in a large house in Pembridge Square, Bayswater, London. They were a clever family. Mr. Gladstone was a professor of science, a widower, and a friend of Faraday. There were four daughters [Flo, Beta, Bella and May]. By a second wife there was another daughter, Margaret, who was a little older than Mabel when we used to stay there. She was the future Mrs. Ramsay MacDonald, Prime Minister of England, and mother of Malcolm, the present Colonial Secretary.

Auntie Emma always sent us a money order for our birthdays; Auntie Maude taught me to use a thimble by offering to give me a silver one. And so on. Each did her helpful bit. We were "like a couple of untamed ponies," as [a friend] said to Mabel not long ago, while talking over old times. We had to drag ourselves up by the "trial and error" method and, were, I think, generally very grateful to those who tried to help us along.

When at last we went to Danesfield, I daresay Auntie Emma was a bit shocked to see what harum-scarum girls we had become. Though perhaps in fairness to ourselves, I may add that we each still had a conscience, and what it implies. Anyway, she really loved us for mother's sake, and, I hope for our own, too. We had a grand time there. Auntie was always so understanding and laughed over our youthful enthusiasm for everything. She led such a comfortable, yet secluded life that I think we added a little spice to it, and reminded her of mother—her first cousin and best friend.

We loved Aunt Amelia, too, but she belonged to the older generation, and sometimes thought Auntie spoilt us, I think.[9] She showed me how to put my hand behind the candles attached to the piano so that the grease would not blow onto the polished wood. She wore a "chatelaine," a sort of open, flatpocket, hanging by her side, with keys, scissors, etc., suspended.

There was part of an old canal at the end of their garden—a lovely wild spot where water rats, moor hens, and kingfishers in their dazzling blue coats were still to be seen. Crossing a little bridge, Auntie would say, "Now, chinnoes (using the old word), what's the latest nonsense?" So we sang:

Tis perfectly true, a revolt in the zoo,
Has just taken place, on my word.
The hip-po-pot-a-mus has gone off in a bus
And is flying away like a bird.
The lion and tiger are off to the Niger
The unicorn's collared the crown.
The ant-eater, I find, is staying behind,
And leading a life about town.

From Arthur we learned:

Dinky, dinky Derby ram, dinky, dinky day.
It was the finest ram, sir
That ever was fed upon hay.
They say it weighed a ton, sir,
The most remarkable ram,
But when they cut its throat, sir,
They heard it shout out _____![10]

Auntie loved these absurd songs.

Of course we went to our dear old friend the Crystal Palace, driving up to the front entrance in state with the carriage and pair, Cedric and Rupert. We roamed delightedly about, visiting favourite places.

We liked to stay with Auntie Maude, too. She was so kind, and Unc such fun. He was a great cook, and loved to fix up tasty little dishes of Welsh rarebit or omelettes in his chafing dish, as he had done at Bromley. They called their house Asgard, which, being interpreted from Norse mythology, means, "The Home of the Gods." Just like Unc!

Mabel and I were very fond of children, and now there were three to play with in their sunny nursery: Lauris, Dorothea (from Unc's pet *Middlemarch*) and Valentine. We played "Dance, Thumbman, dance," and all the dear old games of our own childhood.

Unc sported a "buttons" now, a small boy of twelve to answer the door, clean the knives, polish up the handle of the big front door, and make himself generally useful. In the afternoon he put on his green uniform, with the row of brass buttons—hence the name. His mother was a charwoman and glad to have him kept off the streets. His father went to sea on one of the trading vessels, and brought back exciting things like jars of ginger, or tamarinds in syrup from the West Indies.

Bryant and May's Match Works were near by, in Turnham Green. A large part of match making was still done by hand, and we used to watch the children crowding into the building to do their job of dipping match heads. There was a lot of child labour still and, I am sorry to say, we took it for granted. It might have been a different story if *we* had been the children.[11]

Towards the end of the summer holidays [while I stayed at Asgard], I took it into my head to walk over to Ealing and surprise the cousins. It was quite a walk—through Acton, and finishing with the long, dull Uxbridge Road, which led past Ealing Common to the North Common Road.

61

I always had a good bump of locality, even as a little child, so found my way easily. When I got there, hot and dusty, the whole family was out, except Spanny. We had a good hug, and then waltzed round the kitchen till she sank, laughing and exhausted, into a chair, clutching at her ill-fitting false teeth with one hand, and her beating heart with the other.

"Oh! Winker darlin', aint yer just a terror!," she exclaimed when she found breath. Then, knowing what I liked, she got out one of her lovely Suffolk harvest cakes— an immense round dough bun, too delicious for words. And after that, she cut the whole bottom off a two pound loaf of Neville's bread, the size of a dinner plate, spread it with beef dripping, and with arms akimbo, watched me munch it. This time, I *was* a "caution!"

I could not wait for the cousins, so we kissed goodbye, and away I went. What a character she was.

One night, Aunti Maude came to say goodnight, and gently told me that Mabel and I were not going back to Wellington College. I was devastated, and wept bitterly. Oh, these changes!

It turned out that Miss de la Mare had been made principal of a new school at Folkestone, Kent, called Kent College for Girls, and we were to go there. These decisions were made, and there was no questioning or discussing them for us. We might just a well have been cattle. Grandpapa was now very old and frail, and bed-ridden, I think, so it would be better for us to be out of the way.

CHAPTER SIX

Kent College for Girls, Folkestone 1887 - 1889

We started off in clean frocks, our voluminous pockets bulging with ripe pears, kindly donated by Emily from the store cupboard. At Ashford Junction we had to change, and discovered to our horror that we had sat on the pears, and our frocks were hopelessly stained. A bus met us at Shornecliffe Station, outside Folkestone, and we drove to the school, full of new enthusiasm. It was a fine, new, red brick building of three storeys, high up on the cliffs, on the Bouverie Road. The now well-known Promenade ,"The Lees", ran along the top of the cliffs behind us. The school stood on about an acre of uncultivated land, and the surrounding country was very bleak; hardly a house in sight, and future roads just indicated.[1]

There were only two boarders beside ourselves: Fanny Snow, a parson's daughter, and Lilian Lyle, a rather heavy but very good-natured girl, about my age, whose parents had independent means. She had unlimited pocket money but little chance to spend it. It was not long before more girls came, both boarders and day girls.

Miss de la Mare had secured the two chief staff positions for friends from the Channel Islands: Miss LeSueur, for English, who made history dry as dust—just facts and dates; Miss Voisin, a mathematical genius, who could not impart her knowledge to her pupils, or understand their difficulties because it was all as plain as daylight to her. Miss Julia Atwater, a licentiate of the Royal College of Music, was to teach music and singing. We all loved her at once. She was barely twenty-one, and just a girl like ourselves, but with authority. Miss Smithson was the matron, a martyr to asthma. When she had a bad attack you could hear her screaming gasps for breath all over the school. It was terrible.

We had an excellent drawing master, Mr. Alfred East, who came over from Dover once a week and later became an R.A. (Royal Academician), so we were fortunate. One of the unfurnished dormitories was equipped as a studio, with easels and a few plaster models. We drew conventional rural scenes of thatched cottages and trees, with stubs of charcoal, and Mr. East taught us perspective with books set in "himpossible persitions" (*Punch*). I loved drawing and often made maps and physiological diagrams for fun in my spare time. I longed to go to the South Kensington School of Art, or to the one in Hastings, and even ventured to say so to Grannie, but the idea was received in cold silence.

There were cubicles for the older girls, and those who could afford them. I slept in a dormitory with three others. There were also sound-proof cubicles for practicing music, which were the very latest thing. Because there were only a few girls, I secured a desk by a window. When lessons were dry, I drew the beautiful Downs, with their lights and shadows. Miss de la Mare gave us a thorough grounding in physiology, which Mabel and I loved, and for which we have been thankful. She was a good teacher.

Class distinction was strong in those days. It would be hard to explain without appearing snobbish what it meant to Mabel and me to be sent to boarding school with a lot of shopkeepers' daughters. It was not that we considered ourselves superior in any way, but it was an indignity because the classes did not mix on equal terms. These girls had very little, if any, cultural background. Ours had certainly been shockingly neglected since mother's death, but the seeds of good taste and moral courage, which she had sown, were there, and we had the added help of inheritance. Consequently, it seemed natural that we—Mabel in particular, being older—should take the lead, and try and set the standard for the school life and activities. I say this without conceit; and at the time had no thought that it was so. (It just goes to show how different conditions are now.)[2]

A few of us banded together to exclude the girls who wanted to be sentimental and talk about young men and love letters they received. Some of the girls were like a lot of sheep, afraid to have an independent thought. The two "Oakey's Knife Polish" sisters, Kathleen and Evelyn, were very nice girls, and joined our anti-sentimental league at once.

There was a little girl of about nine, Marion Jay, whose whole soul was in the violin. She was a genius, and you could see her thoughts were far away when ordinary lessons were going on. A small day girl might have just stepped right out of one of Phil May's pictures in *Punch*. She was one item in the large family of the butcher of Hythe. Her mother had just received the Queen's bounty for triplets, which added to the family. Another girl had twice been expelled from former schools, and broke all the present rules with bravado. We were not allowed to use the front stairs, except on special occasions, so she gloried in rushing up or down without being caught, if opportunity offered.—So you see, we were a mixed crowd.

Shorncliffe was a large military base, with permanent buildings, and a tent encampment for hundreds of red-coated soldiers. Miss de la Mare was a great one for long walks, sometimes taking the girls herself. Once, on our way home, she found to her dismay that she had led us right into this camp, with coatless soldiers on every side, polishing brass buttons, or spitting on their boots to make them take a shine. Of course they started to crack jokes about this crocodile of schoolgirls in their midst. There was no turning back, so Miss de la Mare, scarlet in the face and perspiring, hurried us along, saying excitedly, "Look neither to the right hand, nor to the left, girls. Keep right on!" What she thought either we or the soldiers were going to do, I don't know.

We had a real sergeant from Shorncliffe—not young and handsome, you may be sure—to teach us drill, which was an excellent thing. We marched and marched, till we carried ourselves like ramrods, with an easy rhythm, which was aided by the musical drill and marching Julia Attwater gave us. (Julia Attwater was awfully nice to the boarders. She used to play to us during her own free time in the evening, and Mabel and I heard many an old favourite from Mr. Kennedy's day.)

A place for everything, and everything in its place, or there was trouble! Our chests of drawers and desks were inspected regularly. I learned to be tidy at last, for which I have always been most grateful. Miss de la Mare instituted a "fine drawer" for articles found left about. Every Saturday morning out came this drawer and we had to pay 6 pence (12 cents) to regain anything, even if it was only a penny pencil. There was no escape, as *everything* had to be marked with our names. That made us careful.

Once a year the members of the Board of Directors came to the school, which was quite an event. There were the usual recitations, class singing, and drill. The girls also gave a demonstration of fire drill, which was really rather a farce, because only four of us dared to climb out of the third floor windows and slide down a rope without any knots, to a very precarious safety. It did not seem to dawn on the authorities that in case of a real fire the rest of the girls might all be burnt, as there were no other means of escape.

The school gave a benefit performance at Hythe in aid of the Seamen's Institute. We sang "The Spider and the Fly" and "The British Lion", which received a great applause. A little girl of five sang a solo, quite unabashed, before the large audience. You could have heard a pin drop. Another child, disguised with cap, apron and broom, and holding a doll, recited, "I'm a busy little mother, keeping house from day to day; you will never find another half so bright or half so gay." Lily Hart was not a born actress but the seamen loved these simple things, which reminded them of their homes, so everything was applauded manfully.

Four of us older ones played a double duet on two pianos, "Alessandro Stradella," by the English composer Sterndale Bennett, and Marion Jay gave a violin solo. Julia Attwater had got up the whole thing, single-handed, and it was such a success that she was asked to repeat the performance in the large concert hall in Folkestone.

(In view of the present conditions of Europe, with wars and rumours of war, I will quote "The British Lion," who, I am afraid, has lost some of his former prestige.)

The British Lion

Oh, the British Lion is a noble scion,
And proud in his conscious might.
The terror of those he has made his foes,
For he ever defends the Right.
And yet so mild, that a timid child
May approach him and need not quail,
And may pat him on the crown,
And stroke him down,
But beware how you tread on his tail.

His foes at best, are knaves confessed,
Whose malice from envy springs.
And it oft betides his giant sides
They pierce with their gnat-like stings.
But he merely yawns
For the thought ne-er dawns
Such pigmies to assail;
Till grown more bold
His strength to behold
They venture to tread on his tail.

Then up he bounds, and his roar resounds
As he lashes each foaming side.
His warlike breath, hurls fire and death,
And scatters them far and wide.
And great and small, down, down they fall
'Neath the breath of his iron hail,
And repent to their cost
When all is lost—
That they trod on the lion's tale.

(It may be a different tale this time!)

65

Power did not suite Miss de la Mare. She became very autocratic as time went on, and seemed to want to rule by fear. She got the idea that Julia Attwater was in league with the girls against her, and stopped our lovely musical evenings. She also put the cook-housekeeper onto spying on the girls; we caught her listening behind the door.

The food got worse and worse. The first clash came when Mabel and I went to Miss de la Mare and complained that there was no butter on the bread. So each girl was given a minute square of butter to spread for herself, enough to scrape over one slice. As we had nothing *but* bread and butter for supper, we needed five or six slices each. Some of us began to call the potatoe pie "horse pie," the scraps of meat were so tough, secretly hoping Miss de la Mare would hear. We were ravenous all the time. Lilian Lyle joined us in some of these rebellions; she had some spunk, and wasn't afraid because her parents had money. Possibly Miss de la Mare was beginning to find these two girls from Ore Place rather "tough chewing," like the meat she provided for dinner.

We were frequently in her bad books. She wanted a culprit to weep and beg her forgiveness, as some girls did, and then she was all smiles. I laugh still when I remember how Mabel stood up to her. "Speak to me in my private library, Miss Higgs," and Mabel would stalk along the passage, with her head in the air (sometimes I was with her), fold her hands and stare abstractedly out of the window while Miss de la Mare delivered her tirade about some triviality. Then she quietly said, "Oh," and walked out of the room.

We left Miss de la Mare purple with rage, but we did not mind because she had lost the respect of most of the boarders. As time went on, the "fat was often in the fire." What reports she wrote home, I don't know, but feel sure she dare not face Grannie with failure to crush us into subordination.

To try and discredit Mabel before the boarders and some of the teachers, Miss de la Mare called us into a classroom one evening. She started a long harangue on "what an evil influence Miss Mabel Higgs had on us," and so on. I was wild, and looked round to see who would stick up for Mabel. No one moved an eyelash. That was too much! "Don't you dare speak about my sister like that, Miss de la Mare," I blazed at her.

Her jaw dropped, and we glared at one another. There were a few moments of awed silence, then she turned and stalked out of the room without a single word. The next morning I was sure there would be the usual call, "Speak to me in my private library," but to my astonishment, nothing happened. Miss de la Mare never referred to the episode. A pat on the back, and "Well done, little sister," was Julia's comment when she heard of it.

Julia, Mabel and I planned wonderful castles in the air. Julia genuinely intended to start a private school in the north of England. Mabel, having trained as a hospital nurse at Guy's, was to be the matron and teach physiology. I was to go to the South Kensington [Royal College] of Art, and then teach drawing in Julia's school. It really seemed as if we might make it come true, but like many castles in the air, it faded away.

There were the usual holidays when we all packed up and went home, but Mabel and I did much the same things as I have already described. One Christmas, May Gladstone was staying at Ore Place, and brought a book by a new author, Rider Haggard, called *King Solomon's Mines*, which she and Carina took turns in reading aloud in the evening. We had never heard anything half so thrilling, and I did not know how to tear chapter myself away when bedtime came at 7:30, but I was never allowed one minute's grace. I have the feeling now of watching the hands of the ornamental clock on that lovely mantelpiece, creeping nearer and nearer to the fatal half hour chime. But the others were very good about telling me the parts I missed.

For half-term holidays in the summer, one of the teachers took the boarders on some lovely excursion, and how we hoped it would be Julia. Almost any fine Saturday afternoon we could go away up over the Downs, or to Caesar's Camp, but it was a whole day's expedition to go to the Warren by rail, and you flagged the train to stop for the return journey. There was no station. The Warren was a wild rift in the chalk cliffs, a landslide of long ago, where nightingales sang and nested, undisturbed by the ordinary tripper.

It was an almost impossible and dangerous scramble down to the beach, so we made a lovely picnic ground among the bracken fern which, in England, is not looked on as a weed. There is an anonymous little poem which describes the place beautifully:

Wind in the tree tops, wave on the sand
You whisper of things I can understand.
Things remembered and things forgot—
For you have knowledge and I have not.
Long is the way and over long,
To where the sea chants evensong;
Yet echoes of waves forever still
Come to my ears in the inland hill.
And here where the rock is worn away
Is a shell from the seas of yesterday.
When the cliff arose and the waters fled.
Forgotten sea, forgotten waves,
The cliff is a tombstone over their graves.
And the land wind whispering through the trees
Speaks with the voices of vanished seas.

These lines are so true of the Downs behind Folkestone, too, where we used to find shells.

We went so seldom into Folkestone, that I don't remember the town itself. But I do remember one occasion when the boarders were taken to the large concert hall to hear a little boy prodigy play the piano. His name was Josef Hofmann, ten years old. He came onto that large platform quite solemnly, dressed in a black velveteen suit, with a large, white, turndown lace collar. He played, amongst other things, Mendelssohn's "Capriccioso," and his hands were so small that he had to use one finger of each hand for the well-known octave passages, and he could not reach the pedals.[3]

* * * * * * * * * *

During one of the earlier terms at Kent College, 1887, the same year that we heard little Josef, we had a letter from home to say that Grandpapa had died and we were to go back at once. When Mabel and I arrived there was a black hush over everything, and the few people around were talking in whispers. Maids were telling, in awestruck voices, about a large picture that had fallen off the wall a few days before—a sure sign that the Master was going to die. (I have an idea that he would have died, anyway, but there you are.) The Mistress was shut in the library, with Carina going in to see her occasionally.[4]

Mabel and I were hurried into Ore, to be fitted for black dresses of some very thin, cheap material, unsuitable for schoolgirls. Those were the days when people draped themselves in masses of black crepe, and heavy mourning. Even children were put into black frocks and crepe arm bands.

The funeral was quite simple, as Grandpapa would have wished. After a service in the drawing room, the coffin was carried on the shoulders of some of the household retainers, who considered it an honour to carry the Master to his last resting place. The sons and some of the family were there. In slow procession we walked along the familiar drive, two and two, followed by the maids and gardeners, to the cemetery just over the hill. It was a touching sight to see some of the older ones rubbing their eyes with their well-worn caps. Little groups of villagers, with their children, stood sadly at the roadside. Grandpapa was dearly loved by all. "He had an eye that winces at false work, and loves the true." And so that good old man passed into history.

Mabel and I went back to school, where we seemed to spend the rest of the term mending our black dresses, which tore if you looked at them. Miss Smithson took pity on us and helped darn the everlasting slits.

Grannie took a furnished house on The Marina, Hastings, with Carina, and when we came home for the holidays we went there, too. We slept in an immense double bed together, but I am afraid I did most of the sleeping as Mabel did not sleep well with anyone. One night we were rolling about in the bedclothes when she evidently thought I was old enough, and ought to know something about life and its production. She tried to tell me, but it all ran off me like water off a duck's back. I was just sixteen. There never was a bigger simpleton than I in such matters. I was a "dumb egg" as we should say now.

* * * * * * * * *

Leonard was now learning farming somewhere near Andover in Hampshire. To put a long story short, crossing a stile one day he passed a bewitchingly pretty girl: dark brown hair, sparkling brown eyes, and a complexion of cream and roses. It was a case of love at first sight. Leonard let no grass grow under his feet till he had discovered that this little rose was Emmie Batsford, from the picturesque village of St. Mary Bourne. They "walked out" together on Sundays, as is the custom of the country, and it was not long before they were married, in 1888 I think. Mabel and I were still at boarding school in Folkestone, so we could not go to the wedding.

Andover was on the London and Southwestern Railway, beyond Basingstoke. There was an exceptionally long viaduct, which the country folk called the "fire-dox"— one of these "newfangled words". It carried the trains over a road which meandered through beautiful rolling hills and occasional woods. As it wound its pleasant way along this countryside, with human touch it planted little groups of thatched cottages, or a blacksmith's shop, haphazard, by the way, which sat down contentedly to enjoy the quiet life and await the coming of a less peaceful era.

St. Mary Bourne was one of these, though larger than some. It boasted a church, saddler, and Mr. Batsford, known as "the Master", who owned a pretty, creeper-grown house and carpenter's shop on the little River Bourne. There he lived with his wife and three girls: Maude, Miriam and Emmie. Cottages of every description sidled along the main road, or were crowded off at odd angles, peeping into back gardens or pigpens. Geese puddled around, and everyone knew everyone else and their business.

The Master was a tall, fine-looking man, with bushy eyebrows, good features and a long, grey beard. He would have made a typical portrait for one of the Apostles. He had a gruesome story connected with that beard. Turning his lathe one day, it caught in the wheel and in the twinkling of an eye half his beard was torn out by the roots. You didn't call a doctor for a little trifle like that. In fact, I don't think there was a doctor to call. He ran to the woodshed and plastered the raw, bleeding surface with dust-coated cobwebs, torn from the roof. He told me cobwebs were a fine thing to stop bleeding. In fact, while I was there he cut his hand quite badly and applied the same remedy. We knew nothing of germs in those days, but I had an idea it was not a very healthy thing to do. Why he did not die of blood poisoning I don't know. It must have been a case of "kill or cure".

It was splendid to drive along the winding dirt road in a gig behind a stout cob, through the narrowing valley, with grazing cattle on the hillsides, rabbits with flashing white tails, skuttling about their warrens, and sometimes a copse, carpeted with snowdrops in the spring. At last there came into view a distant hill, locally known as "Gallus Hill", on the top of which was silhouetted the remains of an old gallows. Then one knew that the charming little hamlet of Netherton was very near, where Leonard had leased a small farm and quaint, old-fashioned, two-storey cottage, with tiny, latticed casement windows.—Perhaps more picturesque than convenient, but Mabel and I thought it enchanting. [We] spent a never-to-be forgotten time there soon after Leonard was married.

The first morning of our visit I woke to a croaking voice saying, "You're a devil, you're a devil, you're a devil," all in one spurt of words. I sprang out of bed and peeped out of the tiny casement to see our wicked old Grip, with an innocent eye, sitting on a branch of an apple tree just outside. It was a joyful surprise! He had gone to bed when we arrived the evening before, so Leonard had purposefully refrained from telling us he had brought Grip from Red Lion Court. We were delighted to see him after ten years. Whether he recognized our stocking-clad legs as the juicy morsels he used to peck in earlier days, it would be hard to say. He spent his days in the apple trees, swearing the blue ruin, or playing mischievous pranks, which finally led to his downfall.

As Aunt Tabitha remarked in *Hookeybeak, the Raven,* "Your tricks will bring you grief, my friend, before you are aware!" Grip discovered a collection of match boxes—and made a meal of the poisonous heads. The next morning, Leonard found him stiff and cold on the floor. There was great mourning in the family.

Emmie was a little shy of us at first, but it soon wore off. She made the most delicious bread, and churned butter from their own cow's cream in one of the old-fashioned plunger churns. We explored the countryside, Leonard with his gun, ready for the odd rabbit, which made a good stew. Every little handful of scrub seemed to conceal a hare, which loped off across the otherwise open field with Spot in frenzied pursuit, as if they knew they were "out of season." Sometimes we met the two sons of the family who lived in the "big house" out shooting, too. They were known as Allan B. Nosey, and Will'm B. Nosey on account of the size of that feature, and partly because they were a bit nose-in-the air to the villagers.

* * * * * * * * *

Our life at Kent College came to an end with the death of Grannie, from a lingering cancer, in the fall of 1888. Her determination and spartan spirit carried her through months of torment, without complaint. She still took the head of the table and poured the coffee, till Charlie Shaw insisted on her giving in at last and going to bed till the end came.[5]

No one in the family needed, or could afford the upkeep of Ore Place, so the contents were divided among the family, or sold. Ellie had the dear chimes clock, I know. When we went home for the last time, we had the miserable task of going through our few possessions. I remember sitting on our bedroom floor, holding a little wicker doll's pram, which I had treasured since I was one year old. How to part with it?

69

Mabel said, "You can't play with tiny dolls at sixteen! Throw it away!" It was put on the heap of things we were not taking with us, and I looked away. The stuffed kingfisher and little poquatsa owl which Arthur had sent us from America were moth-eaten and had to go, too. We packed our few books, work boxes and desks (a kind you never see, now).

I have heard since that the turning out, sorting, and distributing of the accumulation of nearly thirty years was a herculean labour, and we never knew what became of Grandpapa's valuable library of books, or the organ. That beautiful place was eventually bought by some Jesuits, and turned into a Jesuit College. A huge, ugly brick wing was built onto it, where the darling red squirrels used to dash out from their fir trees to pick up cones. It is fortunate Grandpapa did not know what became of his home, which he loved so dearly.[6]

Once, when Mabel was staying with Ellie at The Gables, she walked up to Ore Place and boldly marched right up to the house and looked around, but a Brother soon asked her to leave. I would rather continue to think of it as I knew it.

Ore Place, showing the two additions built in 1906.
The entire building has been demolished. Photo courtesy S.M.A. Fathers

The Howard Spalding household. Back, l to r, Hilda, Winifred, Mabel and Dorothy. Front, l to r, Lilian, May, Muriel, Aunt Lizzie, Margaret and Ethel

CHAPTER SEVEN

Ealing - 1889

And so we were drift and homeless again. Mabel would be twenty on March 5th, 1889, and I had my seventeenth birthday the 20th of December previously, when Uncle Howard and the Aunts of Ealing offered us a home there. I suppose there must have been a good deal of consultation among the family before this solution was decided on. It certainly was noble to take in two more girls, where there were already seven: May, Ethel, Lilian, Margaret, Hilda, Dorothy and Muriel.

* * * * * * * * * *

Well, eighteen months have gone by since I wrote the last sentence. It is now November 1939. A long spell of illness, followed by the continual threat of war, and finally war itself, seem to have drained me dry. So far, "all is fairly quiet on the Western Front." Owing to a present temporary illness, and for the lack of physical exercise, I will dip into the well of memory again, and see what comes up.

* * * * * * * * * *

St. George's, the large brick house where the Howard Spalding family lived, faced south onto the North Common Road and Ealing Common, so it was a fine, sunny situation, and they had a good garden. We certainly were a crowd: Uncle Howard, Aunties Marnie and Lizzie, and nine girls between the ages of seven and twenty, Old Barpsh in the nursery or play room, and Spanny and her niece "little Mary". So there you have us: fourteen females and one lone male!

Uncle Howard had a large bedroom (where he kept his thirteen pairs of walking shoes, all alike, much to our amusement), to which he could retire if he felt too overwhelmed. But he had that rare gift of being able to concentrate on deep reading with bedlam all around him. He was a martyr to insomnia, and used to take long walks in the middle of the night.

We girls were not allowed in the drawing room, except on "occasions". The Aunts had to have breathing space somewhere. We were full of high spirits and there was very little quarreling. There did not seem to be time to quarrel, we had such fun. In the winter time some of us had to skip in the hall for five minutes before breakfast to work off a little superfluous energy and make us warm.

Both Aunts were artistic and cultivated. Auntie Marnie had a friend, Alice Mold, who was a frequent visitor to the house. They taught Art in London, going up by the day. When Mabel and I had been at Ealing about a year, it was decided that Auntie and Alice should live in London and continue their teaching, leaving Auntie Lizzie in sole control at Ealing.

Auntie Lizzie sat at the head of the table. She was a marvel of tact in managing such a herd of high-spirited girls, so clever at devising means of keeping us within reasonable bounds at meal times without recourse to the usual "don't do this or that." She instituted guessing games or making rhymes, at which we took turns round the table—anything to keep us from all talking at once.

The beautiful old carved chairs had high backs, but we were never allowed to lean back in a chair. It was not the custom for girls to do that; it was considered lazy and ill-mannered. So we had to pretend there were nails sticking out. Instead of saying, "Don't lean back," Auntie would suddenly say, "Nails!", and everyone sat bolt upright, conscious that someone had defaulted.

We had dinner in the middle of the day, so at tea (or supper as it really was), there was just plenty of lovely bread and good gravy dripping, or bread and demerara sugar, with an occasional harvest cake of Spanny's make. The grownups had something a little extra: some fish or eggs. Occasionally, Antie said, "All girls over—(pause)—eighteen may have some fish." Oh, lucky ones! Or perhaps it would be "All those over—sixteen—may have two sardines." There was a sigh of expectation among us to see who would be included in these extras.

Another game was to earn the money for our supper by running errands during the day, but May and Mabel were too old for this, and Do and Muriel too young, I think. There was great competition as the time drew near, when someone discovered she had not enough to "pay for" some harvest cake, or a half penny bun which were Saturday treats. "May I go and fetch your knitting, Auntie?", and that might mean three long, double flights of stairs as she slept at the top of the house. Or, "May I unlace your boots? Or fetch your slippers?" All the money was entirely imaginary, but we were quite conscientious about the amount we had earned, and solemnly ate the extra slice of bread dry if we had not enough to pay for dripping or sugar. Of course, Auntie saw to it that we were properly fed.

There was one great drawback in our lives. We knew no boys, though I, for one, did not care. But it must have affected us all. A year or two later we occasionally saw the only son of one of Auntie's friends, but he was such a milksop that we all despised him. Poor Fellow! Perhaps he was shy of so many girls. (Some of these apparent milksops had hidden fires within, so who was I to judge them?)

Captain [H. Richard] Angel lived next door. He traded in the West Indies, and owned his own sailing ship, *The Torrens*. Occasionally, he came to Sunday tea with us when he was in port and was, I think now, a good deal amused by our chatter and laughter, which got more uproarious when he was there. He was such a genial fellow. He called me "the laughing girl," but we all did our share, that's sure. [1]

Leonard's health had not been very good for some time. The family bronchial asthma was making inroads, so he went for a voyage with Captain Angel to see what that would do for him. Unfortunately, they were wrecked in a storm, but managed to limp into the port of Pernambuco, off the coast of South America, from where Leonard came home on another boat. It was bad luck. [2]

Grandpapa had left Mabel and me shares in the Drury Lane business, which should have brought in one hundred pounds ($500) a year each. But, as things turned out, we only got seventy pounds. We were more fortunate than some members of the family, the residuary legatees, who really had more claim on the estate. Later, our income was still more reduced, and finally faded out altogether from that source. I think most of our money was turned into the family "pot" at Ealing to pay for our board and, in my case, clothing and more schooling, about which more later.[3]

We four older ones (May, Mabel, Ethel and I) had our hair up now. At least it was *supposed* to be up, but mine, growing on such a wild head, was more often down than up. The word "sweet" has been so over-used that I hardly like to apply it to May, but that's what she was, gentle and kind to all, and ready to pour oil on any troubled waters. At that time Do (Dorothy, and now "Carlo") was given to bad attacks of the sulks. She would sit at the meal table, glowering like a thunder cloud, but May could generally get her round. She was little mother to all of them. She had long, fair hair and was so like our mother in features.

Peg (Margaret) was the good-natured butt of the family. Leonard called her "the Papuan" because her wavy, brown hair stuck straight up on end. If there was anything "on", Peg was always discovered to be washing her head. Several years later, when we were all dressed for May's wedding, and the fly (four-wheeled cab) was at the door, ready to take us to London for the ceremony, there was a hue and cry for Peg, and believe it or not she was washing her head.

The family needed a new hat for going out occasions. One hat had to serve for several of the girls. (In fact, later on, when more hard times came, there was one rig out kept: hat, coat, dress, etc., and only one girl could go to London, or wherever it was, at a time.) On this occasion Lilian was chosen to be fitted as she was the dressy one. We thought it "swanky" of her to use a looking glass. Hilda and I went, too. Here, in the hat shop was a young, up-to-date sales girl who knew her business. "What are you looking for, Madam? A navy flop?" That finished Hilda and me. We had to be shooed out of the shop, and "a navy flop" remained a joke forever.

Sometimes Auntie took us in batches to London: Whiteley's, the Burlington Arcade, or the Soho Bazaar. More rarely, to a Christie Minstrel Show, or to hear Corney Grain, the comic impersonator and singer, and we laughed for weeks afterwards. He was very large and very clever. I can still see him pretending to be a woman on a shopping expedition, or a lady of fashion, dressing for a ball and fixing her side curls in front of an imaginary mirror. But Messrs. Maskelyn and Cook, with their unsurpassed and still unsolved magic and mystery, were always the favourites. Auntie had to save the money for all these treats out of the housekeeping allowance from Uncle Howard—The House, as we always called it, as if it was an individual. If "he" was feeling a little flush, "he" might dig down into his pockets for a six penny water ice to top up one of these infrequent, and consequently more delightful excursions, especially if we went to Buszard's.

In the winter there was skating and, oh, the hearburnings to see if The House could provide the sixpence necessary to skate on the private lake. It was sixpence each, so of course we had to take it in turns, perhaps three at a time, and *would* the frost hold? And *would* we get a second turn if it did? The suspense was almost unbearable.

Then there were the new swimming baths in the summer. Sixpence each again. We shared two or three home-made, thin cotton bathing gowns, which were transparent when wet, but we had to wear stockings for decency's sake. Later on, it was discovered that blue serge did not cling like cotton, and people began to wear gowns made of that. You could even buy them ready-made in shops: elbow sleeves, sailor collars, trimmed with white braid, and a full skirt to the knees, buttoned round the waist. And still the stockings! You had to be decent, make no mistake.

There was no filtering of the water, and it was only changed twice a week, Monday and Thursday, so that by Wednesday and Saturday it was a deep, rich yellow-brown. We learned to try and avoid those days.

Uncle Howard was a musical critic for one of the periodicals and attended concerts in that capacity. He had two free passes and used to take one of us girls with him. It was a great treat, as Mabel and I had not forgotten our early feast of music with Mr. Kennedy. Uncle took me once, and I heard the later well-known singer Plunket Greene in a trial performance.

One of the outstanding events of those times was the opening of the Earl's Court Exhibition, London. The first of its kind, I think. It was so successful that it was followed by one for the colonies and others. The House treated some us older ones to a day there; a marvellous day of wonderment. The chief thing that remains fixed in my mind was this new invention called a telephone. I have always liked inventions. By paying three pence you could put a receiver to your ear and hear talking or music playing somewhere else. We tried it. (I must have seen the telephone at Charlie Shaw's in St. Leonards some time after this, when I stayed there.)

One summer holiday Hilda Spalding and I stayed at Netherton. What a grand time we had! It was harvest time and we worked like a couple of men, unloading the sheaves of wheat, or helping to build the stacks. It was rare fun. The extra harvesting hands said they had never seen girls work like that before. I hope that we were not depriving them of an extra shilling or two. We never thought of it in that light.

The morning that Hilda and I were to leave, we got up at 4 a.m. and walked a couple of miles down the road to gather blackberries to take home to Ealing. We picked a huge market basket full, running ourselves so short of time that we had to leave for the long drive to the station in torn clothes, dishevelled hair, and juice-stained, scratched arms and hands. It seemed all right after a week or two of wild country life, but what we looked like when we arrived in London and were met by some neatly-dressed relation I must leave to the imagination.

It was at Netherton that we were first introduced to the curlew, that quaint nocturnal bird, with his long, pointed wings and harsh, distinctive cry, as he flits hither after moths and insects. Leonard used to take us out in the lane after dark and call up into the sky, "Hello, the curlew there!", and we fancied they made an extra dart in our direction.

When Miriam Batsford was married her parents very kindly asked me down for the event, and to stay a week. The girls' sister Maude had died, which was a terrible loss to them all. I had no wedding garments, but the Spalding family turned out what was available, with alterations, and May rigged up a rather elderly wide-brimmed leghorn hat with some fresh flowers and a piece of tulle with which I was quite content. Clothes were not the vital item they are now. As far as I can remember, I was some kind of a bridesmaid at the affair, being "from London", and there was a big spread afterwards.

* * * * * * * * * *

In those days there were very few positions open to a girl on leaving school unless she had had some special training. Those whose parents could afford it might go to Girton or Newnham Colleges, and later be able to take a good position as History or Mathematics mistress in one of the new schools, or Art mistress, if she had been to South Kensington, or Music mistress, if trained at the Royal College of Music. Our poor education had not fitted us for any of these, and there was little else than the hum-drum life of a nursery governess.[4]

Mabel, at twenty, was already very capable. Considering her age, this might be taken for granted in these days, but girls then were four or five years behind the girls of the present day in experience and sophistication. She went to keep house for a widower, known to the Aunts, with several school-age boys. Their housekeeper had either left, or gone on a long holiday, and Mabel was quite equal to the occasion. She made a great hit with the boys. They were vegetarians, so she needed the advice of the cook in order to devise their meals. It was terrible to be parted from her.

Aunti Marnie gave some of us drawing lessons in her spare time, which I loved. I still longed to go to the South Kensington [Royal College] of Art in London, but there was no money for that. Looking back, now, it seems to me it might have been better to put what money was available to that purpose, instead of continuing with second-rate general education, but the Aunts probably had good reason for deciding otherwise. There was never any questioning the decision of the grownups.

Anyway, to boarding school I had to go. I had had enough of school, and one of my worst nightmares was to dream that I was back again, even long after I had left for good. Miss Edna Jackson, of Ore Place fame, had two sisters. Miss Judith and Miss Helene kept a small, private school to which I went: Brandram House, Lee, Blackheath, to be exact. These two fast-aging ladies [were] battling against the infirmities of life, and struggling for existence in the rising tide of modern schools with their trained staffs of teachers. It was a tragedy.[5]

The school was an ancient, tall, slim, once-private house in a row, with a small piece of sooty garden at the back. About twenty steps led up to the front door and first floor. There were ten boarders and perhaps as many day girls. We slept on the third floor, four in each of two bedrooms, and one or two in a dressing room. There was no fire escape. No water was laid on upstairs, except in a minute toilet on the second floor, to which we had to ask in French to go up. We all washed in one basin on a table on the landing, and emptied the water into a bucket. There was not enough for each to have fresh water, so it was a case of first come first served, and one tooth glass served for all.

The day girls and boarders kept their outdoor clothing, boots, and galoshes in what was once, probably, the box room, just below ground level. There was one tiny pane of glass which was never cleaned (possibly to keep people on the street from peeping in), and no ventilation. At one end, a zinc bath, which had seen better days, had been built in. It had an outlet, but no taps for water. In fact, there was no hot water laid on, even in the kitchen. It all had to be heated in kettles or crocks on the range. Once a week we boarders went down into the Black Hole of Calcutta to have a so-called bath.

The first girl got a pail of hot water; the second, half a pail added to it, the third girl half a pail more. Then the water was let out and the process repeated. There could be no false modesty in such circumstances.

The teaching was on the level of twenty or more years earlier. To try and give some semblance of being modern there were visiting Masters for certain subjects. One frousty old man came to give us lessons in elocution. We sat around the dining room table as, of course, there were no desks. He started the first class by a long harangue about pronounciation, and finally made each girl recite, "Not at all, man," and "Not a tall man," emphasizing the difference. And so the first lesson was over. The second week he asked for a blackboard on which he wrote Longfellow's lines:

> Do you think, O blue-eyed banditti
> Because you have scaled the wall,
> Such an old moustache as I am
> Is not a match for you all?[6]

putting all sorts of curly-wiggles, dots, and lines over the words, to indicate the proper inflection of the voice. Again, we took turns in mimicking him as far as possible, but because he was "an old moustache" himself, and a flabby one at that, and looked so ludicrous, we were all convulsed with hardly-suppressed laughter. So ended the second lesson.

Miss Judith had sat in the room on each occasion to act as chaperone. [When the old man did not return] again we were left to draw our own conclusions. His place was taken by a Master for literature—a younger man (but not too young), with sandy hair and moustache, keen on his subject, but utterly unable to inspire us with interest. He mouthed such immortal names as Per-r-r-cy By-s-s-he Shel-l-ey with relish, baring his grimy teeth, and peering at the tips of his cigarette-stained fingers. We were supposed to write an essay on each lecture, but I could only see the funny side of it all, and disgraced myself by writng about six lines, for which I was deservedly reproved. Where the Miss Jacksons dug up these musty old things it would be hard to say. Some poor, down-at-heels literary relics of a bygone day, or one-time "coaches," perhaps, glad to earn a pittance to keep body and soul together.

One thing we really liked were the Swedish drill classes. It was almost the only up-to-date teaching we had, music being the other. Swedish drill was just beginning to get a footing in England, and we had a very nice, properly-trained teacher. There was not room enough, but she made the best of it.[7]

Ridley Prentice, examiner for the Royal College of Music, and author of *The Theory of Music,* which we used at Kent College, came to give lessons to two or three of the senior girls, but I had to learn with Miss Helena. It did not take me long to find out that I knew a good deal more about music and theory than she did. She thought I had a "voice", and very kindly gave me free lessons in her spare time, beating her chest to indicate the method of producing low notes, and she taught me a song of her own composition.

Once a term Mr. Prentice came to the school and gave us a recital. After the senior girls left, I had the honour of turning the pages for him, because I was accustomed to reading music. He explained passages to us, and it was delightful.

When I had been there two terms I won the music prize in competition with his pupils, so next term the Aunts allowed me to take lessons with him. He could be very kind, but had a most scathing and sarcastic tongue. Each girl came down from her lesson weeping *every time.* I made up my mind he shouldn't make me weep. He did his best, without success (though it was a close shave several times), and finally became quite human.

Perhaps the less said about the food the better. You could ask for "not quite so much", but having once accepted a plate of anything, you were expected to finish it to the last morsel of gristle. Our only salvation was in the fact that two girls took turns in sitting at a side table. We maneuvered this to the advantage of each. One girl did not like mutton, which we always had on Tuesday. It was the only joint of the week. So she and I sat at the little table and she surreptitiously passed her mutton to me, preferring to go hungry. Another day it was liver, tough and stringy. The same process. Each had a chance, and so it went on, either unseen or overlooked by the Miss Jacksons.

The bread and scrape for tea became so scraped that it was invisible, even if held slantways to the light. So it had to be taken to Miss Judith. One of the girls went with me, after some persuasion. It improved for a time. When we came in from evening church at 9 p.m., we might have something to eat. All the odd scraps of bread accumulated during the week were soaked in water, with a very small amount of raisins, and pressed into a deep pie dish. (There was no such thing as a flat pie, as we know it now.) This toothsome concoction was served cold and clammy, even in winter, and few were hungry enough to stomach it. There was nothing else. Some of us were desperately hungry all the time.

Mabel wrote to me regularly once a week, and how I looked forward to her letters. Ethel was good about writing, too, which kept me in touch with the family. One day, when the letters were handed round at breakfast there was one for me in almost illegible writing. It was from old Barpsh at Netherton, trying to tell me that Em had a baby boy, October 23, 1889, and he was to be called Thomas Leonard. Tears of excitement filled my eyes, and I was nearly bursting. Everyone wanted to hear the news, and congratulated me on being an Auntie. It was one of the red letter days of my life. Letter writing was not one of Barpsh's strong points, but I gathered that the baby was "the one and only best"; she had never nursed a better.

At the end of the term, each girl voted secretly for the one she considered should have the Good Conduct prize. There was a lot of whispering, giggling and comparing notes. Someone asked me who I had voted for, but I reminded her it was a secret ballot, and would not tell. Everyone laughed. There was some mystery, evidently. When Miss Judith, with due ceremony, pulled the name slips out of a box it appeared, to my amazement, all had voted for me, except myself. I was very touched by their kindness. It seemed to be a turning-point for me. I was determined to do my best at lessons, however futile the teaching was.

Hard work brought its reward. The next term—it seems fantastic to say—I won all the prizes (except the Good Conduct, which one could not win twice): highest term and examination marks in drawing, music, hand writing and recitation. (I once had to inflict the whole of Longfellow's "Robert of Sicily" on parents and visitors at the end of term.) One could only claim two prizes which, of course, was perfectly fair. My only comment is, what ability or capacity for work can the others have had if I could be first? It passes understanding.

We were supposed to talk French all day, except at breakfast, dinner and after evening prep. *"Puis je aller en haut"* was the most correct phrase we knew, and probably the one most in use. The rest was just pidgin French: *"Voulez vous lendez me votre thimble?"* or *"Puis je fetch mon work basket?"*, etc. No one corrected us and we never learnt any more.

Some of us had terrible colds and coughs in the winter; there was no heat, except in two minute grates in the first floor rooms. I can remember, now, when asking to go *"en haut"* meant wheezing up those awful stairs and having to sit down several times on the way.

Perhaps anyone reading this account will think I have just picked out the disadvantages, but the fact is I have minimized them, if anything, and could give plenty more along the same lines. The whole thing was a farce, a travesty of education, not very far removed from the old Dame School. It was a transition time; the last gasp of the old system. Today, one can feel nothing but pity for those who had to eke out a meagre livelihood by such outworn methods. Fortunately, it was not many years before the Miss Jacksons were able to retire, possibly on a pension, to Bexhill-on-Sea, where they became leading lights in church work, Miss Judith and Miss Edna living till they were well over ninety.

It fell to my lot to ring the old cracked bell in the morning on the landing to wake the boarders. I had never been used to waking at a certain time. In fact, we overslept ourselves sometimes at Ealing, and would be wakened by little Mary tapping on the door and saying, in her sing-song Suffolk way, "Mibel, that's ite o'clock!" We shot out of bed to be in time for 8:15 breakfast. So something had to be done about this bell ringing. I wrote 6:30 on my forehead with my finger, and thought of it there, saying 6:30

over and over, till I fell asleep. After a few mornings, I found I could wake to the minute without effort.

Another job that came my way was to look after a little girl of nine and help her with her prep. The patience I had learned in playing with little children in the drawing room at Ore Place, under Grannie's eye, stood me in good stead now. This child and I used to retire to the cloak room after school and, perched on the edge of the old zinc bath, battle with spelling and impossibly difficult texts, such as, "So that they that would pass from hence to you cannot, neither can they pass to us that would come from thence", in reference to the other world. It often took three quarters of an hour for her to learn one text, which could have no possible meaning for her. She was unattractive, but tried so hard and depended on me so much, that I became really fond of her. There were no schools or special training for children [with learning disabilities].

There were two or three very nice girls among the boarders. One came from Keswick in the Lake District. Her mother was staying with a sister in Bromley, and asked some of us over to spend an afternoon in her garden. We had a lovely time, and she was so kind. Her kindness combined with seeing the old familiar streets were too much for me. I howled in bed that night.

* * * * * * * * * *

Another girl came from Southampton, and to my joy she asked if I would like to spend two weeks of the holidays there. She told me her father kept a shop, and they lived over it. Would I mind? Of course I wouldn't, but it was very nice of her to mention it as that sort of thing might have been objected to in those days.

I went home to Ealing first to take my school things and rig up a few clothes. It was all so exciting as I had never stayed with strangers before. A new garment was just coming into fashion called a blouse. It was separate from your skirt, had a turn-down collar, and buttoned down the front—very different from the one-piece dresses we had always worn. Auntie bought a Weldon's pattern and some pretty, striped winsey (like thin flannel), and she and May turned to and made me three of these new blouses, I sewing on buttons, making buttonholes, and overcasting the seams. I suddenly felt in the height of fashion.

Sad to say, these first attempts were not an unqualified success. Auntie was a clever needlewoman, but to save material she cut the blouses too short—just to the waist—not realizing that directly I raised my arms out would come the blouse from under the skirt band. We pinned the skirt and blouse together with a huge safety pin, hoping to have found a solution, but by the time I came back from Southampton the pin had torn great holes in the blouses, and I had spent an uncomfortable and embarrassing time tyring to keep body and soul together, as these were the only clothes I had. It was that or nothing.

A long train journey, especially through new country, was always exciting, and I expect I had a "very jolly time" as we should have described it then. Some of the family met me at the station. The father owned a small, rather shadowy draper's shop in one of the older parts of town, and the family lived over it, using an outside stairway. My glimpse into their home and surroundings was just like a chapter out of one of Dicken's stories come to life. An entirely new experience.

The mother was a capable, buxom lady, with an eye to the economical side of housekeeping, but very kind. There was novelty in everything. I was fascinated by the laying of the table even. They had the old-fashioned metal cruet to hold salt, pepper, mustard and sauce, as you might see in a wayside inn, and a sham, cut-glass butter dish of

80

the same vintage, with bell-shaped cover and water container to keep it cool. I had never seen things like that in a private home. The shop assistant came up to dinner and supper, but never spoke a word unless spoken to. He excused himself when finished and went down to let the father come up. He was apparently on a lower plane, socially, and never took part in their lives.

The father never appeared after supper. He was boxed in his tiny office where, by the glimmer of a small gas jet or tiny sky light, he poured over his accounts and made out orders. No wonder he wore strong glasses. The family never went in the shop; it was evidently not correct. So, though I would have loved to examine everything, I only got a peep if the door was open when we went out.

In the evening we helped prepare vegetables to be dry-salted away for the winter—shelled peas by the bushel and cut string beans. It reminded me of Ore Place.

The first night I was nearly mad with flaming irritation of something biting me. The next morning I ventured to mention it, never dreaming what it was. They were most apologetic. They said that many of the houses were very old and over-run with bedbugs which were impossible to irradicate. I saw them crawling on the ceiling and dropping on my bed. Perhaps the family had become immune.

The family was very kind to me, though they evidently had not much money for extras. Anyway, I didn't want entertainment; it was all so interesting as it was. One day my school friend and I made a trip to Netty Abbey, a beautiful old ruin, and I made a sketch of it. Another day, I went on one of the pleasure steamers (alone, for some reason which I have forgotten), down Southampton Water, along the Solent, quite close to the famous Isle of Wight, with Osborn Castle, Shankin, Ryde and the world-renown Cowes of Royal Regatta fame. There was a silly, out-worn riddle: Why doesn't the Queen ride a horse? Because she prefers Cowes to Ryde.

At the Needles, sharp pinnacles of rock projecting from the sea, we turned, leaving Ventnor, where Grannie used to go, just round the corner, out of sight. We landed at a small place for half an hour, and I picked up some shells on the beach. All the way I made notes and sketches of everything, to be able to tell the cousins when I got home. It was a sparkling blue day which I shall never forget. I would like to have gone down and explored the wonderful miles of docks, but they told me I could not possibly go without a man.

One morning I woke feeling so ill I simply could not stand. Every bone ached. I felt so sorry to put them to the trouble of waiting on me, but more so when a few days later the older sister was also stricken, evidently having caught the infection from me. I got up as soon as I possibly could to wait on her. When I got home, I told Auntie Lizzie, and she said I must have had this new complaint which doctors were calling influenza. So may people had had it that it must be infectious.

* * * * * * * * *

Mabel's twenty-first birthday had come and gone while I was at school, and once Miss Judith kindly invited her to spend a weekend, which was a great joy to me. The girls said our voices were so alike they could not tell which was speaking without seeing.

And so ended my school days, thank goodness! I have put all the Blackheath experiences together, but, of course, we all went to our various homes for the holidays. I must skim over these, though my mind teams with memories of good times.

Back, l to r, Winifred, Hilda, Howard Spalding, Ethel and Lilian
Front, l to r, Muriel, Adelaide with baby Freda, Dorothy and Margaret

Summer holidays, 1893, Vale House Farm, Suffolk

Leonard and Emma Higgs
with Tommy

Tommy Higgs with
Grandfather Batsford

CHAPTER EIGHT

More Changes 1889 - 1896

And then came the Crash. The Drury Lane business, Grand-papa's pride and joy, went broke. After a time it staggered to its feet again, but it was never the same. Its heart was broken.[1]

St. George's had to be given up, and we all had to pack, like sardines, into a much smaller house in the centre of Mount Park Crescent, Ealing. The move took two days. Some of us went the first day and thought it awfully jolly to eat picnic suppers in the kitchen, which Spanny had managed to scramble together, but she would not eat with us. She knew her place better than *that*, though she was quite equal to calling us all by our nicknames: "Do-do darlin'" (Dorothy), or "Don't be so stoopid, Lally" (Lilian), etc.

We thought it a lark to help make up beds and unpack what we could the first night. The rooms seemed so small after those at St. George's, but who cared? The next day the big dining room and drawing room furniture arrived, with the rest of the family, and we lived in turmoil for a few days till everything was straightened out. With a smaller allowance, it must have taxed Auntie's ingenuity to feed all us hungry girls, but old Spanny was not to be done. We could not have meat every day, so she produced the toothsome Suffolk substitute, roly-poly suet, with thick brown gravy. We wolfed it up.

We were allowed more licence in talking at meals now, to give us a chance to form and air our opinions. Auntie's approval or reproof was generally timely, and we took the latter to heart. One day at dinner I was "positive" about something, I forget what, and she said, quietly but firmly, "Don't be so self opinionated, Win, dear. It is not nice in a girl of your age." I subsided, probably a little resentfully, but remembered what she said.

The girls continued at school. Ethel was studying Stubb's Constitutional History of England, and in her spare time attending to her pet rabbit, which she christened Stubbs, in a small hutch in the tiny back garden. All the gardens in the Crescent converged and everyone could see and hear everything that went on, because the board fences were only about five feet high. We used to play hockey, rounders, French and English, and all sorts of games, making the most terrible noise.

We knew none of the neighbours, and nobody "called", as was customary on newcomers. I daresay our menage gave rise to inquisitive gossip, because anyone could see with half an eye that Auntie was far too young to be the mother of such a tribe of girls. She wore her hair short, like a boy, because she had such bad headaches, and that made her look younger.

But one day Auntie received an anonymous note protesting about her "screaming females", and asking that we be supressed. I am afraid we all treated it as a huge joke, but of course we had to try and make less noise.

[When we played hockey we were dressed] in long, bulky skirts, trailing the ground, and very narrow-brimmed, small straw sailor hats. The bodices were boned to make them fit. You bought a set of covered bones and sewed them in yourself. They constantly broke, and tore holes in our undergarments and ourselves. How did girls manage to play in such discomfort? We often came home from a walk with our skirts and petticoats six inches deep in thick mud. These had to be dried and then everlastingly brushed in the garden. Someone devised a clasp to catch some of the folds of the skirt, which were lifted off the ground by a cord round the waist, but they were not much use.

We had the most voluminous pockets, let into the side seam of the dress skirt, into which we crammed an almost inconceivable amount of what we considered necessities. Mine contained the following:

a handkerchief (very large, made of heavy white cotton)
a pair of folding scissors
a pen knife
a fruit knife (with silver blade and mother-of-pearl folding handle)
a pencil (with protecting cover)
a folding pen with little inkwell attached to a chain
an India rubber
a little notebook
a dictionary, for which I made a cloth cover

Then, if we went shopping, the smaller parcels must be stuffed into the pocket, too. Imagine the weight. And yet we accepted these things. They were the custom, then.

Auntie started a family club for us at Mount Park Crescent. Its interests were varied. One thing that remains in my mind was the initial choosing of names. For some unknown reason we each had to be "Mr." somebody: Mr. Stubbs, Mr. Winks, Mr. Lally, Mr. Papuan, Mr. Duggah, Mr. Carlo, and lastly, Mr. Yor-Yor (Muriel). Uncle Howard was asked to become an honorary member, and we gave him the name Mr. Puss. He was so serene, abstracted, or deep in his thoughts, that it hardly seemed to fit.

The meetings generally consisted in games, Pope Joan being the favourite. It was a lovely card game for any number to play, the nine of diamonds being Pope Jone. It was thrilling to see the various pools growing (if not claimed) with small prizes donated by Auntie (i.e., a sugar stick or piece of Callard and Bowser's butterscotch, and other treats), till the end of the game, when we each disclosed our winning cards and the pools were distributed.

Sometimes a member gave a recitation or a reading. Ethel and Lilian once recited "DeLorge's Love", which was well done and most dramatic, and I gave an illustrated account of my visit to Southampton and the trip on the *Solent* to the Isle of Wight. Members had to keep very good account of their money, with a monthly inspection by Auntie. Woe betide us if we were a half penny out.

We loved Auntie to read aloud to us in the evening, while we did our sewing. She had several little books written in the Suffolk dialect, which delighted us, and which she read to perfection, having been raised in Suffolk. Sometimes she would get out Tom Hood's poems, with "The Table of Errata", beginning, "Well! Thanks be to heaven the summons is given/It's only gone seven, and should have been six./There's fine overdoing in roasting and stewing/And victuals past chewing to rags and to sticks!" Sometimes it was Bret Harte's short stories, "The Luck of Roaring Camp" and others, which I feel sure would be readable now. Time for reading was limited and intermittent, and our ages so varied that it did not do to start on a long story.

I have mentioned sewing several times, but have not said what it was we sewed. Sewing was a real business then, and Miss Hughes' teaching came in handy. (The cousins were too busy with their studies to do much in that line. Also, they had not had the training.) I made all my underclothes by hand, and they were not the simple garments that girls wear now, unfortunately. None of your flimsy synthetic cella-silks, or suedines for us, but good, heavy English cotton, manufactured in the Lancashire mills, and made to last:

- a nightdress, with yoke, high neck, long sleeves, and wrist-
  bands, and gored sides to give width
- a bodice of white calico, shaped to the figure and fastened
  down the front with linen-covered buttons
- a white cotton petticoat, long and flounced, with rather
  coarse Swiss embroidery, and buttoned round the waist
- in winter, a flannel petticoat, with deep hem, feather stitched in silk
- a cotton chemise and pair of open drawers (the two legs just
  joined at the waist), with embroidery at the knees)

Multiply these by two, and it represents a bit of labour, so the evening reading-aloud helped one along. Fortunately, I loved sewing and took a secret pride in turning out good work. Over this mass of undergarments we wore the voluminous dresses of the time, with skirts trailing the ground.

I think flannelette was invented about this time. We were rather amused by the name, because it was made entirely of cotton. It was attractive stuff, with fluffy surface, but very inflammable. After a short life people gave it the go-by, as there were rumours of bad accidents. Manufacturers experimented till they found a way out of the difficulty, but it took a long time to overcome people's fear. I was once waiting on a railway platform and saw a young man light his pipe and fling the match down. In one second the girl he was escorting was a flaming torch. The dying match had caught the fluff on her skirt. People rushed to brush out the flames, but though she was unhurt she was white and shaking. I am afraid their day's outing on which they were obviously bent was spoilt by the accident.

I am so sorry I have not space to say more about the cousins individually. May was now grown-up; Ethel deep in history, which subject was to be her life's work; Lilian making the violin her profession, studying at the Royal College of music; Margaret, still the "Papuan" but later to train at Guy's; Hilda, a wag, with Dodo in tow, like a pet dog. They called each other "Master" and "Carlo". The latter name has continued through life. When teaching in Hilda's private school, Queen's Gate, London, she became "Miss Carlo" to avoid the confusion of two Miss Spaldings. None of the girls knew the origin of the name. And, lastly, Muriel in her early teens when Mabel and I came to this country in 1897. She trained at Dartford Swedish Drill College and was a mistress there. Ethel is the only one I have seen since we left the Old Country, sad to say. She came to British Columbia in 1904. They have all grown into fine women, with a deep affection and loyalty for each other.

Being unable to realize her great desire to be trained as a hospital nurse—and what a good one she would have made—Mabel was now working in the Children's Nursing Home, High Barnet, in Hertfordshire. It was an entirely free institution. Everyone except the cook gave their services, and the children, mostly incurable spinal and hip cases, were paid for by private subscriptions. There was never any lack of funds or donations of fruit, toys and clothing. It was run by Miss Pawling, herself a trained nurse, who gave her whole life to the work. She was one of those really good women, not in the religious sense, one may be fortunate enough to meet in a lifetime: high principled, capable and human, an outstanding character, with unconscious influence over all with whom she came in contact. She and Mabel became lasting friends.

Auntie must have been on the lookout for something for me to do because I was now just nineteen. One day she called me into her bedroom and asked if I would like to teach a little boy of seven. I was delighted at the prospect because I loved children. The sister-in-law of a friend of hers wanted a governess for her little boy named Phil. Mr. and Mrs. Hutton (these are not their real names) had a flat in the Albert Hall Mansions, quite close to Regents Park, London. I was to go up every day with a season ticket, staying from nine till some time after one o'clock lunch. For this I was to receive the magnificent sum of twenty pounds a year (about $100) "to begin with", but I felt rich.

Phil was a dear little boy, well-mannered and well-groomed. All his clothes were made by his father's tailor, and everything was immaculate. His sturdy little sister Effie, three and a half, was a picture: light brown curls, deep blue eyes with dark lashes, and bright, rosy cheeks—and a will of her own. She had once sat on her father's knee for four hours rather than say, "Please" to get down, but she gave in at last. A devoted old nanny looked after her. The first morning, Effie stalked into the room and annouced, "Me don't know Mit Hid 'et," took a good searching look at me, and stalked out again.

I set to work to make a timetable and plan lessons, all of which was great fun. I was instructed in just how much the window was to be opened, and to be sure and put the guard in front of the fire when we went out, etc. After 2 1/2 hours of lessons, Phil (all dressed up in his paraphanalia of lanyard, whistle, sailor collar and whatnot) and I went for lovely walks in Regents Park, and he sailed his boat on the round pond, as millions of children had done before and since. Sometimes we pretended we were just acquaintances so that he could practice taking off his cap. He ran ahead, then turned and came towards me, as if we were meeting casually, lifting his hat. He soon caught on.

One day when he had run on, a man sitting on a seat murmured something which I did not hear. Thinking he had asked me a question, I turned towards him, and he said, "You're a very pretty girl, you know." I replied, "Oh, I thought you asked me the time," and strode on. So that was the sort of thing Mabel had meant when she warned me not to let men speak to me. The cad. Paying silly compliments! I had no idea of his intentions. There was evidently more to learn though. I was told never to get in a railway carriage where there was only one man. I remembered that injunction. And get out and into another if left alone with a man. I did that, too. What could all this mean? The warnings were necessary, though, as I found out on more than one occasion. Mabel was my guardian angel, but I hope instinct would have prompted me, if she had not. It was a great mistake to bring girls up in such utter ignorance. At twenty I had not the slightest idea where babies came from, and rarely gave it a thought.

Sometimes Mrs. Hutton sent us shopping, to choose some frilling or whatnot for her saying, casually, "You must use your judgement." Whew! That was something new! Use *my* judgement. I used it, and found more confidence.

Mr. Hutton was a barrister, landscape gardener and art connoisseur. A clever man, with his head in the clouds. He had some fine etchings, well-arranged on the walls of their drawing room. I think he was an architect, too, because he had built a terrace of six very charming, small houses at a seaside town near Ipswich, on the east coast, keeping the first in the row for his family.

We all went down to the cottage in the early summer, and had a gorgeous time. Oh, that east coast air! It was intoxicating. You drank in new life with every breath. We were in the heart of my family's home country, Suffolk, with its sing-song dialect: "Be you a gooin' on t'baich?", or "Yere come Failiz in 'is bo'at!" Mr. Hutton was laying out a property on the cliff and Phil and I used to go along and watch operations. It was most interesting to see what could be done with a perfctly flat piece of rank grassland. Cartloads of soil were brought to make a wind break, trees and shrubberies were planted, and delightful little paths and summer houses made, long before the house was built.

While scrambling up and down the beach I discovered pieces of fossilized bone protruding from the sandy earth. And then began a thrilling hunt. Phil and I scrabbled and dug, never knowing what would turn up. At various times, I found shell, bones, and sharks' teeth, all fossilized—one a real beauty, highly polished. The serrated edges were worn away by the action of the sea, which had receded, leaving the tooth in the cliff. The sea was now encroaching again, washing these fossils out. But the *piece de resistance* was a whelk shell, scrolled the reverse way from those of the present day. How many aeons ago did Mr. and Mrs. Whelk decide to change the then prevailing fashion in whorls?

There were delightful little huts on the beach, from which people could bathe. They were portable, and could be stored in the winter. Each family had their own, and it was most convenient. Kaiser Wilhelm II (Queen Victoria's grandson) had taken a large, furnished house further along for his five sons, and about as many tutors. We used to see them playing on the beach. Prince Wilhelm, the eldest, was about twelve as far as I can remember. They were constantly herded by the tutors and not allowed to speak to other children.

Gerald du Maurier, son of the great *Punch* artist, and his family rented one of Mr. Hutton's cottages. His were the two little boys, twins, I think, who so often appeared in du Maurier's pictures. One could recognize them easily: curly hair, spindly legs, linen or velvet suits, with large, turn-down collars.

I went home for a few weeks holiday. A month was the usual thing. None of your measly two weeks that people have to be content with now. There was no Ore Place for the family holiday, but Auntie had contrived to save enough to take a furnished cottage at Southwold on the east coast. For some unaccountable reason, May did not want to go, so because I had already had a change at the seaside, Auntie decided I had better stay and keep May company, with Uncle Howard coming home in the evening. I thought it would be a lark, as I loved May, but she was often lackadaisical and not at all like her usual self. I tried to jolly her out of it, but without much success. What could be the matter?

One day I heard her ordering afternoon tea for two in the drawing room. Then she appeared "all dolled up", pink and rather flustered. There was ring at the front door bell, which she answered *herself*. Who should walk in but Laurie Shaw, of all people. Laurie had not come by chance. It was planned, and they were in love. Shy, reticent Laurie had won the treasure he had waited for so long.

They had a quiet wedding, May going off for the honeymoon in a bonnet, as was the custom after marriage. She was now a young matron, and hats were left behind with girlhood. Perhaps May knew the lines written in 1828 by Emily Dickinson:

"Midnight, Goodnight", I hear them call,
The angels bustle in the hall.
Softly my Future climbs the stair,
I fumble at my childhood's prayer,
So soon to be a child no more.

Someone raked up the less poetic couplet: "Slyly stealing, he to Ealing/Made a daily journey." And Laurie was nick-named "Slyly"—the least appropriate that could possibly be applied.

When I went back to the Huttons, they had given up their London flat, and taken a house in Putney, a newish suburb, near Wimbledon. It was a longer journey, with "a change" so I only went home for weekends, and looked after Phil all day. Mrs. Hutton was constantly out—generally in London—from early morning till late afternoon. She had promised me a raise when I had been with them a year, but there was no mention of it. Auntie very kindly offered to remind her, but, shy as I was, I felt it would be better to do it myself, because I had to learn to manage my own affairs. Rather reluctantly, Mrs.

Hutton "remembered" there had been talk of it at first, and gave me another five pounds a year, but I saved on the daily train fare.

Phil and I were good friends. He looked up to me as a sort of oracle, displacing his mother in knowledge, much to her amusement. It was always, "I must ask Miss Higgs", or "Miss Higgs will know." It was quite embarrassing at times. We explored the new roads, but they were not half so nice as Regents Park. It was in Putney Village that I could not resist buying the little white china dish for six and a half pence, which is still in my cupboard, fifty years old.

Phil could recite poetry very well, and one day his mother took him to the Hospital for Incurables, standing in magnificent grounds, where he delighted a large audience by spouting all sorts of ditties: "I had a little doggie", and "There once was a naughty young kitty called Puff." He was not the least bit shy. (This home was built by Grannie's father, Andrew Reed.)

This was the winter of the first terrible influenza epidemic, which swept England like a prairie fire (1891-92). The previous attack was just a foretaste in comparison. Now, whole families were stricken at once. Doctors were run off their feet, till they, too, fell victim to it. You couldn't get a nurse or help of any kind for love or money. Phil and Effie went down with it.

Phil was delirious, and kept calling for me. Mrs. Hutton asked if I would stay over the weekend. I lay in bed beside him, holding his hot little hand all night, which seemed to be the only thing he wanted. After being up with him for three nights, I got a letter from Auntie Lizzie, saying I must ask to go home and help as they were all ill, except Peg. I tore myself away from Phil and dashed home—he was on the mend now.

Poor things! Aching bones, flushed cheeks, unmade beds. "Please give me a drink of water" on every side. Three in one room, two in another double bed, Auntie Lizzie in her room, and little Mary in the attic. Spanny and Peg were on their last legs. The next day Peg had to give in, having done nobly, and just as some of them were able to help themselves a little later, I had to roll into the dressing room myself, my bones and head on fire. Well, all things come to an end, and we survived it.

Now, I will make a note of a second dream that came true, though it will probably be scoffed at. (The first was before the death of Auntie Wahr.) One Sunday I dreamed I was waiting on the platform at Ealing when, just as the train came in, a horrid-looking man dashed out from the shadow of the tunnel and made a grab for my purse. I snatched it away and sprang into a carriage. It made a great impression, but more so when, to my astonishment, it actually happened that morning. I have never forgotten that man's face.

The next time we went to the cottage at Felixstowe, Mr. Hutton could not go, but he had taken pity on an impecunious artist and entrusted him with the job of painting the children, to help him out. He lived with us. First he made a full-length portrait of Effie, standing in a corner, to get his hand in. Then he painted a full-size portrait of Mrs. Hutton. I sat for the figure as there was a baby coming. We returned to London, and soon after Phil and I were sent to stay with his grandparents (maternal) at Datchet, near Windsor. The new baby arrived, another boy, at Putney.

One day Phil and I were walking along the road to Windsor when I saw a carriage and pair, with a postillion coming towards us. The Windsor Greys! That indicated Queen Victoria. I had hardly prompted Phil to stand, facing the road, and lift his cap, when the carriage was already passing us. In the hurry of the moment I quite forgot to curtsy myself. I daresay the old lady saw what was happening, as she gave us a nod, but she was a stickler for etiquette.

While there I read a short life of Michael Faraday (applied science of electricity), and found there was something to read other than just stories, or the sentimental trash that the boarders used to blubber over at Blackheath in the evening. I knew I would rather read nothing than that. I was not "a reader", but Faraday started me off on a new track. Alfred Wallace's book on evolution was fascinating, with illustrations of the unborn young of monkey, man, pig, calf and rabbit, all practically the same at one stage. That *was* an eye opener! [2] They evidently did not arrive in a doctor's black bag, or from under a cabbage leaf. Later still, I read a good deal of Darwin's *The Origin of Species* but it was too deep for my utterly untrained mind. It only left a lasting impression, a desire for more.

One day our peaceful existence was shattered by a telegram, addressed to me. It was from Mr. Hutton, and read, "Do not let Phil out of your sight for a moment". I was stunned, but obeyed his instructions to the letter, trying to put two and two together. I think I wrote to Auntie and Mabel, and they wired me to go home at once.

How could I leave Phil and poor Mr. Hutton in the lurch? He was very hurt that I should desert the child in such a crisis, but Auntie insisted that I must not be mixed up in a scandal, and go I must. I intended to return if I could, but was not allowed to. I daresay Auntie did what was right, according to those times, but I have always regretted it. I never saw Phil again. Mrs. Hutton deserted her husband and children and, after divorce proceedings, married the artist.

Just before Mabel and I left England to come to British Columbia, I heard by chance where Mr. Hutton and the children were living in London, and determined to try and see them. The only opportunity was about ten o'clock in the morning, so it took them by surprise. Mr. Hutton and Phil were not there, unfortunately. Effie was lolling disconsolately in the window, her pretty curls all dishevelled, and the little boy, about two and a half, was sitting in a high chair, eating his breakfast in his sleeping suit. They both looked too neglected and dirty for words. They were in charge of a hospital nurse who looked rather putabout that I should find them so. And well she might.

Effie remembered me at once and flung herself on me, clawing my hands and imploring me to come and live with them, or take her away with me. She was about seven and a half. I was heart-broken, and had hard work to keep back the tears. It was terrible to have to tear myself away and leave her, but I could do nothing as we were leaving for British Columbia in two days. (For obvious reasons I have had to substitute names for this sad episode.)

There was a sequel, more than twenty years later. I was in the waiting room of one of the doctors in Victoria, British Columbia, when I suddenly recognized the signature of the artist on one of the pictures [on the wall]. I casually remarked on the fact to find that the doctor knew the former Mrs. Hutton and her husband, and their grown-up daughter, "Maisie", very well in England. The tragedy that I had witnessed meant nothing to him, so I said little, but the fate of those poor little motherless children has often haunted me.

* * * * * * * * *

Leonard had parted with his little farm in Netherton, and had gone to join Arthur Spalding on Pender Island, British Columbia, leaving Emmie with her parents till he had made a home. She had lost a baby girl, and when recovered brought Thomas, now nearly two, to stay with us at Ealing. Emmie and I spent a lovely day at Richmond Park. We made Thomas a new frock of all-over embroidery, with a scalloped edge and a hat to match for the occasion. (Imagine a boy of two dressed like that now.) I was as proud and happy as Lucifer to lead my little nephew around by the hand, or hold him while one of those street photographers made a grotesque picture of the three of us. It was set on the glass negative, with a thin piece of copper round the edge for a frame. We looked like blackamoors. Thomas was wide-eyed and solemn with amazement at everything, never having been away from the village where a tame goose acted as nursemaid.—If he got out of the gate onto the road, the goose would flap him to the side and hiss at passers-by.

In 1892 Emmie showed her inherent pluck by blindly starting off alone with Thomas to join Leonard in the then practically unknown new world, a tiny island on the Pacific Coast.[3]

* * * * * * * * * *

The summer of that year Auntie had taken a large, furnished house at Walton-on-the-Naze for a month, and Spanny came to cook for us this time. We had a lovely holiday bathing, collecting wild flowers and shells and sketching.[4] Auntie took a botony book, and we roamed the country lanes, getting specimens, pressing and naming them. The east coast rollers are gigantic and marvellous to bathe in. Great combers, away over your head, knock you down and drag you out with the under-tow, but you have to be strong to battle with them.[5]

There were lovely things to sketch: an old mill with a water-wheel, built just for that purpose you might think; shells in abundance along the north beach. Auntie offered prizes for the largest and smallest pecten shell and the best general collection, and so on. She had brought a book on shells, too. We were so keen about everything, and competition was good incentive and always friendly.

The sea air made us hungry, and we came home after bathing for what Spanny called "'levenses", a Suffolk expression for a "bit" at eleven o'clock. One day she saw me coming across the green for a piece of her harvest cake, and made her historic remark, "'ere comes that Winker! Aint she suthen crule?" It was a great compliment. If there was any family disagreement, Auntie would say, "Now, children, no ructions!", another Suffolk expression.

That summer 1892 Carina and Mabel had stayed at World's End Farm, Chiddingly, Sussex. It was owned by young [Alfred] Cornford, who had married Ruth, an ex-maid from Ore Place. They had a delightful time, but Mabel came back full of terrible stories of London slums, where Carina was digging into the mire of semi-starvation, large families living in one room, underpaid work, and other horrors which we had never dreamed of.

Uncle Howard had been coming home less frequently for some time, and one day announced he had married again. This meant a big change for all. Auntie Lizzie, having devoted the best years of her life to keeping house for her brother-in-law, and looking after the family (her sister Maria's children), now retired on her well-earned laurels to a little cottage in Wendover, Buckinghamshire, taking our love and gratitude. It is sad to remember that I hardly ever saw Auntie again. People did not travel as much as they do now; it was expensive and, of course, there were no motor cars.

A baby girl arrived at Mount Park Crescent—Freda—followed later, in succession, by Olive, Phyllis, Cicely, and, at long last, a boy, John Howard junior. But the last three came after Mabel and I had gone to British Columbia. That made *eleven* girls and one boy living (little Tommy had died long ago).

December 20th, 1892, was my twenty-first birthday. It was always somebody's birthday, and because mine came so near Christmas I was accustomed to little notice being taken of it. A few days before, old Barpsh, who was staying with us, asked me to go into town with her, as she wanted to buy a thimble for someone about my size. We looked at several and I tried them on, protesting that what fitted me might not fit the other girl. She finally bought a heavy silver one for two and six pence, a large slice out of her hard-earned income. I never gave it another thought, but to my absolutely genuine surprise there was the very same thimble on my breakfast plate. I always was a dud at seeing through transparent glass.

Uncle Howard gave me that delightful book, *The Vicar of Wakefield* by Oliver Goldsmith, bound in calf, and I am sure there were other nice presents which I have forgotten.

The ceremonies over, we girls went for the usual afternoon walk. When we came in they said they were going to change for tea. "Nonsense", I said. "We don't dress up for birthdays." They insisted, however, and persuaded me to put on my best frock. Finally, we went down, after rather obvious and puzzling delays. But instead of going into the dining room, where I began to suspect there must be a birthday cake or some surprise, someone suddenly threw open the drawing room door. The room was a blaze of light. I was dazzled for a moment, and completely taken aback.

Sitting and smiling on couch and chairs were Unc and Maude, Laurie and May, Charlie and Ellie (who were now living in London) and—Mabel, whom I had not seen for months. I was in such a transport of joy that I fell on her shoulder and wept. The surprise was very kindly meant, but the shock was too great. I was dazed all evening. We all managed to squeeze round the fine old carved oak table for supper, with much laughter and merriment. I will never forget my twenty-first birthday and the kindness of everyone.

The summer of 1893 we all had a lovely holiday at Vale House Farm, near Dunwich, Suffolk. The sea was encroaching so fast that cottages were vacated almost overnight, as they began to tumble over the cliffs. One was just splitting in two when we were there, and part of it went down. It was said there were the remains of eleven churches, some only just covered at low water, and we saw the ruins of one as the waves slowly disintegrated it. The farmer's wife cooked for us, and she must have thought she had an army billeted on her, judging by the amount we ate.

A good strong cob and two-wheeled chaise made a lovely addition to our fun. We took turns driving the three or four miles to the beach, while the rest footed it. We roamed the countryside, did the usual sketching and reading aloud, and poked around the farm buildings and cart horses. Adelaide was busy with baby Freda, now about six months old. We missed Auntie Lizzie very much, because she had always taken part in our fun.

I think it was the autumn of that year, 1893, that I went to High Barnet. Dr. and Mrs. Reginald Ryle, who lived at Hadley House, Hadley Green, wanted someone to look after their four children: Effie, who was then about eight; Jessie six and a half; John four; and Margaret two and a half. Their former devoted nanny, who had done the spade work in their infancy, was leaving. Grammar and "aiches" were not among her strong points, and the children were learning to imitate her. It was easy to make friends with them when I went to be inspected. I only had to make a circle with my thumb and finger and invite one of the children to see if "Mr. Fox was at home", to gain their interest. "Dance, Thumbman, dance", followed and the trick was done. I was engaged.

This idea of having a lady nurse was something quite new, and some of the older generation in our family were quite shocked that I should take such a position. Auntie Marnie wrote, protesting, saying I could have no idea of the "degrading duties" I should have to perform. She belonged to the old school to whom class distinction was vital. It took her many years to get over that prejudice. In a letter to me from Ethel, Auntie suddenly sent me her love. I wrote to her then, just as if nothing had happened, and we corresponded from then on, till her death in 1939. She had been doing what she thought was the right thing, I am sure of that.

The Ryles had a rambling house—in fact it was two houses connected by a passage—and a waiting room for patients. Mrs. Ryle, serene and madonna-like, devoted her life to her family, teaching the children and doing household duties. At breakfast she cooked a new preparation called "rolled oats" over a spirit lamp in the dining room. Friends dropped in to see her frequently, but she rarely returned their calls, and never went to what might be called a "tea fight"—a social gathering for the sake of it.

I loved the life and the children. There was something so solid and dependable in a family like theirs. I kept the nurseries clean (they only had one maid), washed the woolen garments, darned endless stockings, and took the children for walks. Their clothes were of the simplest [style and material]. Winter dresses, which Mrs. Ryle taught me to make, were always made of Miss Frank's serge, a hard-wearing material in a few, but artistic colours: brick red, sage green, and a pretty blue. It simplified matters just to add an inch to a yoke and sleeve, and three inches to a hem, but was very dull, I thought. I wanted to branch out into something new.

Punctually at nine o'clock Prentice drove up with the high-wheeled gig, for Dr. Ryle lived in the horse and buggy days of the country doctor. He had a pharmacy attached to his consulting room and dispensed his own prescriptions at a shilling, or at most one shilling and six pence for a bottle. When Mrs. Ryle was ill I helped him fill the bottles from the tap, while he made humorous remarks about the credulity of some patients who only needed a little coloured peppermint to cure them. He found a welcome in every home. Laurie Shaw had been a student at Guy's hospital with Dr. Ryle, and when he and May had their first boy they named him Reginald after Dr. Ryle.

Dr. Ryle remained quite unruffled and unhurried when an urgent message was brought by a breathless maid. He knew his patients and their nerves and needs. Life was not the rush it is now, so there were few accidents that might call for immediate attention. He was a home-loving man, gentle and devoted to his children, always managing to give some time to them every day. The Ryles were agnostics, but Dr. Ryle read parts of the Bible to the children from the point of view of it being an interesting old story, and they loved it. Before they went to bed he read *Swiss Family Robinson*. When a certain chapter reached a climax, Jessie, thrilled and pink with excitement, could stand it no longer and gasped, "Oh, father! That's enough! Let's have a bit of the Bible!"

Dr. Ryle's hobby was astonomy. He had quite a sizeable observatory in the back garden, with a domed, revolving roof, and powerful telescope. He was kind enough to show me the heavens sometimes, taught me to find the constellations, and gave me two beautiful books on astronomy: Sir Robert Ball's and one with fine black and white plates, showing the planets and constellations in relation to each other.[6]

In those days working people were called "women" and those of a higher social standing "ladies". It was a loathsome distinction. Mrs. Ryle rebelled. All females were to be called "ladies" by her children. A shabby and uneducated woman who kept the toll gate, which led from the church to the Common, was always spoken of as "the gate lady".

High Barnet was an interesting, old world country town, probably little changed in a hundred years or more. Once a year a large horse fair was held in the fields at the foot of Barnet Hill, with breeders and fanciers from all over the country buying and selling horse flesh. It was a pretty tough place for a week: pickpockets and other hangers-on did a roaring trade. One was well-advised to avoid the town.[7]

The High Street, with its quaint old shops, taverns and the inevitable "Coach and Horses Inn", straggled up to Hadley Green, and there, under a tree, were the remains of the old village stocks, where scoundrels of both sexes were baptized with the abuse and rotten eggs of their more fortunate associates.

The Battle of Barnet, during the War of Roses, was fought on April 14, 1471, when York was victorious and the Duke of Warwick killed. A stone monument had been erected, called the High Stone, to commemorate the event. St. Albans, the site of another battle, was a few miles away, on the old Roman Road.

Next door to the Ryles lived three maiden ladies, known to all as the Miss Tudors, descendants of an old Tudor family. Then came the large house of the Elliots, well-known photographers of the firm of Elliot and Fry in London. They had a lovely garden with an ornamental pond, and had given permission for the Ryle children to go in there to play. Play sedately—no romping. I took them several times without encountering any of the family. And then, one day, young Elliot appeared with a camera and tripod. Taking not the slightest notice of me, he began to pose the children under a tree, addressing his remarks to them as if I were not there. Having taken several pictures, he walked off, without so much as "Good afternoon".

Once, when the children and I were poking round the pond we spied a bird's nest full of babies in the boat house. The distressed cries of the parents rattled the babies to such an extent that they came fluttering out of the nest into the water below. Now what to do? The children were thrilled when I pulled up my skirt and jumped in up to my knees to the rescue. Things like that didn't happen in their well-ordered lives. *Too* well ordered to my own way of thinking. No one had ever fooled with them, or "pulled their legs". They evidently had no young uncles to josh and tease them. Old Fold Manor was the home of Miss Lucy and Miss Mary George. They had a married brother with a large family living in Wapella, Saskatchewan. Mabel and I stayed there on our way to British Columbia.

Widowed Mrs. Nixon and her three daughters Lily, Gertrude and Dora, lived opposite the High Stone. Herbert Church came courting, and carried Gertrude off to his log cabin on the Prairies, twenty-five miles from Calgary, where he and his brothers, Dick and Teddy, ran a horse ranch. They were the sons of Professor [Alfred John] Church. We also stayed at the Calgary ranch, and a few years later Gertrude stayed with us [at South Pender] while they were moving to Comox, Vancouver Island, bringing Elsie, Madge and Dolly.

There was a fine old Norman church, with square stone tower, and almost next door the Callard family of Callard and Bowser's butterscotch fame had their home. But we didn't see any butterscotch when [the] children went to tea with Rudy and Leibie Callard.

Alfred Noyes, the artist and illustrator of children's books, lived a secluded life on Hadley Green, and was rarely seen. The Wilbram Taylors lived securely behind the stone walls and wrought iron gates of their estate on the Common. They took no part in the activities of the Green.

Behind the Common were beautiful Hadley Woods, where soldiers must have skirmished among the parents of these fine old trees, taking cover in the hollow. And then the land rose to the little hamlet of Cock Fosters, with Lord Strafford's Place, Wrotham Park, beyond. There were a lot of nice families around: the Petries, Hodgkinsons, Jenkinsons, Draysons and others.

Kate Stevens was a frequent visitor at the Ryles. We became good friends. She and I attended a series of evening extension lectures in London one winter on electricity. It was awfully interesting. We had to write up each lecture and work out problems alone, sending them in each week for correction and criticism. We had practical work, too. The final great moment arrived when Kate and I managed to make a bell ring ourselves, in the sitting room. After that, we fixed a permanent bell from the kitchen to a bedroom in the other part of the house. It was a triumph.

Another winter, Ethel and I used to meet in London on Thursday evenings, and go to lectures on "Old Trade Routes of the World" by Mr. H.J. McKinder. I was transfixed with interest. If only we could have had teaching like that at school. He had a huge, almost blank map of Europe, and traced the routes taken by the old Phoenecians and later traders in the most absorbing way.

London was full of facilities for education and broadening one's mind, and I only regret that I had not more opportunities for excursions in these realms. I went to the Royal Academy several times over a period of years and saw the well-known picture by Luke Fildes, "The Doctor". Millais's "The Huguenot", made a deep impression. Burnes Jones was at his zenith with pictures of languorous, red-haired females draped and posed in "himpossible persitions", as a picture in *Punch* expressed it.

I saw George Alexander and the famous Mrs. Patrick Campbell in "The Second Mrs. Tankerey", a stupendous piece of acting which I shall never forget; also, Forbes-Robertson (later Sir Johnston) as Hamlet, another wonderful performance. May Shaw and I went to hear Paderewski, and she had to suppress my applause as the audience was carried away by his playing. He was young then, with terrific power.

At the British Museum I saw the original Magna Carta, and wonderful exhibits at the South Kensington Natural History Museum. I also heard Pachmann. Then, of course, there was the delightful zoo in Regent's Park, where old Jumbo reigned supreme, and Madam Tussaud's Wax Works were quite amusing. I heard Charles Brandram, the Dickens impersonator, in "The Christmas Carol", and the poor "Cheap Jack". They were most moving.

But serious things were looming on the horizon. Social problems that had begun to cross my path. Sometimes Mabel and I met Carina at Holloway, a shopping district on the outskirts of London. While we had tea in an Aerated Bread Shop, Carina poured out shocking tales of her work in the slums.[8] Of three and four families living in one room, each occupying a corner. Of babies being born in these conditions. Of sweat shops where women and girls worked eighteen hours a day in dark, unsanitary, unventilated cellars, doing piece work, making blouses (supplied to them already cut out) at one shilling a dozen, and supplying their own cotton, while children sewed on buttons at a penny a gross. We were horrified and made a stand never to buy a ready-made blouse. It brought to mind that stinging indictment of those conditions: "Stitch, stitch, stitch/In poverty, hunger and dirt" from "The Song of the Shirt" by Tom Hood.

Carina was particularly interested, just then, in a family with five or six children. There was one bed for the lot, a few cracked cups and plates, and the only thing the mother had been able to provide to receive her new baby was a yard of glazed calico. Carina was taking her one egg at a time, because experience showed that if it was not eaten while she was there, the little ones found its hiding place and gobbled it up raw, shell and all.

The two oldest girls of eleven and twelve were trying to cope with the family, and battling with life, never having seen grass growing or a live cow, and always hungry. Mabel and I determined, then and there, to take these little waifs down to World's End Farm for our holiday treat, and show them the country. This we did, and Carina came with us, and if those two children had the time of their lives, we certainly did, too. The huge brick oven turned out the most delightful bread, and we had home-made butter from real cream. We explored the farm. "Ow! Miss! Look at the pig! (pointing to a calf). And, "Ow! Miss! See them apples a 'angin on a tree!" (What a joke! They ought to have been on a coster-monger's barrow!) Alfred Cornford showed them what he called the 'og 'ouse, and they saw flowers growing and picked them with wonderment for the first time in their lives, not knowing the names of any.[9]

Carina, Mabel and I walked over to beautiful old Herstmonceux Castle, and I made a sketch of it while they wandered around. We stayed a fortnight, and if ever two pounds ($10) was well spent, it was then. The following year, the little girls were so sophisticated in country life and travelling that they were able to go alone, and we gladly footed the bill. London children are so quick witted.

* * * * * * * * * *

On my afternoons or evenings off [at the Ryles], and generally on Sundays, too, I went down to the Children's Nursing Home on Park Road, and took part in the life there—sometimes wheeling crippled children out in company with others, or learning the intricacies of hospital bed making and management.

Friends called Miss Pawling "The Reverend Mother", or "The Venerable Bede", which Mabel and I shortened to Bede.[10] It was very good of her to allow me to go there so often. She always made me welcome, and we three (Mabel, Bede and I) had cosy little suppers together after all the children were settled for the night. I can't describe Bede. She was—well, just too nice for my pen.

The children at Bede's Home were mostly cases from the slums: babies that had been dropped in infancy and developed curvature of the spine, under-nourished children with rickets, children of diseased parents, crippled for life. But cases of tubercular hip disease were the most common. Little mites of four and five were so clever at feeding themselves from a drinking cup, or balancing a plate of food on their chests, while lying flat on their backs. They were all happy, each new one joining in the chatter and singing after a short spell of home sickness for the slums they had left.

Bede was so clever with them. They were not allowed to grizzle for their own good. And to see them smile and call, "Sister, sister", when she went into the wards showed she knew what she was about.

There was Lucky George, four years old, flat on his back, never to know what it would be like to run about and have fun. His world was bounded by his cot, and watching the other children through the bars. Bede would come in and say, cheerfully, "Well, George, aren't you the *lucky* boy? It's your turn to have the horse to play with." And this "lucky" boy gave a wan smile of pleasure and proceeded to wheel a skin horse up and down his shrunken little chest.

Lying in the big arm chair was "little woman" or "Voomansh" as we called her, about three years old, with a hydrocephalic head, and inclined to whimper at first. "Now, Voomansh, make a *nice* face. Make a nice face for Sister", and she, too, curled her lips to order.

People may say, "How cruel to make a sick child smile", but if so, it was "cruel to be kind". It formed a habit, and the habit became natural. Far better than having fifteen or sixteen sick children wailing and crying all day. Many of them were not in pain or suffering in any way. The whole atmosphere of the place was happy and wholesome, and every corner spotlessly clean.

But there were some cases beyond even Bede's capacity to make them happy. I went down to the home one afternoon to find Bede and Mabel gingerly washing a new arrival, a little boy of two, who had been kept in a box since infancy, and had somehow survived there, his big head and little stick arms and legs growing and shaping themselves

96

to the angles of the box. It was the most shocking sight. He was just alive, bald, and entirely devoid of any intelligence or even ability to cry. Bede had to be very careful not to break his fragile bones. He needed the utmost care, but within a week he began to show signs of intelligence when we said, "Hullo, Boxer!" [He was] the wreck of what should have been somebody's dear little boy.

There was a motherless little girl of three named Maudie Vale, who was so clever with the other children, taking plates and mugs round, and making herself generally useful. She had no home, so Bede finally adopted her, and Maude called her "mother", and Mabel and me "auntie". As years went by she took a greater share in the work.

Lord Strafford gave a fine piece of land on Hadley Green, and a beautiful new home was built, with large sun room, and a garden. Eventually, when Bede passed on, Maude Vale was asked to become the matron, and made a most efficient one.

* * * * * * * * * *

Now baby Peter arrived at Hadley House. It caused some amusement that agnostics should choose two Biblical names for their sons. When the monthly nurse left, Mrs. Ryle was still not very strong, so, to my great joy, she instructed me in bathing and dressing Peter from her bed. After a day or two, I could do it alone in the nursery.

I loved these "degrading duties" and as I was to be a mother myself some day, they were of inestimable value. I called Peter "my baby". Now there were five to do for, but as things worked smoothly and punctually, all went well.[11] We lived according to schedule. The children were conscientious and could be trusted. As the children's birthdays came round I gave them each an individual cup and saucer, with plate to match. They were delighted. (I used the set I had had as a little girl at Anerley.)

Dr. Ryle was the son of Dr. Ryle, D.D., Bishop of Liverpool. There were two other sons: Arthur, a jolly bachelor, and an artist by profession; and Herbert, who followed in his father's footsteps, and later was made Bishop of Winchester.[12] The Bishop was probably about sixty-five or seventy, and belonged to a social age and followed the customs from which Dr. and Mrs. Ryle had broken away. So when he invited Mrs. Ryle and the children (which would include their nurse, as a matter of course) to visit him in Lowestoft for a holiday, Mrs. Ryle evidently felt she should say something beforehand of his attitude towards the working classes, of which I was now a member. It was rather an embarrassing job for her, because the Bishop was her father-in-law. After the experience with Elliot, and a few others, it did not worry me at all. "A cat may look at a king", anyway, even if he does wear a Bishop's mitre.

Lowestoft is one of the chief fishing ports on the east coast. Hundreds of fishing smacks come sailing in between the twin piers of the harbour, making a pretty sight, with their brown sails. Men in oilskins and hip boots waded about among the mountains of fish, mostly herring, on the wharf, and girls shovelled them by the ton into baskets. The whole waterfront smelled of fish, and there were fish scales everywhere.

Our children were not allowed on the beach because it was crowded, and the home and breeding place of many germs. We generally walked along the Esplanade. Peter could now join us in our walks, sitting up in the pram. We made a regular procession. There was a certain amount of rivalry as to which of the children should walk beside me, holding the ends of the handlebar, leaving the other two to hold the front of the pram. So we had to arrange that they took it in turns.

I told [the children] the stories of books, as Carina had done for Mabel and me, only mine were simple for children. This led to the idea that we would act a scene from *Alice Through the Looking Glass*, and they could learn their parts as we walked along. We kept it a secret as far as possible from Mrs. Ryle, because she and the Doctor were to be the audience. It reminded me so much of my own childhood. I chose the scene where the Red and White Queens quiz Alice on general knowledge. Effie made a splendid Red Queen, with cardboard head-dress; Jessie, round-eyed, looked the part of Alice; and John was a solemn little White Queen, anxiously waiting for his cue to say, "She can't do sums a bit". The parents were delighted, and I think the children gave a repeat performance with a few of Mrs. Ryle's friends invited to see the show.

Once or twice the grandfather ordered a carriage and pair, and invited the family to go for a drive with him. He was not really fond of children, so I went along to keep them quiet, and see they did not fidget. Of course there could be no introduction under the circumstances, so I sat down opposite the Bishop, between the children, but he did not see me. He and Mrs. Ryle carried on a desultory conversation on "safe subjects" as the drive progressed.

[When the Ryle family returned to London] we came to an agreement that rather than leave them, Mrs. Ryle would pay a girl to do the nursery work and laundry, while I looked after the children in return for a home. I was *so* glad to be able to stay on.[13]

* * * * * * * * *

My eyes gave out that winter, 1896-96, and I was not well. This entailed several visits to Charlie Shaw for glasses and so on. Perhaps it was my more-or-less present enemy, but high blood pressure had not been discovered then.

While staying at Upper Wimpole Street with Charlie and Ellie, they were asked to dinner with the well-known Royal Acadamician Alma Tadema and his wife. Ellie asked if she might bring me, so an extra young man was provided to complete the table. I think he was rather amused at my lack of the usual small talk, but we got on finely with experiences in country life and animals.[14]

There was the usual sign for the ladies to retire to the drawing room, and I think Ellie was glad to make me the excuse for not staying very late. She called me "Princess Picklemehoff" in my fur-collared coat.—Leonard had sent me some coon skins from British Columbia.

About this time, when I was at Wimpole Street, Ellie heard that Mr. Ralph Grey from the Gulf Islands was in London, and asked him to tea. It was interesting to think he knew Arthur and Leonard, but we found it rather hard to get details of island life from him. Little did I think he would be my good husband!

Effie, John, Margaret and Jessie Ryle

"Mrs. Hutton", Phil, a relative, and the "impecunious artist"

England's pristine beaches contrasted sharply with the Gulf Island landscape that greeted Winifred and Mabel in 1896

Polly Payne, Saturna Island, is seated in a native dugout canoe, near a beach strewn with sandstone boulders and overhung with arbutus trees.

CHAPTER NINE

Westward Ho! 1896

Leonard wrote to us at intervals. Em had been to Mayne Island where she had a baby girl—Amelia Winifred ("Bay")—with Mrs. Robson to look after her. Thomas was "a big fellar in overalls" now, and could handle an axe.[1]

He sent a little sketch of their log cabin at The Kloshie Illahie (the good land in Chinook) and a photograph of himself, Em, Gerry and Harold Payne, and Warburton Pike on the beach at Saturna Island. We had never seen a beach like *that*! Old tree roots and trunks lying about, and Gerry rolled in a blanket, lying on the shingle. What a queer place! And *then*—"How about Mabel taking a holiday and making a trip to see it all?"[2]

We were enthralled with the idea, and Mabel finally decided to go. She certainly had a good, long holiday coming to her, having worked for years without any remuneration. My heart ached to go with her, but of course I could not say anything, and so looked forward to her return, to tell me all about it.

And then one day Mrs. Ryle, perhaps having guessed my thoughts, asked if I would like to go, too. She could get their old nanny for three months to help look after the children.

Can anyone who reads this guess the half of what that meant to Mabel and me? To go together! We were walking on air, on golden clouds of anticipation for the next few months, till all the arrangements could be completed. Leonard wrote, saying he would build a new bedroom for us; or we could sleep outside or on the beach if we liked! Not knowing the first thing about long-distance travelling, we decided to go under the auspices of a Society, which provided a matron and cheap fares for girls who, as a rule, were going to take positions as domestic help in towns or on the Prairies.[3] Leonard was on the first through train to Port Moody, ten years previously, 1886, and had told us how the engineer had stopped the train on the Prairies to shoot a coyote. Someone lent me a book with an account of a journey across Canada by C.P.R.—of being hosed with dust and cinders in the open observation car. It all sounded most exciting and, like John Gilpin, we were "all agog to dash through thick and thin!"

The day arrived; we left Euston Station (London) and sped northward. Never having been in the Midlands, the country was most interesting. The train ran through a patchwork of fields and hedges, embroidered with towns, villages, and an occasional bridge. Through Rugby, with its famous school, past "smoking chimney and murky cowl" of the Staffordshire pottery district, and on to Crewe, a large junction. We thought of the popular song: "Oh! Mr. Porter, what shall I do? I want to go to Birmingham; they've taken me on to Crewe." Reference to a map will show that she was a bit off her route.[4]

And so to Liverpool at last. Vast docks, wharves, and shipping noise. We saw nothing of the town or cathedral. Here we joined our party and, boarding a tender in a whirl of new experiences, were taken out to our "liner", the S.S. *Vancouver*.

The *Vancouver* had been a cattle boat for some years, and then re-converted to take passengers again. Down in the bowels of the ship, where the cattle had been, the company had erected rough wooden bunks, in tiers, just boarded off from the hold, with the most deplorable washing and sanitary arrangements. The matron had about eight girls for domestic work in tow, and two others on their own, as we were. One was going as a governess, and the other, she told us later, was a reporter on a newspaper (the *Seattle Post-Inteiligencer* I think). We four girls were assigned the two least desirable Second Class cabins, which had not been taken by regular passengers, but we were in luxury compared to the others; Mabel and I had a porthole.[5]

The matron gathered her charges round her, sitting on the bare deck, and would not allow them to wander from her or speak to anyone. She tried to make us do the same, but we refused. After she got back to London 'e reported us for insubordination, but who cared?

We were steaming slowly out through the Mersey, when the bell rang for supper. Down a very steep little companionway we found three tables, covered with oilcloth and laid with knives and forks; no ventilation. A so-called waiter—at any rate he had on an apron, if that constitutes a waiter—plunked a plate of meat and vegetables in front of each of us and retired. Mabel and I eyed each other. Certainly we knew nothing about ocean travelling, but perhaps this was not quite what we had anticipated. We were hungry, and so choked down some of the meat, which was smothered in greasy, fried onions. A "nice rice pudding" followed, with well-boiled, strong coffee. We climbed the ladder, rather amazed, but ready to laugh it off.

It was calm the next morning, so we went down to breakfast. Tough steak, greasy fried onions and strong coffee again! For *breakfast!* Well, we had started out with the intention of squeezing every ounce of pleasure out of the trip whatever befell; so we asked our stewardess if she would bring us what she could from the Second Class dining saloon. She was not a bad sort, and promised to do her best. But fate decreed that food of any kind would not tempt us for some time to come. That old tub heaved and plunged and wallowed after we left Moville, in Loch Foyle, Northern Ireland, where we picked up mail.

At last we found our feet on the tiny piece of deck allotted to us. One day we heard a Swede exclaim, "Eke-bairg! Eke-bairg!", and followed his pointing finger. We saw a glorious big iceberg, glistening in the morning sun. Then we ran into thick fog off the Newfoundland coast, and the engines almost stopped, which felt so queer and silent.

At Rimouski the pilot came aboard to take us up the St. Lawrence, framed in the Laurentian Mountains. It was hard to believe that vast spread of water was a river, but it gradually narrowed till we saw Quebec City crawling up the hillside. Crossings were not made in five and a half days then. The *Vancouver* took two weeks to reach this old, historic town. Mabel and I debated how much we ought to give the stewardess. She looked a bit huffy when we finally gave her five shillings ($1.25), which we had thought would be generous. As we came off the boat, hawkers stood at the gate, shouting their wares: "Apples two for five!" Two for five what? "Five cents!" How much is that? We were afraid of being fooled at every turn.

We climbed the steep, winding old streets to the Heights of Abraham, marvelling at everything, and sat down, listening to children chattering French as their native tongue. The train took us to Montreal, where we gladly shed the disgruntled matron; a feeling that was probably mutual. She was just a little Jack-in-office.

102

We were puzzled to see the houses roofed with coloured "slates" as we thought, which the Seattle girl said were made of wood, and called shingles. What would she try to "stuff us up" with next? From then on we didn't believe anything she told us!

Travelling "colonist" involved in stocking up with some food, amongst other things, enormous bananas, which were a great novelty. I don't think I had ever eaten one. We each had an enamel plate, a mug, a knife and spoon, a tiny saucepan, and a little tea-maker spoon. (I had my sketch book and made little sketches, mostly in pencil, all the way, but they are all lost.) We could make a cup of tea on the little stove at one end of the car, and had one meal a day on the diner. Our cabin trunks went under the seats, which had no padding; but we each had a cushion for a pillow at night. The seats were jointed and we pulled them out ourselves to make a bed, having paid $2.50 each for the use of so-called matresses of ticking, filled with hay. At the end of the journey these had to be returned and, with fumigation and fresh hay, were used again, indefinitely. So the CPR did pretty well on that deal.

At first Mabel and I jumped off at every little wayside stop, but soon learned that "Board! Board!" was a warning to be heeded, if you did not want to be left behind. The washing arrangements were primitive in the extreme. A triangular corner of the car was partitioned off and contained a small basin and limited supply of water. There was just room for one at a time. All our old ideas of so-called modesty had to go to the winds, with both sexes in the car—which was perhaps a good thing.

It was strange to try and adjust one's eyes to the clear atmosphere and long-distance views and the immensity of everything. Coasting along Lake Superior, I pointed out to a fellow passenger what I thought was a little island covered with bushes. He smiled and said, "Do you know that island is about ten miles away, and the "bushes" are tall trees? The whole of the British Isles could be dumped in Lake Superior and hardly make a splash.[6]

A railway guide, with map and timetable, helped us follow every mile of the way, and to know when and where to expect a stop, and for how long. In these days of easy travel, movies and picture magazines, there is nothing comparable to give more than a faint idea of the revelation which unfolded before us as we crossed the Continent. Quaint little wayside stations, with a burley-looking backwoodsman waiting for the mail, his buckboard or democrat hitched to a post, and no other sign of habitation; level crossings, with people walking unconcernedly on the tracks; the gigantic locomotive, with its wide, open-mouthed funnel; the strange, plaintive howl of the whistle and tanging bell, and cowcatcher—all these and many more were new to us. Gophers popped out of their burrows, and there were unbelievable acres of wild flowers: tiger lilies, lupins and many we could not recognize.

Then came Winnipeg, with its wide Main Street, and the one and two-storey shops, with false square fronts above. There was a General Merchandise Store here and I bought a queer little cap, which took my fancy, for Thomas. A few sidestreets and scattered houses, all "frame", on the outskirts completed the Winnipeg of 44 years ago. No street cars or paving, just board sidewalks. I wonder what it looks like now?[7]

Mabel and I made friends with the engineers and stokers, and they often let us ride in the cab with them, which gave us a much better view of the country than peering out of windows. At Wapella, Saskatchewan, we got off, bag and baggage, to stay with the George family who were farming there. They were most hospitable. Their boy of fifteen understood all the management of the farm, and we were amazed to see Percy, nine, swarm up the mane of a cart horse and go off alone to harrow. Some of the children went to school in the morning, a big and little one riding on a bare-backed horse. Mrs. George had been an operatic singer and still had the remains of a good voice. They were anxious to show us off to their friends; but I am afraid that we did not come up to the expectations as "fashionable young ladies" from London.[8]

I must skip over the details of this visit or we shall never reach the Coast. At the station, stumbling around in the dark, we saw a glimmer of light in the waiting room and heard a strange noise. Stretched out on the bare board table was the station agent, snoring like a grampus. How we laughed as we slipped away again. Indian Head, Moose Jaw, and Medicine Hat were fascinating names, each with a history; and then we came to Calgary, our next stop.

We arrived in the middle of the night this time, so we took a room at the little railway hotel, hoping for some sleep. But railway hotels were the meeting and drinking places for the countryside at train time, whenever that might be. We got up early, leaving the smoke-filled saloon (which we had to pass through) to its patrons, and strolled along the one street, with its board sidewalks.[9]

Coming to a cake shop with tempting-looking pies and buns, we went in to get something to eat. A customer was just asking for a "jelly cake" and it intrigued us to know what that would be. It turned out to be what we should have called a "Victoria sandwich," though not so good.[10] We went back to the hotel to wait for Herbert Church, who soon appeared with a democrat and pair of fine horses. Our baggage was piled in and off we went.

At Calgary, Mother Earth was already beginning to roll and crumple towards the foothills, preparing for the final, mighty heave. Far away on the horizon rose the first snow pinnacles of the Rocky Mountains. There was no road to our inexperienced eyes; it seemed as if Herbert just drove away into the trackless, rolling prairie. It was incredible what he did with those horses and buggy. The democrat behaved like a double-jointed insect, crawling up rough hillsides at impossible angles, and then careening down into gullies and across river beds. After 25 miles of this, we swung round a good-sized log cabin, to find Gertrude, with baby Elsie, and the brothers outside to welcome us.

From a mass of interesting experiences, I must choose just a few. Our first surprise was in the kitchen, where Teddie was kneading a huge pan of dough. He was breadmaker. We were shown the cattle corrals, with post and rail fences and home-made gates, and the shed, where in winter they hung up a whole beef carcass. It froze solid and they chopped off pieces with an axe, as needed.

They took us on lovely, and often breath-taking drives along the Bow River, which was at [high] water then towards the end of June. The horses thought nothing of crossing with the water almost in the buggy, so that we had to lift our feet, and I think the boys did these stunts on purpose to try and get a rise out of Mabel and me. Herbert sometimes took a twinkling, sidelong look in our direction, but we weren't giving him any change!

There was some kind of "Horse Fair" about ten miles away, to which we all went. Dick rode, and they put Mabel and me each on a beautiful horse; while Herbert drove Gertrude and the baby in the democrat. I say "put" advisedly, because neither of us had ever been on a horse before, and didn't even know which side to mount. Of course we rode side-saddle. All went well on the outward journey. It was a fine sight to watch all the different buggies and horses of every description converging on the appointed meeting place, the men in ten-gallon hats. I was so busy watching, as we trotted down the last hill, that I nearly ran over a man on foot, quite forgetting that I was in charge of my horse. He sprang to one side, and was about to use some language, but, seeing I was a stranger and greenhorn, too, he refrained. It was evidently a rodeo, with which everyone is familiar now, so I won't describe the buck jumping, steer riding, and Indian races, which enthralled Mabel and me.[11]

When we started home our horses, which were a little ahead, suddenly remembered important business in their stalls, and started to race. Away we flew, mile after mile, and away went our hats and hairpins. Dick came thundering after us, but the nearer he got, the faster went our horses. It was a case of holding on to anything like grim death. At our last gasp we came to a hill and managed to slow down, and Dick made a grab at my reins. We [had] come about six miles at top speed. And it *was* speed; because Herbert told us afterwards, with a rather guilty but wicked twinkle in his eye, that the horses were two of their best, and accustomed to racing against each other. Dick had intended to trot home with us, but we had started ahead and were off on our breakneck race before he knew it. Anyway, they said we were pretty plucky to have held on as we did, and, I think, were secretly relieved not to have two smashed-up girls on their hands.

The three brothers raised thoroughbred horses for racing and carriage work, and when they had a shipment ready, took turns in travelling with them on a cattle boat, to sell in England. Years later, Herbert wrote an amusing and interesting little book on their early start in this country.[12]

One day Dick said he as going to round up some stock and would I like to go with him? Needless to say, I jumped at the chance and away we went. How he knew where to find a bunch of cattle in that wilderness I could not guess, but presently I found myself galloping along behind a herd of perhaps thirty or forty, while Dick kept them rounded up. He shouted orders to me, which were impossible to hear through the din of snorting beasts and thud of pounding hoofs. The ground was riddled with gopher burrows, but I had to trust to the sagacity of my horse to avoid them. Somehow I had got right in the middle of the cattle, when he did put his foot in one and tripped, nearly throwing me over his head as they thundered past. Poor fellow. He must have wondered, "what thing upon his back had got."

Dick maneuvered the panting beasts into one of the corrals, and Herbert shut the big gate. After a breathing spell they both went in and cut out the yearling calves for branding, letting the remainder go. We were thrilled to see all this.

Again we had to move on and board the train for British Columbia, regretfully leaving our old friends at Hadley Ranch. There were no enclosing doors on the coaches then, so Mabel and I spent hours sitting on the steps, or in the open observation car, where we were duly "hosed with dust and cinders," as predicted. All the next day, we seemed to crawl towards the mountains, apparently so near and yet so far off. Up at 4 a.m. the next morning, we were determined not to miss a minute of daylight. The train threaded itw way into The Gap, past the Three Sisters, and so to Banff. There was no dining car, but the train stopped at stated places, where a meal was ready to be served. You had to bolt it and dash off at the now familiar "Board! Board!" I shall never forget Field, where the hotel dining room was so prettily decorated with sweet peas, in the heart of the mountains.

We rode the whole way through the mountains in the engineer's cab. Nearly all the bridges were of trestle construction then and, winding and rocking down the Corkscrew, we peeped out into space, looking back at the five tiers of tracks which formed the spiral.

Kicking Horse Pass, the beautiful Illecillewaet River Valley, Revelstoke, the Shuswap Lakes, and many other scenes are imprinted on my mind forever. Kamloops, Hell's Gate, where the train stopped to allow passengers to see the raging mad Fraser River below; Yale, Hope, the Fraser Valley, and—at last—Westminster Junction, where Leonard was on the platform to travel with us to New Westminster.

What a meeting! He took us to the old Guichon Hotel, and we had dinner, much amused at the number of little dishes which surrounded our plates. [13]

The next morning we went to the wharf where, after introductions, Leonard persuaded Captain Jaggers, a most genial man, to take his steamer, the *R.P. Rithet* (an old sternwheeler) to Saturna Island, which was not on his route that day. You could do that sort of thing long ago. Time and delay didn't count for much, and two girls didn't come out from England every day for the Islands. There was a current saying, which was very applicable: "We're never in a hurry in this country. When we get there, we get there." So the other passgners merely wondered at the change in route, and smoked while watching people coming on board. [14]

Leonard said, "Oh, here's Pike!" "Where?" "Right here, coming up the gangplank." We looked in amazement. A moment later there was a hatless man, in shirt and overalls, with a gunnysack slung over his shoulder, being introduced to us as Mr. Pike, of whom we had heard so much. He was just returning from an exploring trip, and was always one of the most courteous of men.—We made one more re-adjustment from old country conventions to the new. [15]

Hadley Ranch, the Herbert Church homestead southwest of Calgary.
Gertrude Church shows off baby Elsie.

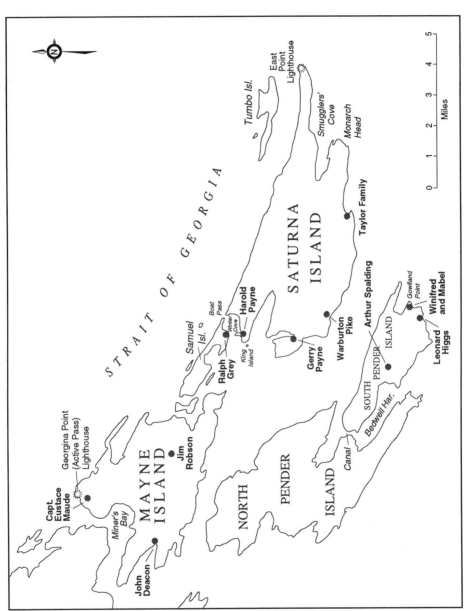

The Southern Gulf Islands of British Columbia

N

STRAIT OF GEORGIA

Tumbo Isl.

East
Point
Lighthouse

Smugglers'
Cove

Monarch
Head

SATURNA
ISLAND

Taylor Family

Miles

0   1   2   3   4   5

Boat
Pass

Winter
Cove

Samuel
Isl.

Harold
Payne

Ralph
Grey

King
Island

Warburton
Pike

Arthur Spalding

Gowlland
Point

Winifred
and Mabel

Gerry
Payne

SOUTH
PENDER
ISLAND

Leonard
Higgs

Georgina Point
(Active Pass)
Lighthouse

Capt.
Eustace
Maude

Miner's
Bay

MAYNE
ISLAND

Jim
Robson

NORTH
PENDER
ISLAND

Canal

Bedwell Har.

John
Deacon

107

CHAPTER TEN

To South Pender

The *Rithet* whistled—a shrill, prolonged blast—or was it the alluring siren of adventure calling? I should like to hear that magic sound again. We chugged down the Fraser River and across the Gulf of Georgia. It was not a clear day, so there was no view, but we did not realize that. Through the swirls and eddies of Plumper Pass the boat churned her way, and then down Navy Channel to Saturna Island.[1] As it was low tide, the *Rithet* could not tie up at the wharf, so several rowboats put out in answer to a warning "toot" to take off passengers and baggage.

Mabel and I clambered over the side, to find ourselves in a small dinghy, with Leonard and Harold Payne, whose name was so familiar. Mr. Pike was taken off by his rancher, Fisher[2] and Mr. Arthur Drummond took our trunks. I spied a little canoe drawn up under the trees, and on the beach were Gerry Payne and his sister Polly who was spending the summer there. We were introduced and Leonard explained how he had wheedled Captain Jaggers into calling at Saturna. It was getting late so Gerry Payne said quite casually he would put us up for the night, and Mr. Drummond would take us and our baggage down to the Kloshie in the morning in the plunger. We were at a loss to understand how anyone could suddenly ask three people to stay the night, but everyone appeared to take things for granted, and just naturally did what was wanted. There were no social formalities, either in manners or dress, and no one seemed to expect any thanks.

We were in a new world of strange and unexpected, though delightful experiences. Gerry (I speak of him as Gerry, though, of course, he was Mr. Payne then) rowed us round the point to Breezy Bay. We climbed the steep bank to see his pretty little frame house, painted white and green, standing about 200 yards back. He was a bachelor, living alone with his farm helper, Jack Blantern, but when he later showed us to a bedroom upstairs, we found the bed made, basin and jug of water, towels, and every convenience, and were told to make ourselves at home. We were amazed.

Mabel and I were up early the next morning, being too excited to sleep much. Gerry had "fixed" a good breakfast of bacon and eggs, coffee and toast, which we ate in wonderment at his capability. We helped to wash the dishes—a novelty for us—left our bedroom tidy, and then all set off for the wharf, where Mr. Drummond was ready with the plunger.

In loading up, one of our cabin trunks toppled into the water, but was quickly hauled out.[3] A little accident like that only added to the thrill of everything. The sail was hoisted, but of course we knew nothing of there being a "fair tide," or "tacking with a light breeze" down to Blunden Island. Leonard realized there was a limit to what we could absorb, so wisely left us to drink in as much as we could, without constantly saying, "There's such and such a place," or "this is so and so".

Through Blunden Channel, we crossed Camp Bay, passed the Green Hill and Fern Point, soon to be so familiar, and turned into the Kloshie Bay. At last Leonard said, "There's Emmikins and the kids!" We could see a little log cabin on the bank but no people.—Nearer still—yes, there was Em, hurrying down the path, while Thomas and Bay jumped from log to log and over the rocks in bare feet. They were not expecting us, but it was such a happy meeting. The children suddenly turned shy, and Thomas discovered he had "a flea or something" in his shirt, which needed a lot of attention. It was an absurd little nervous habit of his, we found. Sometimes it was a barnacle in his toe, or a button off his pants. He was going to be seven in October, and Bay was just three that July. Sad to say, another little dead baby had come between them.

Mr. Drummond stayed on, finally having lunch with us without being invited. Another thing "taken for granted". Evidently, we must rearrange our Old Country ideas still more. There was plain, home-made cake, with jam for lunch, which tasted so good after food on the train. In fact, we chose it every day, it was such a change. Sometimes Em could spare a little cream to go with it, as they had a cow, and made butter in the old plunger churn from Netherton.

Leonard had kept his promise and added a large bedroom to the house, so Mabel and I could unpack in comfort. When [the weather permitted] we took our blankets and slept against a log outside. It was such a thrill to look up at the stars and wake in the morning to see a hummingbird whirring over the patchwork flowers on our coverlets.

Em had a store room in which we were surprised to see so many "pickle bottles" as we thought. It looked as if they must *live* on pickles. But Em explained they were for preserving fruit for the winter. [This system was] far in advance of anything of the kind in England. It was the same with the stoves we saw. They stood out from the wall, so that you could get all round them conveniently, whereas the English ranges were built flush with the wall. (Years later, when Malcolm Shaw came out to Samuel Island, he was dumbfounded to see one of these stoves in our kitchen. They were "the very latest thing in England, just coming into use," he said.)

[Johnny, a young Japanese man, helped Em with the heavy work and the laundry.] The latter he did in the garden, in tubs mounted on boxes, heating the water in coal-oil cans over an open fire.[4]

Leonard wanted to show us "the field" at the back of the house. It was his pride, because it had involved a lot of heavy clearing, sawing down immense trees and burning the brush. "Where is it?," we asked, looking around among huge, blackened stumps, four or five feet high, with some grass between, and stepping over the occasional log. "Why, *here! This* is the field," he explained. I suppose we had been expecting acres of lush meadowland, as in England.

They had a piano, which Em had brought from the Old Country with her "settlers' effects," and which had never been tuned since; but in the evening we used to have a sing-song. Em had quite a good voice and could sing alto, without having been taught—just by ear. She had a book of old songs and I had brought several from my school days: Molloy's *Masks and Faces*, and *London Bridge*. Leonard could pick out an air with one finger and would, no doubt, have been able to play well if he had given his mind to it earlier in life, because he could do anything he chose.

Mother Nature has a curious way of dividing the spoils of inheritance. She dipped in her Pandora's box and handed Leonard an exceptionally large share of brains, but failed to give him the necessary desire to make the best use of her gift. He could do anything he put his mind to without any effort, which is sometimes a man's stumbling block towards any real achievement in life. If he had gone to college, I have no doubt he could have taken a position afterwards where brains were needed, but he would have none of it. He followed Arthur Spalding to the Gulf Islands and carved a home out of the back woods. He built a good frame house; boats, small and large, without any instructions; and made a forge where he devised wrought iron gadgets, pokers and whatnot. When Auntie Emma died and left Mabel and me some money, we gave Leonard a new piano, and he concocted wonderful things from the keys and vitals of the old one. On one occasion he went over to the American side (Friday Harbour) to defend an old smuggler who had been caught. By the use of absurd technicalities about tides and boats, he got the presiding judge so tied up in knots that the prisoner was acquitted, though undoubtedly guilty. Later in life Leonard wrote poetry—"Freedom's Slave" and other verses, which were accepted by the *Spectator*, a most particular periodical. His poems about nature and wildlife appealed to me more than anything of the kind I have ever read.

All Leonard's life was hampered by ill health, bronchial asthma being the family failing. Even that could have been alleviated to some extent if he would have consented to live in the Upper Country, where he was free from it, but he preferred to stay at the old Kloshie Illahie home and put up with his disability.

There was no Forestry Department in those days, and forest fires raged [unchecked], filling the air with smoke for weeks on end, and blotting out all views of the mountains and islands. That summer, 1896, we had a good deal of rain, which was fortunate in a way, because it kept the fires in check.   In the early morning of the second day after we arrived, Leonard took me by the shoulders to the open door, and pointed eastward. The smoke, which we had not realized was there, had lifted in the night, and revealed the lovely islands "casting down their golden crowns around the glassy sea". Towering over them, on the horizon, the magnificent peak of Mount Baker rose eleven thousand feet high above the Cascade Mountains. A lump came in my throat, and tears filed my eyes. It was unbelievably beautiful. No words of mine can paint the picture, or express the impression it made on me. Leonard again had refrained from telling us what enchantment nature was holding behind that man-made smoke screen. South Pender Island faced the Strait of Juan de Fuca, the dividing line between Canada and the United States, so the Kloshie had the full benefit of the whole grand range of the Olympic Mountains [and the Cascade Mountains] in Washington State.

The adjoining ranch to the Kloshie was owned by Arthur Stanford, whom we had known as a boy in the old Bromley days. His father was the well-known publisher of Stanford and Company, makers of maps and charts. (Ralph had been to their headquarters on several occasions, and Mabel and I got a chart of British Columbia and the Islands before we came.) He had a good, large, but unpainted frame house, and had brought out a young farm lad of the simple, gullible type, to help with the work. This youth was known as Amos—his name being Elijah. We heard that the poor chap was wading through a batch of what was known as "sinker" bread (heavy) which he had made, Arthur Stanford thinking it the quickest road to learning. It probably was, but pretty tough on the boy.

Beyond Stanford's place was Bilk Point, named by Arthur and Leonard ten years before. They were green then and "bilked" into rushing out in a boat, after dark, to rescue someone who was not in any danger, merely showing a light. They crept back, hoping they had not been seen.

Arthur Spalding and his family lived about two miles inland, so we all walked over to see them. There was no road, of course, just a single-file, rough trail through the forest. We passed a group of large glacial rocks, and further on a monster known as "the Big Rock"; over the hill we stumbled, on loose boulders and roots of trees, down into Arthur's valley (or flat) of fields and cultivated land, divided by post and rails, or snake

"Kloshie Illahee",
South Pender Island, British Columbia

Washday for Em Higgs, Johnny and Tom

111

*Lilias Spalding with l to r; sister Agnes McKay, Charlie Long,
Gerald Payne, Arthur Spalding and Arthur Long. BCARS 40621*

fences; past his barn, and then the final steep climb to the house—a nice frame building, with a large verandah covered with a vine and creepers.

There we found Arthur, who we were so glad to see again; Lillie and her two younger sisters, Gertie and Aline; and the three little girls, Hetty, Bessie and Bea, the latter about two years old.[5] They showed us round the place, and their lovely flower garden—a fine display of polyanthus—and then Aline disappeared to get tea, while we all sat on the verandah and talked. In about half an hour she appeared with tea things and "jelly cake", which, she said, she had just made "right now" (a new expression to us). Mabel and I were astonished to think of a girl of sixteen being able to make a cake at a moment's notice. We walked home later, wondering how anyone could find the way with so little trail, but we soon came to know it well ourselves.

Arthur and Lil were terrific workers. They had acres of cultivated land, which Arthur ploughed with a yoke of oxen—great, clumsy brutes—using the old terms, "Gee!" (right) and "Haw!" (left) to guide them, which sounded very quaint.[6] Lil kept the three little girls so tidy and clean, and their long hair curled. They wore cotton dresses, rough-washed, as she had no time for ironing. She was a good shot, too. One evening she went down onto the flat and shot a deer that had been devouring their crops.

Arthur grew wheat for his chickens, and used a flail on the barn floor to thrash the grain from the chaff. Of course they longed for a boy, and when Mabel and I returned the following year their wish was granted, and Herbert arrived—named after Arthur's oldest brother.

Charlie Long lived in Bedwell Harbour with his partner Gerald Richardson, an exceedingly nice fellow who had just come out from England, and a young chap named Brantford. We walked over there to see them, and it was jolly to meet Charlie again; he was always good fun. These bachelors were quite equal to giving anyone a cup of tea, with a loaf of bread and butter to help youself, even if it was just on the bare board table. (There were plates, of course, and milk, known as "canned cow".) They didn't go in for "frills".

All the Islanders raised sheep and lambs to be shipped and sold in Victoria. It was quite a trip for those on Pender, to row them up to Saturna to be put on the steamer. It was dull for the sheep, calves or pigs, too, because they had their legs tied together. Arthur Stanford's cow broke her leg, wandering among the logs, and had to be shot, of course; but he wasn't going to be "done in" by that. He got out his wash boiler, and he and Amos cut up Mrs. Bossycow into convenient pieces and boiled her down till she made meat essence, like Oxo. This he cut into squares, wrapped them in grease paper, and sold them to his grocer in Victoria.

From the Koshie one looked right across to Stuart, the westernmost island of the U.S.A. group, with Turn Point foghorn and lighthouse. Flash, wink-wink gleamed the light, which seemed to be a friendly welcome each evening to us on the Canadian side. The foghorn was not so pleasant! How he blared! But he served a useful purpose.

Eastward was Flat Top Island; then Waldron, with a long, distinctive, bare, sandy promontory, and behind them the twin rounded mountains of Orcas Island. Rising above these islands were the snow-clad Olympics, in ever-changing light and shadow, with the gulch of Port Angeles visible on clear days.

"Old Burke" the smuggler ventured across the Straits (about 20 miles) from Friday Harbour on San Juan Island, very occasionally in calm weather, in his old, shallow skiff, stained grey-black to escape detection. There was no "feathering" when he pulled, for fear the sun would glint on the wet oars.[7] He generally crossed in the small hours of the morning, starting near the end of a flood tide, and dropping back to the Kloshie on the first of the ebb. He had to keep a sharp lookout to see that Mr. Drummond's boat (he was the police constable) was not on the beach. If not, he showed up with chickens, or a little tobacco, or whatnot to sell. But what he wanted was *wool*, after sheep shearing. He could pay a good price for fleeces and make a profit on the other side, but it was a risky business for the old fellow.

The beach was an endless source of interest and Mabel and I often went beachcombing with the children. You never knew what you might find, from a canoe to a bundle of stair carpet, or a crate of lanterns. If you [needed] some lumber for a pigpen, or rabbit hutch, you hunted along the beach, and would be sure to find what you wanted.

We saw steamers of all kinds plying their trades: an occasional four-masted schooner from Australia, with her sails still set if there was breeze enough, and big ocean-going liners, which passed majestically down the Strait, glittering white on the blue water. A lovely sight.

Thomas knew each one because he and Bay played all day on the beach. They paddled along the shore astride logs which, in their happy imagination, became the *Empress of Japan* or *India*. They turned over rocks to find "mangers" (crabs), or whittled boats out of chunks of beach wood. I was horrified to see Bay run into the house and come out with a butcher knife nearly as long as her arm, but Em was quite unperturbed. Their feet were constantly poisoned by pieces of barnacles—or "barkinal" as Bay called them—but some kind Providence watched over them and they never came to serious harm, which was a miracle. Thomas was always so nice to Bay, helping her turn a big rock or climbing a tree to get something she wanted. We were very struck by that quality in him.

Thomas could handle a small axe quite well, and was supposed to chop a box of kindling every morning; but, boy-like, he scamped it if he could. Leonard: "Where's Thomas?"

"On the beach."

Thomas appears, looking crestfallen and wriggling in his shirt.

"Have you filled the kindling box?"

"No."

"No, who?"

"No, Sir."

"Well, then, go and do it at once.

And away he goes, his shirt giving him a lot of trouble! Half way through his job, Bay dashes up. "Fushie is barkin' at a minka' under a log on de beach!" The axe is flung down and away they go—soon followed by the whole family at the sound of excited yapping—the kindling forgotten.

Fuskie was a grand little dog, a fox terrier, so game—she had no fear in tackling these ferocious little animals. In and out of holes in rocks, dashing along logs, up the bank, down onto the beach again, scent lost; no, here it is! Off again, then a plunge into the water where Fuskie tackled him swimming, but the mink got her by the nose and held on. Now onto the rocks again, and along the beach, where I actually got him by the tail, but he wriggled loose and was off again. By this time we were nearly as far as Camp Bay, and were all so blown, and Fuskie was nearly all in, that we decided to give the rascal his well-earned freedom, and watched him scamper up the bank, while we returned to the kindling. (Fuskie had once belonged to Ralph Grey, but when he went up the River he gave her to Leonard.)

Nowadays, I don't suppose people can realize the feelings of hard working Islanders when animals destroyed the fruits of their labour. To go to the chicken house and find that a mink had somehow squeezed in and killed a dozen of your best laying hens

114

by biting the backs of their necks, or to find that a deer had jumped a seven-foot fence and eaten the vegetables that were to keep you through the summer—it made you boil, and something had to be done about it. But I couldn't hunt them now, especially a mink, after having our darling little Choo-choo as an almost human pet.[8]

Leonard was careful only to shoot to kill; he never wounded a deer and let it get away, as some did. He never set a trap either if he could catch a thief by any other, more humane means.

****

South Pender had no wharf in those days, and no steamer called. People either sailed or rowed—pulled as they called it. Arthur had an old tub he called the *Sussex*, which he kept in Bedwell Harbour, but rarely used. He was not much of a boating man. Leonard called his little rowboat the "Winifred". The nearest store and post office was at Saturna wharf, a long, three-mile pull, almost invariably against a head tide.

Arthur Drummond frequently came in his capacity as constable of the Islands. "Here comes Nummon in his boat!," Bay would call out. It did seem strange that a scion of Drummond Castle in Scotland should be policing the Islands in a rowboat, but nothing was too fantastic to be a reality.[9] It was said that Ralph Grey had some ancestors up his sleeve, too, but, of course, they all kept these things dark. "Duke's son, cook's son, son of a hundred kings", all were on an equal footing. Mabel and I were swallowing almost anything now, "hook, line and sinker," to use a local expression.

Arthur Drummond had two brothers, Bertie, known as "Red" Drummond; and Walter, known as "Old Black," who ran the post office and had a little store at Saturna wharf. He would deliver an order by boat if it were large enough to make the trip worthwhile. It meant a meal and a chat at the Koshie, which was always welcome to the bachelors. They got to tired of pork and beans, or bacon and eggs. In spite of our having fresh milk, [Arthur Drummond] always beat his spoon in his cup, saying "Used to canned milk," as the reason. So Bay beat her spoon, in mimicry, "Ooost to cahnd moonk!"

Mabel and I settled down to absorb island life, though it was not normal, because there were picnics, hunting, and camping parties as often as they could be arranged, and everyone scamped their usual work to take part in them. Arthur and Lillie were not keen on camping. Also, it was difficult for them, with three little children and quite a lot of stock and crops to get away. So they only went on picnics.

Arthur Drummond was a good messenger as he went his rounds. Through him a huge camping party was arranged at Fiddler's Cove on Saturna. Mabel and I had never rowed a boat in our lives, but Leonard put us, alone, in the little boat, and told us to follow the rest. There was only one pair of oars, so we took turns. Our muscles, unaccustomed to that form of exercise, were tired in no time, so we kept changing places, but were determined not to give in.

It was the greatest joke! On and on we went, mile after mile; and how the others laughed at the way we handled the oars. Across Saturna Channel, past George Taylor's quarry, and the Seagull Islets, we laughed and groaned by turns. "Put it to the paddle wheel Aunt!," yelled young Thomas, cheeking his striving aunts from another boat. (An expression which meant you were swinging your oars like a paddlewheel.)

We rounded Monarch Head and, at last, when nearly dead, saw the leading boats begin to turn in to Fiddler's Cove. A good six miles for a first trial! But of course there must have been a fair tide or we could never have done it.

The camp at Fiddler's (Smuggler's) Cove, July 1896.

East Point Lighthouse, Saturna Island

Some of the Saturna people were there ahead of us, and were already putting up tents, and chopping down fir branches to be piled to form a fine spring mattress to sleep on. The beach supplied planks for a good, long table and mill ends made seats. There was a little creek, and as a cup of tea was always the first requisite, someone made a campfire, surrounded by rocks, and fixed a pole to support the "billy".

Polly Payne, Mabel and I decided to make a "bedroom" on the bank, near a huge log. The men helped us fix our beds, and we shoved our spare clothes and lantern under the log in case of rain. Em and the children had a tent on the beach. After a most welcome supper, at which we fed right royally, we all sat round the campfire, and Polly Payne, who had brought her guitar, sang. Her repertoire was rather limited—the familiar "Che Faro" and two or three others—but it sounded cheerful in the firelight. Strangely enough, the men did most of the cooking, frying bacon or making flapjacks, and so on, and we took turns in washing the dishes, each one having brought his or her own.

Then came bedtime, and we all turned in to the glow and sparkle of the huge log fire. The stars looked down through the branches of the dark trees, but there was little sleep. After a long time of silence, we heard a gentle footfall and light crackle of twigs. "What's that?", and, at the sound [of our voices] away sprang a deer, crashing through the bushes.

We were all up early the next morning, about 4:30, except Em and the children, and Polly Payne, who did not care for long walks in the woods. After a good breakfast and packing up a lunch, we started, single file, up the steep bluff: Leonard, Gerry and Harold Payne, Charlie Long, Gerald Richardson, Arthur Drummond, Mabel and myself, some of the men carrying rifles. We tramped about five or six miles, through thick forest, up and down steep bluffs, over logs and through swamps, every now and then seeing deer, but somehow no one seemed to be able to hit one. The fact was they did not fancy carrying a hundred pound carcass over their shoulders such a long distance—but we learned that afterwards, by more experience. At one place we had a beautiful view of about ten deer, which had been startled by our approach in the valley, and in their confusion they chose to climb a bare mountainside, in full view.

As we were nearing camp on our way home, a deer was spotted in the valley and so someone shot it. I feel so sorry now to write about it, but at the time it was such a thrill. Anyway, it meant meat for all to take home, after it had hung, and people had to live. Mabel and I were pretty dead beat when we got back to camp, and even the men were quite tired, having been gone about twelve hours.

Another day some of us rowed over to Skipjack Island, the rocky, almost treeless home of thousands upon thousands of gulls. We clambered up, but one could hardly put a foot down without treading on an egg or baby bird, they were so wonderfully camouflaged. The air was full of beating wings and the harsh cries of the parent birds, so angry at the intrusion.

Leonard soon took Mabel and me in hand to teach us to row correctly, keeping time, and "feathering" our oars, and we were very glad he did. Some Islanders were content to just "paddle-wheel" all their days. We even had to learn how to get in and out of a boat properly. Skirts were still rather long and cumbersome, and one had to be careful not to expose more than a minimum of leg.

The third night it rained—and how it rained! We three women huddled our bedding under the log as best we could in the darkness, lying head to feet, trying to keep dry. But the heavens let loose a deluge which dripped off the trees, poured down and round the sides of the moss-grown log, finally dampening all our blankets. The next day there was a great array of bedding strung round a huge campfire, which soon dried it.

We climbed Monarch Head one day, and walked for miles through thick brush, till even the men were fairly lost in the forest; but eventually we found our way back to camp. Em, Polly Payne and the kids had amused themselves with fishing to replenish the now empty larder. A camp always started out with good grub—pies, cakes, bread, bacon, and a roast of meat—but with such a crowd we were soon reduced to flapjacks and salmon three times a day.

Some of us walked to East Point lighthouse, at the southeast tip of Saturna, and Mabel and I made the acquaintance of Mr. and Mrs. Georgeson, their little girl Joan, and two boys, Andy and Harry. They were Shetland Islanders and most kindly. We were shown all over the lighthouse and its working—the big reflector and machinery. And then Mrs. Georgeson gave us a friendly and most welcome cup of tea, with biscuits.[10]

That night we heard a great disturbance among the folks on the beach, and the next morning saw the remains of a burnt tent and scorched blankets strewn around. The men had slept so soundly that they never knew the tent and their bedding were on fire till it burnt through and fell on top of them!

More rain. So we all figured it was about time to break camp and go home. What a gorgeous time we'd had.

* * * * * * * * * * *

There was an Indian Reserve or village of the Siwash tribe on the point, near Bedwell Harbour, in those days, but it has long since disappeared. Leonard was good friends with the Indians, and they called him sma-hahl-ton—"the long one". It was they who named the Kloshie Illahee—"the good land"—which was shortened to "the Kloshie".[11]

I took my camera over to the Reserve one day to try and get some pictures with Leonard's help, because the Indians were very camera-shy. There were two withered old kloochmen hunched against a wall, so old they were just bundles of crumpled bones and rags. I got out my camera—unfortunately the old-fashioned tripod affair, which took time to set up—but at the sight of it they squirmed away, disappearing in a moment into one of the houses.

After some persuasion, a young [man with his wife] and baby agreed to be taken for a consideration. But they had to go and put on some finery first, which spoilt it; I wanted to get the genuine article.

The Portage, at the head of Bedwell Harbour, Pender Island, was a sort of half-way place for Saturna and Pender folk, and we had a lovely picnic there after rowing up the Harbour. The first thing we saw, on running up the beach, were two dead bucks, their horns interlocked in ferocious combat, and both entangled in a fisherman's neglected net, which had been strung out over posts to dry. Poor fellows! They must have died a slow death from starvation.

The Spalding crowd came to this picnic, and after lunch Mabel and I were amused to see Lillie roll Bea up in a rug and put her down by a log to have a mid-day sleep.

Stump cricket was always in favour on these occasions, if someone could produce a ball. Mixed bathing was not in vogue yet, so we went off in different directions for a cool-off in the water. (There was a lake up in the hills, with an outlet at Charlie Long's place. In the old days beavers used to dam it, but they had all gone. We bathed there, with Gertie and Aline MacKay sometimes, but it wasn't very nice.) On the way home we saw a mother otter and her babies cavorting about in a little cove. A very rare sight. One day we went hunting; young Brantford with Mabel taking one side of the lake, and Mr.

Richardson the other, with me, agreeing to meet at an appointed place at the other end and go down to tea at the Kloshie. The lake was only about three-quarters of a mile long, but travelling in thick brush was a slow business. Mr. Richardson and I walked on and on, wondering why we didn't come to the meeting place, or see any signs of the others. We had heard no shot, nor seen any deer ourselves. We were puzzled. Suddenly it dawned on us that we had gone right round the lake and were back at the starting place. Poor Mr. Richardson! I shall never forget his dismay; he was always so chivalrous. To think he could have been so "green"! We were both green!

I readily agreed to his request that we would not let on what happened, because, he said, he would never hear the last of it. We hurried on to the Kloshie to be greeted with exclamations and questions as to why we were so late. The others had got to the meeting place first, and after waiting a while had gone on. I did the lying, such as it was.

Another time, having left Em and the children behind, we climbed Jackass Mountain, picking up the Bedwell Harbour people and Arthur Drummond on the way. It was a glorious climb, and a lovely view from the top, but a sudden wind got up on the return trip, getting worse and worse till it amounted to a gale.

We walked single file, as trees were beginning to fall in every direction, and it was very dangerous—more so than Mabel and I realized. Charlie Long was leading, his feet in moccasins, picking the way and setting the pace. Then suddenly, there was a mighty crash and down came a tree, right across our trail, only a few feet in front of our leader. Five seconds between life and death. On we stumbled to Bedwell, and then the last lap to the Kloshie. What a wreck of fine trees. We counted sixty-nine down in sight of the trail between Bedwell and home.

And now for the Pioneer dinner. Leonard, Arthur, and Gerry Payne had all been on the Islands ten years, which made them pioneers—a purely local title, of their own choice—and Em got up a dinner in their honour, to celebrate the occasion.

Mabel at the Pioneer Dinner

As the folks at home in England had an idea the Islands lived in a very primitive fashion, sitting on boxes, and no tablecloth at meals, etc.—possibly dressing in woad—we thought we'd show them a thing or two. Mabel and I laid the table with Em's best damask (kept for state occasions), and all the usual "fixings," knives, forks, table napkins made to stand in fancy shapes, tumblers, tea things, and a centerpiece of flowers. (Islanders had tea at every meal.) It really looked very pretty. Then Em put on a nice black dress, with lacy fichu, and we dipped into our trunks and found something suitable. The men wore suits, and when we were "all set" I took a photograph of the table, with Mabel reading a book in the window; and another, with the pioneers, Em and Mabel, seated round the "festive board". We had a haunch of mowitch (venison)[12] with vegetables and cold ham; a Christmas pudding and a flat pie. (They never made the deep English pies in Canada>) That made quite an impression at home, and they revised their ideas of Island life.

* * * * * * * * * *

The *Rithet* or *Yosemite* called at Saturna on Wednesday afternoon and Saturday morning, and some of us generally rowed up for mail, or to get stores. No one knew what time the boat would come, because there was no time schedule. It depended on the amount of freight to be put off at the other wharves. Often it meant hanging around the beach or store for a couple of hours.

Warburton Pike had a pretty little, well-furnished bungalow there, and often had visitors from Victoria. All the flat as far as the Taylor's quarry was his property. I got a photograph of a group, with him included, on the steps of his house, which was quite a feat. He generally "vamoosed" at the sight of a camera.

Mr. Pike was a most reticent man, and never talked about his exploits. They said he just bundled a few belongings into a boat and went off into the unknown, returning to Saturna months later (as he did at the time of our first arrival), quite unconcerned and unheralded. He had probably been on an exploration trip into the "barren grounds of northern Canada" (the title of a most interesting book of his, which I have), or "through the sub-Arctic forest", another book.[13]

Just by chance, one day the men were talking about what chances one had of surviving if upset from a boat in rapids. Mr. Pike casually remarked he had "always found it was best to cling onto a sack of flour, as it floated a longer time than anything. A sack of sugar soon soaked and sank quickly." He was evidently speaking from varied, personal experiences, though no one had known of these things before.

Old Black Drummond was very hospitable if the boat was late. We all piled into the store and he supplied tea, bread, and butter or jam, and a pan of baked apples which we ate as best we could with his limited supply of plates and silver. Sometimes Mr. Pike put up tea for the wharf crowd, and Em made cakes for the bachelors.

One day a party of us went up Prairie Hill, starting from the wharf. It was a very hot day, and we climbed the 1000 feet right up the bare face, on dry, slippery grass and projecting rocks. It was not too bad to begin with, but got more and more perilous. At last we came to a dead stop. It seemed impossible to go on, and equally impossible to go down again. You gripped a rock and it came loose, and bounded down to eternity; you tried to dig your toes into the dry grass—they slipped, and you nearly followed the rock.

At last Leonard reached a piece of bedrock and, leaning over, caught the next man's hand, and so we formed a chain and reached the top. It seemed good to sit down and admire the view. Over the tops of the islands the Olympics formed a towering

121

background, [and one could see as far as] Sidney on Vancouver Island, eighteen miles away.

Seeing the Taylor's place [almost] 1000 feet below, we all suddenly thought a cup of tea would be fine. And there was Mrs. Taylor—a tiny figure, like a little old woman in *Water Babies* when Tom went down over Harthover Fell.[14] But how were we to get there? There was some discussion among the men, as no one wanted to return the long way we had come, so Mabel and I, in our daring ignorance, said, "Come along, we can get down here," and straightaway started to plunge headlong down an almost perpendicular precipice, leaping from rock to rock, sliding down loose gravel, clutching at saplings or bushes, unable to stop, having once started. We just kept going till we landed hundreds of feet below, and looked around. The men were following, rather reluctantly, and arrived at the bottom quite suprised to find we were still whole. They were "knocked" to think we had attempted such a dangerous descent. Perhaps it appeared foolhardy, but we knew no fear and were ready for anything, without a self-conscious thought. It may have been the pent-up energy of years. Anyway, there we were.

[In 1938 Arthur Drummond and his wife came to tea at Kensington Place, Vancouver, and one of the first things he spoke of was that "Smuggler's Leap," still quite awed by it. We had taken their breath away, he said, and confessed that not one of them would have dared to go down, but were obliged to follow where two girls led the way.]

Mrs. Taylor was a tall, wirey, hard-working Lancashire woman, with three children: Chrissie, Valley and little George. Asked the reason for the name Valley, she laughed and said, "Oh, we live in a valley, and so we thought Valley'd make a nice name."

We visited the quarry, and were shown an outcropping of coal in the hillside. The children could go with bags and collect enough for their stove; but the difficulties were too great to work the vein for commercial purposes.

We got our longed-for cup of tea from kind Mrs. Taylor, and then walked back along the flat, past Fisher's place, to the wharf; and so home in our little boat to the Kloshie.

* * * * * * * *

I must skim over the trip we made to Moresby Island—Mabel, Leonard, Thomas and myself—to see the family there. One of the boys, seeing the boat approaching, came down to their landing stage. The father was eccentric, and had built two hexagonal houses, connected by a large, common dining room. He occupied one section with possibly his wife, but the children were not allowed in its sacred precincts. They lived in the other section, where they could make a noise without disturbing their father. It was not a bad idea, really, especially as he was a crank.[15]

We had sit-down tea with the family, the younger ones very shy as they seldom saw strangers. The father had flown high in the choice of names for his children. Horatio, the eldest, ran the farm very efficiently. Then came two very pretty girls, Tina and Agnes, who were never allowed outside without heavy veils to save their complexions. There was Darwin, George and Hypatia, and I forget how many more. Hypatia didn't know what to make of Thomas. I don't think she had ever seen a little boy before. They stared at one another, and at last she screwed up enough courage to point a finger at him and say, in a supulchral tone, slowly, "Can—he—come and play?"

They went off together, and when it was time to leave they had reached a stage when she managed to ask, "Does—he—have to go *right now?*" We had a good five miles to pull home, so were obliged to go "right now".

Previously, the father had bought some land on South Pender at the western point of Bedwell Harbour, and brought an action against Arthur Spalding for allowing his range sheep to feed there. Ralph Grey was a justice of the peace at that time, and tried the case at Mayne Island. Of course the man hadn't a leg to stand on because he had not fenced his land.

* * * * * * * *

A feeling had gradually been consolidating in our minds, Mabel's and mine, that life in England was going to be very tame after this experience, even allowing for the fact that everyone had been in a holiday mood and life was not quite normal. In fact, the seed was sown the day we arrived and had gradually been growing. The thought of drumming away for the rest of our lives tied down to jobs, however congenial, seemed impossible now. We would make a home on the Islands and go back to England to see all the relations every few years. The thought of possible marriage never crossed our minds—not mine, anyway. There was no school for Leonard's children, and here was Thomas nearly seven. We felt we might serve a useful purpose by teaching him and Bay; and at the same time lead a happy, unconventional life ourselves.

Leonard was wise enough not to press the point, but the time came when our minds were made up and we all began to make plans and choose a site for a little house, which Leonard said he would have built for us, to be ready by the following spring. The other side of the Green Hill there was a dear little bay, with fairly good beach for a boat, and fine garden soil, a grand view, and only about seven to ten minutes' walk from the Kloshie. There we bought five acres of land from Leonard, and he drew up plans for a house for us, which was to cost $500.00. No plumbing, of course. No one had any plumbing or water laid on. All water had to be carried from a well.

A piece of alder bottom was to be cleared and fenced for a garden, with fruit trees planted. I asked for some "wood" to be left over for carpentry—shelves and whatnot, at which Leonard groaned in protestation. "Wood! Wood! Don't talk of wood out here. It's lumber!" But "lumber" to us was such things as old trunks in a "lumber room". (I was keen to learn carpentry.)

CHAPTER ELEVEN

One Last Camp

Our holiday was drawing to a close. There was to be one last big camping party at the Pass; this time with a half way stop at Saturna for one night, as it was too far to make the trip in one day. Mr. Drummond brought the plunger to the Kloshie, and the Bedwell Harbour people joined us in their boats. At Saturna our party was enlarged by Gerry and Harold Payne, Polly, Red Drummond and Mr. Pike with his sloop. A goodly crowd!

We rounded Old Point—against a head tide, of course—peeping into now-empty guillimots' nests in water-worn holes in the rocky bluffs. Young gullies were still hanging around the old home. Across Elford's Bay, with a glance down Boot Bay (named for its shape), past the Lunch Islands, through The Gap, where cormorants (commonly known as stinkers) were basking lazily on the rocks; and round to the beach on the Saturna side of Canoe Pass. It was fine, so no tents were set up. Mabel, Polly and I slept on the beach, or tried to, but we were devoured by fleas. (Some beaches were alive with fleas in those days, but they all mysteriously disappeared.)[1]

At daybreak, about 4:00 a.m., when kingfishers were beginning to wake and hover over the water, ready to dive for an early morning breakfast, we hunted along the beach for skids, as the tide was ebbing, and launched one of the boats. In crossing to Samuel Island we saw, framed between the rocky points of Canoe Pass, Mount Baker "in all his glory," Point Roberts, on the mainland, was reaching out a long, dark finger into the Gulf. As our boat grounded on the muddy shore of Samuel a "she-she-gar" (heron),[2] who had had his eye on us, rose protestingly on his immense wings, trailing his long legs, and flew off, squawking, to another fishing ground. We hoped to get some sleep, but the fleas were in our blankets, so we gave up, spreading them in the sun to encourage the fleas to seek shelter, which they did, fortunately.

We walked across the semi-cleared flat, scrambling over the burnt logs and past one huge old tree, still standing, to the bay on the other side, where we feasted on Ralph Grey's raspberries and early plums in the old orchard, and investigated his queer-looking house, which had never been finished. The main framework was there, with rooftree and bare rafters, but only the leanto was shingled and the sides boarded. He lived in that. It would have been a nice little house, if it hadn't stuck half way.[3]

Ralph Grey was away up the Fraser River, fishing, and I don't think we saw him on this holiday. He left Billy Trueworthy, who was part Indian, to look after his sheep while he was away.[4] Billy was a character. Always good-natured. Most of the ranches had sheep turned out on the range to fend for themselves, but every now and then they had to be rounded up for ear-marking the lambs and so on. Billy was a master at this job. No one could touch him. He could run for hours on end, up and down hill, through the woods, till he miraculously got a band of sheep into a corral, with the help of his little mongrel dog. He never seemed to tire. In fact, he said he wasn't tired till he "saw double."

Well, we went back to Saturna, carrying with us some queer things we had found in the mud when getting our boat off. They were like lampshades, made of sand glued together and were, I suppose, the former home of some marine animal.[5]

A pair of fish hawks were circling round their nest, perched high on top of a tree, which had been broken off short, in the gulley leading up to Mount David. Year after year they built there, just adding a few more branches and twigs each season, till at last the tree, which was rotten, blew down.[6]

After a good breakfast, everyone piled into the boats and started off for the Pass, by way of north Samuel Island, on a strong flood tide. Out into the Gulf, round Point Comfort lighthouse and hotel, through swirls and tide rips, till we reached a beach near Mayne Island wharf. Here a big camp was made, as at Fiddler's Cove. Tents pitched, rowboats drawn well up on the beach, to be out of the way of "wash" from passing steamers, and the plungers moored at the wharf.

Someone always hunted around for a rotten log containing a core of pitch, to split for kindling, and to make fire lighting easy in case of rain. There was great fascination in finding a good chunk of pitch. (I love it even now.) It smelt so good and shaved easily with a butcher knife, and was proof against the heaviest rain.

There was quite a settlement around Mayne Island wharf. Tall, lean Mr. Collinson was the postmaster, and held the record for having the largest feet, and being the island's champion liar—or shall we say, Romantic. No matter what the topic of conversation, he could lie, and lie interestingly—as long as anyone would listen—about his experiences and utterly impossible exploits in that particular line, with a perfectly straight face; and then tell the same episode next time, with varying circumstances. It was a real gift.[7]

Three families, the Robsons, Bennetts and Deacons, were among the [early settlers], and peopled the island with their descendants. Mr. and Mrs. Robson, Old Country people, kept the hotel, a frame building, near the wharf; called nearly everyone by their Christian names, and kept open house to all and sundry. Such characters! People like that have passed out of the world forever. When Mrs. Robson's cooking was praised, her husband said, proudly, "Yes! My wife's a very good 'ousekeeper, but 'er grammar's 'orrid." She knew her class distinctions, too. Fellows crowded in the parlour, and she wanting to pass through: " *"Ex-cuse* me, Mr. 'iggs. *Get out of the way there, Wagg!"* Her grammar *was* a bit 'orrid. "He never said nothing to nobody, but went straight out!," speaking of some man.

Dances were held in the hotel dining room. The old-fashioned kind, with a local fiddler, and someone to call the figures in a square dance. "Doe si doe and allerman goose" (*Dos a dos, a la main gauche).* La Valse a Vienne became "Suevienne," and so on.[8]

Mr. and Mrs. Bennett, such kindly folk, were farming inland, and raising a large family of red-headed sons and daughters. They took summer boarders and Mrs. Bennett, a frugal soul, allowed her guests the run of the orchard before meals.

The Deacons had a large farm rather out of the way of the usual traffic, and we hardly knew them.

Our party had gone to the Pass to fish, as the salmon were running. It was thrilling. Two or three boats put out, with one rowing and one trolling in each. You hardly had your spoon, line and sinker overboard before there was a bite. How firmly was he hooked? Yes, he's on! You played the line, and then came the ticklish job of getting him into the boat. He flopped about and covered us with scales and water before he could

Robson's Hotel, Mayne Island

William Tompkins Collinson, Mayne Island

"One Last Camp" at Mayne Island

Georgina Point Lighthouse, Mayne Island

be silenced. Out went the line again, another nibble, No, he's gone! Nibble again. Yes! Pull him in! Sometimes we got into a tiderip, and were tossed about for a bit. So each boat caught three, four or five fish in an hour, and sometimes more, if they were running well. [9]

The Siwashes had taught Leonard how to spear rock cod in shallow water, standing up in the bow of the boat while someone gently guided it about till he saw one. He was soon an expert, though it was most difficult because of the refraction of light under water. I think he was the only white man who could do it, but the water was too deep at the Pass. He could rake herring, too, another tricky job the Indians taught him. The rake was about five feet long, with sharp nails driven through to form a comb. He took Mabel and me to the herring rock in the Pass, where you could stand right at the edge of the water. The herring swept past in thousands on the flood tide. He dashed the rake into the water like a paddle, and soon raked a bucketful for supper.

Some of us walked along to Point Comfort Hotel, kept by the Mawdsleys then[10] and on to the lighthouse [to meet the keeper and his wife, Henry and Sophie Georgeson]. Passing Robson's hotel on the way back, we saw a young fellow, a visitor, on stilts, walking around, and figured we would have a try at it. The men made several pairs, and we practiced up and down the road. It was good fun.

We were running very low on food. In fact, we had had nothing but fried salmon for two days, and were heartily sick of it, and longed for bread. So a detachment went over to the wharf, armed with several salmon as a thank offering, to see if Mrs. Robson would bake us a pan of biscuits, or some bread. Kind soul. Of course she would. Getting out the stilts to pass the time while she baked, we paraded 'round, seeking whom we might devour. Out came the youth on his stilts and eyed us. That was a bit too much. I charged up and challenged him to mortal combat, while the others stood by to see fair play, laughing. We whacked and tripped and circled round, but as he was an expert and I only a novice, it was not long before he had me down, all fair and square. That broke the ice, and we all had several jousts, till our clumsily-made stilts gave way, and we had to quit.

It did not take us long to wolf up the bread and biscuits Mrs. Robson had made, and we hadn't the nerve to ask again, so it was decided to strike camp and all make for home once more.

* * * * * * * * *

Island Lore

1. Always put out a fire on the beach or in the woods when finished with.
2. When you jump out of a boat, take the painter with you, and tie it to a log or rock, to prevent the boat from drifting away.
3. Never sail while wearing gumboots. They fill with water and sink you if the boat upsets.
4. Never leave oars in row-locks; they float away.
5. Always take food and matches, even on a short trip.
6. Always pull a boat above high water at night.
7. Always leave a gate as you find it; either open or shut.
8. Visitors are more welcome if they help with the chores.

Mabel and I had learned a lot of things which would come in handy when we returned in the spring to live on South Pender. In addition to the above: to draw water from a well—a very tricky job—to light a campfire, and a fire in a stove or an open hearth with a back-log. It sounds simple, but fires have a trick of going out on you if you don't fix them properly to begin with.

We had learned the difference between oars and sculls, to feather, to steer a sailboat, to never point a gun at anyone, and to beware of putting it in or taking it out of a boat, even if you know it isn't loaded. Never take chances with a gun, and never stand up in a boat—crouch to change positions.

Reluctantly, out came our cabin trunks, half empty, as we had brought a lot of clothes and oddments for Em and the children. Into them, now, went huge clam shells, sea urchins, purple starfish (dried), eagles' feathers, Indian arrowheads, stone hammers, a snake's skin, beaded moccasins, deer's antlers, seagulls' eggs, and a very precious puffin's egg.—All of which made the Custom House officers stare in amazed amusement when we got home. There didn't seem to be anything very contraband in *that* lot, so they let us pass.

There was no connection between the Islands and Vancouver in those days, so it meant going to Victoria. We bid a grateful farewell to all who had helped to give us such a good time, and then Leonard went with us as far as Victoria, where we had to stay a night, as the boat from Saturna did not make the connection in time. Em and the children were waving towels tied to sticks, standing out on the bluff, as we passed South Pender on the *Rithet*.

A dirt road led from the old wharf at Victoria to Government Street. Where the Empress Hotel now stands were tidal mud flats, fishermen's cabins and rickety wharves, all standing on stilts to keep out of the sludge. A narrow, wooden trestle bridge crossed the flats, built for the horse and buggy days. There were a few small streetcars, and "hacks" with drivers in heavy capes and lashing whips [plying] their trade.

We walked round the old Legislative Buildings (behind the present fine stone structure), which looked more like a schoolhouse or lecture hall—a lumber building, painted a dull red, with no attempt at architecture, most unimposing. The door was locked, so we could not go in, but I daresay we didn't miss much, if the inside was on a par with the outside. [11]

The McKay family lived not far off, near the Dallas Road, so we went next to see them: Mr. and Mrs. McKay, Agnes, Gertie and Aline. Mr. McKay had been an old Hudson's Bay Factor. [12] Someone asked, "Well, what do you think of Victoria?," to which I innocently replied, "Oh! It's a funny little place, isn't it?," which was received with such surprise that I knew I had put my foot in it.

We stayed the night at the famous old New England Hotel (Mr. Young was the proprietor) on Government Streeet, and breakfasted at the still more famous Poodledog Restaurant on Yates Street. They gave us each a steak, large enough for three people, fried potatoes, coffee and the fixings of toast and marmalade, for 25 cents each. We could have had mush, too, but declined. [13]

Then "Good-bye" till the spring; taking the boat to Vancouver, where, I think, we docked at Pier D, then in its infancy. [We] boarded the train at the old CPR station. The trip across the Continent and the Atlantic was made under better conditions than our initial journey, and then Liverpool again.

Even three months had changed our viewpoint on everything—the small train, frequent stops, strange, shrill whistle. And as to the country, it seemed like a toy land, with toy bridges and fields. Outward bound, across Canada, we had been the pygmies; but now, back in England, one felt as Gulliver must have done—afraid to tread for fear of crushing a whole town with one footfall.

Warburton Pike (7th from right) with vacationers, Point Comfort Hotel
Pike owned the hotel

Point Comfort Hotel

CHAPTER TWELVE

A Final Good-Bye 1897

Mabel was welcomed back at the nursing home, and I went to Ealing to replenish my dilapidated clothes; and then back to Barnet. It was nice to see them all again. Mrs. Ryle had got on very well without me, because Effie and Jessie went to school now, which made it easier to break the news that Mabel and I intended to return to British Columbia in the spring. Plans were already in the air for Dr. Ryle and the whole family to move to Brighton. He was far too good a man to be wasting—or giving his ability and culture—to such a small community. At Brighton the girls could go to Rodean School and there would be an outlet for all, though they would be very much missed in Barnet.[1]

There had been talk for some time of this new horseless carriage which someone had invented, and which Mr. Daimler was building. One day, just after I got back, there was a strange sort of throbbing noise on the Green and, running to the window, we saw a weird contraption chugging slowly along the main road. What a queer looking thing! It made us laugh to see it wheeling along without a horse. What was it going to be called? "Horseless carriage" was too much of a mouthful. Dr. Ryle said "auto-car," which was not correct English. You couldn't have a "self car." "Auto-mobile" seemed to fill the bill, but was rather long, then came "motor car" and finally just "a car."

Going down the High Street one day I saw Barnet's first automobile, the owner trying to coax it into stopping outside a shop. He dared not turn off the engine for fear it would not start again, so he and his passenger got out, and while the latter waited on the pavement the snorting monster bounced up and down, collecting a small crowd of inquisitive onlookers.

There was a new baby coming at Hadley House—number six—and Mrs. Ryle told the children they could choose the name this time. With one accord they wanted a girl, which should be "Winifred," which warmed my heart, I must confess. In due course the eventful night arrived. The children were all asleep. The nurse promised to come and tell me, even if I was asleep, but I lay wide awake, listening and wondering. Presently, a quiet step on the stair. Which is it?—A girl. After turning things over in my mind, happily I went to sleep.

It seemed a good idea to learn a few useful domestic arts that winter, before plunging into housekeeping under island difficulties. Blouses with immense sleeves and frilled fronts were being worn with stiff, starched, stand-up collars and ties, like men. It never occurred to us that we might modify these, or even invent more sensible garments. Instead, we took lessons in clear starching, boiled starch, and ironing from a dear old washer woman in her little cottage near the Highstone—like Mrs. Tiggy-Winkle, the Hedgehog, in Beatrix Potter's darling book. "Always do your sleeves and fancies first," she told us. (Of course we paid her.)[2]

Then I thought boot mending would come in handy. So I went to the cobbler on the High Street, and he let me work in the back of the shop with his two helpers, among scraps of leather, tools, and oddments of all kinds and a lovely smell of tanned hides. They were very amused at a girl wanting to do such work but taught me thoroughly. Sitting on a cobbler's bench, I learned to thread a pig's bristle, quite a difficult job, "eat my sole," and split the leather to set it on. Also, to nail soles on with brads, a much easier job; to put on all kinds of patches, and use "'eelball" for the finishing touches to the heel—black or brown. I bought a supply of leather from the cobbler: awls, bristles, brads, hammer, an iron last—in fact the whole equipment, and it certainly saved us many a dollar after we got to South Pender, and was lots of fun. (See photo. I sent a copy to the men who had taught me.)

It was good to see Bede, and to go down to the Nursing Home again, because our last few months were slipping away. She liked to hear of all our doings, because little was known of America, even then. The difference between Vancouver and Vancouver Island puzzled everyone. And where were these islands we talked about? About a year later, when our postal address was Saturna Island, Do (Arlo) confused it with Samoa Island in the Southern Pacific, and addressed a letter to me there! But I capped it. When she was studying in Germany she sent me a card inscribed, "Gruss aus Glucksberg" (Greetings from Glucksberg). As there was no address, I concluded that must be it. It reached her, but what a laugh the German post office officials must have had over it.

We dredged through catalogues for kitchen and household necessities, blankets, house linen, curtains and so on, and Bede spent days with us at Jones Brothers, Holloway. We each bought a round-topped wicker trunk, covered in leather, and had everything stencilled with our names and "Settler's Effects, Saturna Island, British Columbia."

Bede's brother and sister-in-law needed a holiday after illness, and wanted someone to look after their three children while they were away. I think Bede must have suggested me for the job because Mrs. Ryle could spare me now. Mrs. Pauling was very nervous of the children's welfare, so I was to take them to a sanitarium at Bournemouth, where there was a resident doctor and nurse. They were hearty children, but I was instructed to give them Wincarnis, a prepared wine tonic, twice a day, "to build them up."[3]

Bournemouth was what you might call a salubrious place or climate. The parade was the meeting place for discussions of every kind of ailment, and bath chairs jostled each other for position. Children were not really admitted, so we had our meals at a separate table, and I had evening dinner with the boarders, after the children were in bed. There was little for children to do but go for walks, as they might not go on the beach. It was a case of coats, scarves, hats, gloves, shoes and galoshes if the pavement was at all damp, multiplied by three, twice a day. The well-known Chines were very picturesque, rugged, tree-lined clefts in the coastline, but rather far for our daily walks. I thought of Thomas and Bay, barefoot in all weathers, catching mangers and riding logs in the Bay. What a contrast!

Most of the patients or boarders were nose-in-the-air to me, thinking I was a governess, I suppose. Someone to be looked down on; but others were friendly. It was quite a novel experience anyway. There was a youngish mother, with two grown daughters. One was a mulatto, with fuzzy, black hair, the other very fair. No father was in evidence to give a clue. It was very intriguing.

I was reading in the public drawing room one evening, when a young fellow came over and asked what the book was. "Sir Robert Ball's *Astronomy*," I said, and confessed to being very ignorant about the moon, and was trying to study its workings. He was fond of music and played once or twice, but as I had charge of the children and they were not allowed in the drawing room, it was only sometimes in the evening we spoke of topics of mutual interest while fusty people of both sexes discussed their gout and operations in detail.

Once, he came down into the basment sitting room, where I sewed or knitted while the children played. We talked of astronomy, he sitting on one side of the fire, and I, about ten feet away, on the other side. Suddenly, the door flew open and the proprietor's head popped round. I looked up quietly, without moving, and asked if he wanted me. He looked very sheepish and retired, saying, "No," but, to my surprise, I had seen suspicion in his first quick glance. What he expected to find, I have only since been able to conjecture, but I was on my guard after that.

A day or two later, as people were leaving the supper table, a female busy-body hissed in my ear as she passed, "Don't flirt with an engaged man!"

"Don't you dare speak to me like that," I flashed back at her. She passed on, shocked and murmuring condescendingly, "Oh! I was only meaning it for your good!" I suppose she expected me to be crushed and ashamed, but I had nothing to be ashamed of. He was engaged, and I knew it, but saw no harm in speaking to him, even if he were. Some of these families who frequented sanitoriums evidently had little but malicious gossip and sickness to talk about.

One day a lady said to me, "Are you by any chance a relation of Amelia Spalding?"

"Yes," I said, "she was my mother."

"I thought so. You are so like her in appearance, voice and manner. I used to go to Mrs. Pechey's. We all loved Amelia; she was the life and soul of the school."

She told me her name, but I have forgotten it, and I never saw her again. "Ships that pass in the night."

My only claim to notoriety at Bournemouth was the fact that I was going to Vancouver. "Where is that?" Some had never heard of it, or British Columbia.

When the parents returned, Mrs. Pauling wanted to pay me, but of course I would not hear of it. I was only too glad to have been able to do something to accommodate the family, whose various members had shown me so much kindness. So she insisted on giving us a set of silver plate—forks and spoons, and a soup ladle—to take to British Columbia, which was a most welcome and generous gift. Bede gave us the tea set which Mabel still has, with very few pieces broken. And the dinner service which she uses we bought and had packed by Jones Brothers. I think it is still almost intact, after forty-three years of constant use.

We had to face the kind disapproval of practically the whole family in our decision to go and live on South Pender Island; though all were sympathetic and understanding.

One beautiful spring day Herbert Spalding (our uncle and Arthur's older brother) asked Mabel and me to spend a day on the Thames. He kept a boat at Molsey, in the country. It was one of these elegant, highly varnished little pleasure boats, with sculls and sliding foot-board; cushioned seats and back rests—all correct. We thought of the way we had scrambled in and out of island boats, heaving in bundles of blankets and sooty "villies," or smothered in salmon and herring scales, and laughed to ourselves.

Herbert pulled leisurely along, and we enjoyed the lovely rural scenery: country estates with gardens and beautiful green velvet lawns running down to the water's edge; boat houses and houseboats; other pleasure boats like ours, villages and wharves, till at last we came to Maidenhead; quite a little town. Here we had lunch, about 2 p.m., at a tea house. Herbert left the boat to be taken back to Molsey by a man, and after wandering round a bit, we took the train back to London, having had a lovely day.

Of course we went down to Danesfield, to say good-bye, taking all our photographs and sketches which Auntie Emma poured over, wanting to know the minute details of everything. I think she was more interested than anyone. She was always so keen on enterprise, though her secluded life and other reasons deprived her of taking part in these adventures. I am sure there was always the thought of mother at the back of her mind, and for her sake she liked to know of all our doing.

Unc and Maude most nobly gave a farewell luncheon for us in their pretty Elizabethan house and garden at Bedford Park, inviting as many of the family as could possibly come. Dear old Unc was in his element. For days beforehand he was making galantine. (The dictionary says, "white meat boned, spiced, tied, boiled, and served cold," but I am sure Unc added a lot more than that, of his own invention.) He ought to have been a chef.

There was chicken and veal set in aspic jelly; a boiled tongue, glazed and decorated with dice of beetroot and frill of white paper in the correct style; a wonderful trifle with real "booze," jellies and claret cup, served in a glass bowl with silver ladle. But to them the *piece de resistence* was a piece of cold, boiled salmon at—I hardly can say it— four shillings a pound. Of course we could not be so cruel as to tell them that we had eaten salmon three times a day and could buy a whole one from the Indians for 25 cents (a shilling) or go out and catch one ourselves for nothing. Perhaps the flavour would not be so rich as Scottish river salmon.

Carina was still plodding away in the London slums; but after many years of self sacrifice, seeing what an utterly hopeless task it was, she went to live in the country, near friends, and gave her energies to good works in the village, where she could make more headway. She, too, had been caught in the maelstrom of the Drury Lane financial situation.[4]

Mabel knew a widow with three young children, who was finding it hard to support them. After a good deal of discussion among ourselves, Mabel suggested that perhaps she would like us to take the little girl, Janet, out to British Columbia. We would clothe and educate her till she was old enough to decide on the career for herself.[5] Kate Stevens was interested in the proposal, too, and after Mabel had got Mrs. Wilde's sad but wise consent, Kate generously offered to pay Janet's fare. Of course, she was to live with us, and call Mabel and me "Auntie." She was ten. We outfitted her with clothes and other necessities, and gave her a little travelling bag when the time drew near.

I spent some time at the Knox-Shaws, 19 Upper Wimpole Street, London, getting my eyes and teeth fixed. With great difficulty, legal and otherwise, Charlie managed to get permission to build a bathroom—on a ninety-nine year lease. And even then, the water had to be heated in a patent geyser with gas. Their house was one of these old-fashioned, sky-scraping buildings, all in a row, built generations ago, before people thought of baths. There was an area, and basement kitchen, and other rooms with four floors above that. Stairs, stairs, and more stairs. Always trays and water to be carried up. Even all the meals had to come up a most awkward, dark stairway; and afternoon tea another floor above that, and nursery meals another floor still! The ceilings were so high that it took a double flight of stairs to reach each floor. Ellie had what was called a "little tweenie girl," whose legs and heart were young, to do some of the running between floors.

Their drawing room was about thirty-six feet long, with a tiny fire grate at one end as the only means of heating it. We didn't notice it ourselves when we lived in England, but those going home from Canada simply freeze in these huge, vaulted rooms. (Ralph had to wear two suits of underwear when he visited friends.)

While staying with [the Knox-Shaws], I went to the first moving picture in London being shown at the Polytechnic. It was quite astonishing, though it flickered and

134

wobbled terribly, which made your eyes ache. But there it was. Figures actually moving in a picture. It showed troops coming down a gangplank, off a steamer. They walked right at us, getting larger and larger, till they reached the camera, I suppose, and flashed off. That was all there was to it. No story. And, of course, no sound, except the whirring of the projection machine.

But it was the beginning of a new era, just as seeing the first electric lights, hearing the first gramophone record, listening to the first telephone, and seeing the first automobile had been. Five inventions of major importance to the whole world in less than twenty years. And how about the typewriter, wireless telegraph, turbine motor, x-rays, and gliders forecasting aeroplanes before the end of the century.

One day, wandering round back streets near Upper Wimpole, I came upon an antique shop and spied a darling blue and white bedroom jug, which had lost its basin. The lip was cracked, so I got it for eighteen pence. The dealer said it was "genuine Minton china," but I had my doubts about that, though it always went by the name of "the Minton jug." I took it to a riveter, who promised to deliver it not later than June 23rd, because the 22nd was a holiday for the Jubilee, and we were to sail on the 23rd.

We went back to Barnet for last packing. I went to Ealing to say goodbye to the cousins, and then off to London by a very early train to see Queen Victoria's Diamond Jubilee Procession. Laurie secured a window in a medical research building connected with Guy's Hospital, and most generously gave Mabel and me seats.[6] It was on the south side of London Bridge, on the west side of the street, so we should have a magnificent view as the procession approached and passed the windows. There was a long wait, and to pass the time one of the doctors had arranged to demonstrate this new discovery by Roentgen, the x-ray. It was most exciting. We took turns putting a hand into a sort of box, then he photographed it *through the wooden lid*, and later, when developed, there was a picture of the bones of a hand, rings on the fingers and studs in the blouse cuff!

It was a roasting hot day; the crowds were terrific, and the poor soldiers, standing at attention with their heavy rifles, were dropping like flies. Women were fainting, too, in dozens. We looked down on a first aid station and had the full benefit of scores of casualties.

At last we heard the cheering, far off, but a rising crescendo coming nearer and nearer. There was a flutter of excitement, everyone craning necks and standing on tiptoe, but the solid wall of soldiers held firm in that narrow street. Louder and louder, till with a wild roar the outriders came into view.

The Queen, dressed in black, was riding in an open landeau, drawn by the famous Greys, with postillions in medieval costumes. Queen Victoria, the widow of Windsor, was bowing mechanically on a spring-filled seat, with little Prince Edward, her grandchild, three years old, beside her, solemnly saluting and gazing at the cheering multitude.

Behind rode the Prince of Wales, Edward VII, a most imposing figure in Field Marshall's uniform, and his two sons, Prince Albert and Prince George. And then followed a brilliant array of the crowned heads of Europe: the Kings of Norway and Sweden, Italy, Spain, Greece, Bulgaria; Kaiser Wilhelm II of Germany, and the Czar of Russia, all in bright uniform, glittering with medals, plumed helmets, cockades, swords clashing, shining top boots and spurs, riding three abreast, mounted on magnificent chargers, with gilded trappings. Then came gorgeous Indian Princes: the Nizam of Hyderbad, the Rulers of Gevalior, Nepal, Patiala and Travensore, in their national costumes of shimmering satin and velvet, and swords sparkling with priceless jewels. Behind them rode the "Princes of Blood," crown princes representing their countries.

Bands blared, drums crashed, pipes skirled, crowds waved and cheered themselves hoarse, and people fainted in the crush.[7]

There were detachments of Scarlet Lancers, carrying pennants on long staves, Dragoon Guards, Black Watch, Scots Greys, Coldstream and Grenadier Guards in full regalia, all mounted on beautful horses. Then came regiments of soldiers in scarlet uniforms, dark-skinned Sudanese, sailors, marines, kilties with bagpipes, troops from India, Australia, Malay and other colonies, Crimean veterans and Yeoman of the Guard, who marched past almost endlessly in the grilling heat.

It was a stupendous sight, a picture of gorgeous colours, such as had never been seen before, and probably never will be again. That already over-taxed new word, "colourful" describes the scene, because it was full of colour, but it does not belong to that period. it was an era of picturesque pageantry and beautiful horses, and these Kings and Princes had the pick of the world.

Well, it was all over at last, and while the crowds milled about below us, the remembrance of tomorrow and what it held suddenly sprang to life with a sickening feeling. Our last night at home in England. I didn't regret the decision, and I am sure Mabel did not either, but it was horrible to think the last few hours had come.

Mabel and Janet had been staying a day or two at Wimpole Street, and Ellie very kindly put me up for the last night. The next morning the growler appeared, our last baggage—or luggage, as we should have called it—was put in; goodbyes were said in a hurry, though it never entered my mind it was "goodbye forever." Maude had come up that morning and she and Ellie were standing on the steps when we saw a man running up the street, waving—the Minton jug! Nothing could have been more opportune as it gave us all a laugh. There was nowhere to pack it, so, believe it or not, we carried that jug by hand all the way to South Pender Island. Six thousand miles!

We drove to Euston Station, Mabel always businesslike and efficient, tipping porters, counting trunks, finding a carriage. Then came a wonderful surprise—Ellie and Maude hurrying along the platform! They had followed us at the last moment in a hansom, loath to let us go. It was most touching, and nearly caused a breakdown. We waved out of the window to the last, as the long train drew out of the station. I can picture them now, both still quite young, Maude thirty-six, and Ellie thirty-two, but I never saw either of them again. Mabel was twenty-eight that March 5th, and I had been twenty-five the previous December 20th, 1896.

CHAPTER THIRTEEN

The Second Trip West

The railway carriages in England were very different from the Canadian and American coaches of today. Each one was divided into five compartments, with a separate door to each, and the seats lengthways, facing each other. Some people disliked "sitting back to the engine," and said it made them feel sick. Over the door inside was printed, "To Seat Five," and some foolish wag always scratched out the "S" so that it read, "To Eat Five." The first class carriages had upholstered seats and dividing arms, so that not more than five could be seated. But most people travelled second class, where six could be squeezed in—although it was a tight fit if one happened to be "stylish stout."

There was generally a rush to secure the four window seat corners, if the train was at all crowded. The windows in the upper part of the doors let down with a strap, and if anyone dared to open one, someone began to sneeze or shiver, and ask for it to be closed again. Janet needed the window down as she was train sick all the way, poor child.

We made the boat trip in eleven days this time, as there was no fog. We had second class cabins and ate in comfort in the dining saloon. At our table was a mother and her schoolgirl daughter of sixteen. They thought I was sixteen, too, and just naturally called me by my Christian name; and later were amazed to learn I was twenty-five. They were from "Bal-v'l[1]," Ontario. We were amused when the mother said, "Don't b'lieve ah'll *take* my tea this morning," but I don't suppose it sounds funny now. They were probably making mental notes of things we said, to repeat to friends in "Bal-v'l."

Going up the St. Lawrence we stood right up in the bow to try and get a breath of cool air; but it was like facing a blast furnace. I have never felt such heat before, or since. Montreal was like an oven. We simply sat in a darkened room in the Windsor Hotel, with the perspiration running down our faces. In the later afternoon, as it began to cool, the doctor from the boat very kindly asked if we would like to shoot the famed Lachine Rapids in a pleasure steamer, offering to take us. It was a thrill plunging through the boiling, tubulent waters, the steamer swinging from side to side.

We travelled in a tourist coach [to British Columbia], so that we could do a little cooking this time; and had our beds made up at night by the black porter. Janet was really very poorly all the time, which was wretched for her. Mabel and I could not ride in the engine cab this trip, partly because Janet was so seedy, and partly because already regulations were stricter in the matter.

We took every opportunity of getting off the train for a breath of air, even if it was only for a few minutes. At one stop we understood there would be fifteen or twenty minutes. We longed for exercise so walked a little distance along the road with one of the passengers. Suddenly, to our consternation, we heard "'Board! 'Board!" We had quite a distance to go, so the man grabbed Janet under the arm and Mabel and I helped the other

137

side, and we fairly raced along140. The train was already in motion before we reached the platform, and gaining momentum with every second. Our good friend simply heaved

Janet onto the step and jumped on behind to keep her from falling off backwards, rightly leaving us to wait the length of the coach and scramble on as best we could, as by that time the train was going quite fast. It was quite an experience and one we did not repeat, you may be sure.

At Calgary we stopped off again at Hadley Ranch for a few days, where Madge was now the baby. Teddie was bull cook in a camp somewhere, and Dick was also away, so we never saw either of them again. It is sad to have to relate that Teddie and Dick were drowned in the Athabaska River [on June 17, 1898] while on a prospecting trip.

There were two elderly ladies in our coach after Calgary; their first trip, going to visit relatives. If they had known what it was going to be like, they would never have come. Going through the Rockies, making hairpin turns and crossing breathtaking trestle bridges, they took one occasional peep, then covered their heads with wraps, moaning and rocking backwards and forwards. Poor old things! They had probably never been more than a few miles from their native town. Possiby some little Prairie or eastern Canadian settlement, where they had no idea of the [mountains.] We tried to comfort them, and I think it was some relief to know we had been before and were still alive.

* * * * * * * * *

So we reached South Pender, and the dear old Kloshie again, with everyone pleased to see us and we them. One of the first things we did was to run over and see our own little house. We were charmed, of course. Everything was perfect. It was painted white, with red roof and black window sashes, and there was a good pile of "wood" left over for various purposes, as I requested. Only now we were not so green, it was "lumber." There was a nice, large sitting room, about 20 x 15 feet, with three windows and open fireplace, and built-in woodbox to the left, and shelf above; two good-sized bedrooms for Mabel and me, and a small one for Janet; kitchen, store-room and woodshed, with wide verandah across the front of the house. It was all delightful and we could hardly realize it was our home—to live in.[2] Leonard had given a contract to some Japanese to clear and fence a fine piece of alder-bottom land for a garden; and there were actually raspberry canes already planted at one end, fruit trees just coming into leaf, and small fruit bushes—red and black currants.

We all stayed at the Kloshie. Janet had a gorgeous time on the beach with Thomas and Bay. They were as happy as clams, and I can say, now, without exaggeration, that we never heard a cross word between them, which is a pretty good record.

Of course we had no furniture. Some packing cases, with china, curtain material, kitchen utensils and all sorts of stuff, and our little fireside chairs were coming 'round the Horn, but it would be several months before they arrived, even in Victoria. Freight came by sailing ship then, as it was very cheap. Leaving Janet with Em, who was awfully good to her, Mabel and I made a trip to Victoria to buy necessary furniture: beds and bedding, a stove, dining room and bedroom chairs, and a small hearth rug. A deck chair, which we had brought from the boat, was our only easy chair, but we were not accustomed to lounging. The Japanese had made us a dining room table, so we bought a kitchen table with drawer, pots and pans, a bread pan with cover for raising dough (and we, like Amos, took our turns at making batches of sinker bread); a preserving kettle, fire guard, axe, tools and nails. We also stocked up with food at Dixi Ross, on Government Street, where we dealt in for many years: a hundred pound sack of sugar, fifty pounds of

Blue

flour, and all the necessities; 100 cakes of Sunlight soap, clothes pegs, etc., etc. The whole lot to come up by steamer. And did we have an unpacking when it all arrived.[3]

Then came the question of a name for our place. Leonard used to come round in the little boat and spear rock cod and tarpon in our bay. He called them "blue tarpon" which, I think, was a flight of his imagination. There certainly were small fish, different from rock cod, and good to spear at low water, but a blue tarpon is an enormous fish, weighing goodness knows what, that sporting fishermen play for hours on a thread of fish line and rod in semi-tropical waters. Anyway, we thought "Blue Tarpon" sounded just right. It was not long before this was shortened to "Blue" by everyone.[4]

Blue. What a magic word that still hold for me, even now! Memories of dashing down for a very early morning dip, without a stitch on. The ice cold water was so invigorating in those conditions. Of pulling leisurely along to Blunden Island to scramble up the rocks and wander among camas and lilies—a carpet of flowers where no deer came. Of picnics in Camp Bay with a crowd. I can see Gerry Payne balancing a thick slice of plum cake in one hand, while he spread it with butter topped with jam! Picnics on the Green Hill, where we played stump cricket; or perhaps Tusky scared up a mink on the ledge below, and we went headlong down the bluff to help her root among the driftwood. The bachelors sometimes brought over a piece of mowitch or a brace of grouse, and Mabel and I were glad to have them to a meal, or send them home with a pot of jam or a loaf of bread. When we hadn't any meat, Mabel made what we called a "vegetable godge," which soon became famous. These were the most carefree, and perhaps for that reason, some of the happiest years of my life since childhood. The past was left behind, and there was no future. No thought of change.

Arthur brought over his Japanese [helper] Ishida, and they and Leonard put up a picket fence the other side of our house, after searching our source of supplies, the beach, for a cedar bolt from which to split the pickets with a maul and froe.[5] They cut us a good, wide pathway down to the beach, too, as the bank was fairly steep at Blue.

Winifred and Janet in the garden at Blue. The wheelbarrow was purchased with birthday money from Aunt Emma. BCARS 95451

Aunt Emma Edwards

Winifred and Mabel and "the good ship Argo"

Of course we had to start our little school, having brought a blackboard and books 6,000 miles for that purpose. Books oall sorts—history, geography, the dear old "Reading Without Tears," drawing and mapping books, Mr. Sonnenschein's arithmetic, with box of cubes and staves, a book on pysiology—in fact, all the "fixings." And we kept regular hours, with a timetable. No scamping or coming late. I did all the teaching, except geography and physiology, which were Mabel's pet subjects. She did practically all the cooking, and she was a born cook and manager. With the help of Mrs. Beeton's *Household Cookery*, and experience she had had at various times at the nursing home, she soon had it all at her fingertips.[6]

I had never even cooked a potato or boiled an egg when I came to this country, I am sorry to have to admit. It was nothing to be ashamed of, because girls simply couldn't learn these things unless they took a domestic science course or went to the Norland Institute for training girls in nursery and simple household duties. Cooks would not allow the family to meddle in the kitchen. The mistress ordered the meals and went through the stores, but that was all, as a rule. Even Spanny put her dear old foot down: "No, Winker, darlin', you cannot cook. You get out o' my way now. You fuss me." And it had to go at that. At Barnet I don't think I even went inside the kitchen more than once or twice. It wasn't done! [At Blue] I chopped most of the wood and kindling, and Janet carried it in. She had her own chores every day.

The committee of the nursing home had presented Mabel with a beautiful chiming travelling clock in a red leather case, in grateful recognition of seven years of useful work, and this stood in the middle of our mantlepiece. Then there was the lovely Dresden china cup and saucer which mother had won as a girl at Ore Place for table decoration in a flower show competition, and the White Friars Venetian glass standard dish, from our Anerley home. [We had also brought with us] the ebony elephant Uncle Howard brought me from Colombo, Ceylon; the white china goat and horse that came in the Chinese tea chest at Anerley; the Devonshire jug Mabel bought in a village for two pence; the two figures from an Egyptian tomb, Ank-et-maat and Re; Bevi Ugo, the jug from Italy, and other treasures, each holding a memory.

Our sitting room looked very pretty and bright. The Buscots had given us Turner's "Fighting Temeraire" and "Gypsies" as a parting present, and we had the picture mother had painted of French fisherfolk on the beach. Mabel had been given the rare and valuable portait of Mr. Gladstone, and we had the enlargement of mother, aged eighteen, and framed photos of Ore Place and the St. Helen's Ponds, so our walls were not bare.

Em often strolled over to get vegetables from our garden, because it was more fun to have a talk into the bargain than to go out to Fern Point alone, where their garden was. Sometimes, Lil brought the children over for tea on the verandah. Bea was now about three and a half, and very sturdy.

Auntie Emma gave us ten pounds to buy a boat, which was an absolute necessity. Leonard sent specifications to Andy Linton, the long-time boat builder on Pender Street in Vancouver, and in due course she was shipped by steamer to Saturna, and Mr. Drummond nobly towed her down to Blue behind his own boat. It was a great day for us. She was a real beauty, sixteen feet long, broad beam, square stern, with two pairs of ash oars and brass oarlocks, rudder, tiller, painter, mast and sail, painted white with blackgun'le—complete in every detail. We were more than delighted, and had to go over all her points again and again. Then she had to be photographed with us beside her to send to Auntie Emma. The Japanese built us a boathouse in the corner of the bay, with "ways," and she was christened "The Good Ship Argo." She served us well for many a year, and was looked on as one of the family.

Now we had the Argo we could pull up to Saturna every week for mail and supplies. While everyone was waiting around for the *Rithet*, we often played a game of hockey in one of [Warburton] Pike's fields, with improvised sticks. Sometimes on a Saturday some of the fellows would come down from the Pass to join in the game. The Burrell brothers, Fred and Joe, who kept the store on Galiano, young Scoones, and others. The latter made an historic remark which everyone remembers still with a laugh. He was new to such furious play and, at last, being completely blown, he gasped out, "By gosh! I'm bust!" He was a keen little fellow.[7]

Then we all took to having periodical games on Fern Point at the Kloshie, coupled with a huge picnic. It was all good fun. Ralph Grey had come back from the [Fraser] River and often joined us. Once he and I came into collision and knocked each other's wind out. It was quite embarrassing.

The fishermen had asked [Ralph] his name, and he said, "Grey." They protested they couldn't call him Grey. Everybody was Bob or Bill or Jack. What was his name? R.G. he told them. "Oh. Archie. Alright, we'll call you Archie." So everyone around the Islands began calling him Archie or R.G. We did, ourselves.

All the South Pender folk spent Christmas Day at the Spaldings and stayed the night, sleeping on the floor or any available place. Mabel and I slept on the dining room floor. The children had a grand time.

In February, 1898, Gerry Payne, Archie Grey, Fred Robson (brother of Mayne Island Hotel proprietor Bill), and Mr. Winstanley of Galiano Island joined the Klondike rush to try their luck at prospecting for gold. The whole expedition was financed by Gerry. He and Archie came down to say good-bye to Arthur and Leonard, as no one knew what the outcome of these dangerous trips would be. I photographed them against a big rock on the beach at Blue. R.G. wore a pointed beard then, and was no more than just one of the crowd to me.[8]

It was a period of wild speculation and general stampede to the gold fields. The Eldorado and Bonanza Creek mines had been discovered, and everyone thought there was a chance of making millions. The number of lives lost and valuable equipment strewed and abandoned along the various routes could never be estimated. Needless to say, our party made nothing, but they came out with their lives.

[In the] spring Gertrude Church came to stay with us, bringing pretty, curly-haired little Elsie, Madge and baby Dolly. They were giving up the ranch at Calgary because Herbert could not run it alone, and were moving to Comox, Vancouver Island. It was great fun seeing her again, but with three little children we could not take her around much. It was all washing and cooking, and feeding babies, but we enjoyed it.[9]

In the summer Lucy and Mary George came to stay some weeks. They had been to their brother at Wapella where we had visited, and we begged them to come on to us. Lucy and Mary loved the island life, and took to it like ducks to water. Mary fetched kindling from the woodshed in her red flannel petticoat and no dress, which she thought was the height of freedom! She sat on a pitchy log, and was so good when we couldn't remove the pitch without taking the colour out of the skirt. They brought us all the Barnet news; and it was like a little piece of home to have them.

One day Mr. Pike came down in his sloop and took us all for a sail in the Straits, towards the American Islands. He pointed out John's Pass, and Lucy asked, with interest, "Oh, who goes there?"

"John," answered Mr. Pike laconically, without so much as a flutter of an eyelid.

People sometimes stopped in at our place to ask directions or wait for the tide. One day, a man arrived as we three were having lunch on the verandah, so we asked him to sit down and join us. He replied, in an off-hand way, "I don't mind if I do," which

Ralph Grey, Gerry Payne, Edward Winstanley and Fred Robson bound for the Klondike, February 1898. PCAPS G1 248.

Tom and Winifred Higgs

Lilias Spalding with daughters
Hettie, Bessie and Bea

struck us as a very queer way for a stranger to accept an invitation, as the expression was new to us.

There was a logging camp in Bedwell Harbour. The boss was taken seriously ill, so one of his men brought him round to Blue in a tiny skiff, to see if we could flag the *Rithet* and get him on board to go to Victoria. Mabel did what she could for him, and he sat over our fire for several hours. When we judged the steamer was nearly due, we helped him down the bank, got him into the Argo, and pulled out into open water. Presently, rounding Blunden came the *Rithet*, and when Captain Jaggers saw us waving a cloth on a pole, he gave the well-known "toot" and slowed down, knowing something was wrong. Deckhands hauled the man on board and we pulled back to the beach.

The good captain died in the winter of 1898. It was a great loss to the island community because he was always so obliging, genial and a friend to all.

The long winter evenings gave us lots of time for reading, knitting and sewing. Mabel and I each had a Frister and Rossman sewing machine, and we made all our clothes and Janet's. Blouses were still very tricky to make from a pattern, and we were at the stage of making two sleeves for the same arm in spite of care. I knitted Tom and Bay each two pairs of combinations with wool from Scotland. Leonard often came round and read aloud Kipling, Artemus Ward, and articles from London papers. [He] sometimes read verses or stories "by Kipling," and when we had commented on them, confessed they were by himself!

We generally read to Janet before she went to bed: Dickens, *Westward Ho,* and *The Beggars* by de Liefde, a fine historical story about William of Orange.[10] I was battling with *The Origin of Species*, and a book on the derivation of words, when we were alone. We wrote voluminous letters home, too. The large garden took a lot of time. We bought a wheelbarrow with our birthday money from Auntie Emma. And so the time slipped away.

Johnny was very anxious to learn English, so I offered to teach him in the evening. I must confess he was very bright. He could learn two or three words in half an hour or so, but he was practical. They were to be words in constant use, like "cross-cut saw, wash tubs, make jam" and so on. One evening, it was "Easter time, picket fence," I discovered, with some difficulty, by comparing his Japanese picture dictionary with what he was trying to say. He went off in triumph, murmuring, "Easter time, picket-er-fence, Easter time, picket-er-fence," over and over again. Presently, we heard him stumbling up to the back door again, giggling, and "My sorry. My fall over log, too muchie dark stop, my forget-er word. You please tell me one time more." Fresh giggles. So away he went, primed once more.

When he visited Japan later, he made himself a grey flannel suit by hand, and started from Vancouver on one of the Empress ships, which passed South Pender. He wrote me a most devoted letter of thanks and mailed it when they docked at Victoria, finishing up with his touching expression of his feelings as he passed Blue.

Christmas Day 1898 we all spent with the Spalding family again. Mabel and I put some absurd little nicknacks on the tree for the bachelors, just to make some fun. Archie Grey was there this time. We wanted to get a rise out of him because he always seemed so depressed. So, in lieu of a present I paraphrased a popular song of the day, "I'd Have Waited for the Missus, but I Quite Forgot!" It read: "Santa Claus is very sorry he's forgotten Archie Grey,/He had a little present, which he bought the other day./It was a pocket tombstone—Christmas novelty—he got/To put in Archie's stocking, but he quite forgot." R.G. couldn't help laughing.

After Christmas the Bradley-Dynes issued a carte blanche invitation to all the Saturna and South Pender people, to go and stay at their place on Saanich Inlet,

146

Vancouver Island. Mrs. Dyne was Gerry Payne's sister. We had a royal time. There was lots of room as the bachelors rolled up in their blankets on the floor of one of the bedrooms, so we women folk had beds. We fed like fighting cocks and hockey was the order of the day, weather permitting.

Mrs. Dyne had kennels of Scottie dogs at this time. She was also raising turkeys, and had a magnificent gobbler. One day, Mr. Dyne grabbed him by the tail feathers for fun, and to everyone's amused horror they came out in his hand. Mrs. Dyne was duly put out, naturally, but he said, laughing, "Oh, I'm sorry Katie. I thought he was solid behind!" We hardly dared to laugh as the atmosphere was rather tense. Chicken and dog food was cooked in the kitchen. You might go in some time and see a whole cow's head, horns, hair and all, sticking out of a coaloil can on the stove, making soup for livestock.

When our little colony of islanders went to [Victoria] they always stayed at Mrs. Howard's boarding house. She was an old timer and called the men either by their Christian names, or surnames, without "Mr." An adopted niece lived with her, Florrie, who helped serve the meals or sat down to eat with us. There was a good deal of speculation as to whether she could maneuver to ensnare one of the bachelors into marriage. But eventually she married Frank Rattenbury, the architect of the Parliament Buildings.[11]

Old Burke slipped over from Friday Harbour one early morning with six barred rocks for us. We named them after places in the current mining news, such as Yukon, Fort Steele and Similkameen, but I fear they were already past their prime as egg layers. We had a lot to learn about livestock, evidently.

When Harold Payne went to the mines he left us his good, brown Leghorn pullets, and we did well with them, having learnt by experience, sometimes quite bitter. Katie Bradley Dyne gave us some turkey eggs which I "set" under Similkameen by removing her own eggs, with a coop over her, which we shut at night. She was my pet and was so tame. One day the eggs started to hatch, rather unevenly, so we left them overnight. Oh, fatal night! The next morning the nest was destroyed, grey feathers scattered around, darling Similkameen's mangled body had been dragged down the bank; five terrified baby turkeys were hidden about in the grass and one was dead. We knew at once who was the culprit: Mr. Mink. Perhaps the same one we had allowed his freedom after the wild chase. He had dug under the coop, so his doom was sealed this time. We put the carcass back in the coop with a trap in the entrance, knowing he would return the next night. Sure enough, in the small hours of the morning we heard the well-known "chee-ee-eese" of a mink in trouble, and the dog nearly burst herself with barking. Mr. Mink stole no more of our hens or anything else.

We raised the five baby turkeys by hand, a most ticklish job, as young turkeys are notoriously delicate. Mabel's was named "Toodie (Tudor) Tiederman," after a small boy she met in Victoria and whose name amused her. I called mine "Persephone" and Tom named his "Big Pin," for no reason we could ever discover. I forget the names Janet and Bay chose.

When small, we had to take the turkeys wherever we went in a covered basket, to the wharf or for a picnic. Then, by making a little corral on the beach we could turn them loose. Persephone died when half grown, and Big Pin made a reluctant but excellent Christmas dinner; but Toodie Tiederman became the pet of the family. He gobbled to order and did what Mabel called conjuring tricks—jumping up for a piece of bread held just out of reach of his long neck. He passed away in time, as is the fate of all pets, and Leonard wrote an absurd epitaph, in rhyme, which began: "Toodie Tiederman, the conjuror, has dusted up the spout; we were very happy with him; but we're happier far, without."

Warburton Pike and Mabel (front)
with Red Drummond,
Leonard Higgs, Polly Payne
and Harold Payne

Winifred and Janet mending shoes.
This photo was sent to the
cobblers in Barnet who
taught Winifred her craft.

Two ships familiar to Winifred and Mabel: The R.P. Rithet, a sternwheeler, and the Iroquois. Both photos courtesy Ruth Chambers

CHAPTER FOURTEEN

Courtship and Marriage

I couldn't help noticing that Archie Grey made sheep's eyes at me occasionally, but I put the idea aside. I never intended to marry from the time we first came out. One day he got an awful wang on his ankle at hockey, and the game came to an end. It entailed hot fomentations and lying on the couch for a couple of days. Sometimes I was detailed to take his meals in to him. Once, he actually tried to take my hand. I felt I must be very matter of fact with myself and him, so I said, "Don't be grumpy" when he looked tragic, which has been a joke with us ever since.

Archie pulled all the way from Samuel Island to Blue nearly every Sunday, but I don't think he actually asked me to marry him. I used to retire to the woods and sit on a log, to think this thing out. It meant leaving Mabel, a terrible thought. It meant leaving Blue and, most of all, my responsibility towards Janet. If I knew Archie was coming I always put on my old miner's brown drill jacket, which he disliked, because if he wanted me, he must take me for what I was worth, not for what I looked like. Eventually, we just took it for granted that we were engaged.

His full name was Ralph Geoffrey Grey, and I should liked to have called him Geoff, but he preferred Ralph. So I was going to marry a man named Geoff after all, which I decided to do when I was a child at Ore Place.[1]

Perhaps it will not be trespassing on Ralph's life before I knew him to say that his mother died when he was an infant. Some years later his father married again. Ralph was then sent to boarding school at Darlington at the age of eight. At thirteen he joined the *Conway* training ship, and at fifteen went to sea in the merchant service, as a midshipman on the sailing ship *Miltiades*, bound for Australia. After this, his four sisters, Hilda, Marian, Constance and Adelaide, all older than himself, died, one after another in early life. By the second marriage the children were Charlie, Beryl and Dorothy, who died childless some years ago. Charlie and Beryl are married.

Though we sometimes joked about it, I always felt inwardly that it was no wonder he was depressed, and hoped I might live up to the lines: "When love is kind, cheerful and blind,/Love's sure to find, welcome in me./But when love brings heartaches and stings,/Tears and such things, love may go hang!"

* * * * * * * * *

Mabel got a letter from Auntie Emma, asking her to go home (expenses paid) and look after her for a while because she was not well. Of course she went. After all arrangements were made, Ralph and I pulled her down to Sidney on Vancouver Island, in the Argo, about twelve miles, but we were all accustomed to that. It was our way of getting to Victoria easily. Ralph packed her trunk on his back up to the station for the twenty mile run to Victoria. It was a horrible good-bye. The great "Andy" blew his very important whistle, and away she went.[2]

We started home at once, because we wanted to catch the flood tide, and the sky looked ugly. Leaving enchanting Shell Island on our left, we came to the beacon on the long Sidney Island sandspit, past Jones, Domville and Hill Islands, and Arachne Reef, heading for the shelter of Fairfax Point on Moresby Island. We were sailing close-hauled, and shipping more and more water with every mile, but after leaving the temporary shelter afforded by Moresby we were out in the open, between that island and Wallace Point, South Pender Island. By this time it was blowing hard, the wind coming down the channel, hitting the flood tide, and we took on water at each "plop." At last Ralph said we couldn't make it, and would have to put back to Moresby. He lowered the sail and made the turn quickly, while I baled.

It was now quite dark and we were pretty wet. Searching along the coast for some place to land, we found a tiny cove, hauled up the Argo, lighted a fire, and reviewed the situation. It was bad, though unavoidable. Leonard was in the upper country with Harold Payne; Em would be anxious when we did not turn up; we had nothing to eat since a picnic lunch on the way down, and the only food in the boat was a small piece of cheese and a few unripe, green apples. We sat on a log, chewing these, [aware of the gossip] our predicament would cause if the news got around. Ralph hunted for water, but could find none in the pitch blackness. There was no moon. Presently, [with no] warning, I fainted. Poor Ralph! He thought I was dead, not having had much experience in that line.

The night dragged on. Daylight dawned, and with it, to our great relief, the wind dropped. At 4:00 a.m. we made for home, about four miles. Ralph dropped me at Blue, pulled up the boat, and turned in at the Kloshie. When Em appeared we told her what had happened and begged her to keep it dark, which of course she did. The children thought we had come late the night before. This will probably sound strange and even absurd in these days of freedom [for courting] young couples, but it was not so then. It would have been good meat for gossips.[3]

In May 1899 R.G. joined a survey party going up the Stikine River, not knowing how long he might be away. It was a sad day for both of us when they left, to put it mildly. We kept in touch by mail as far as possible. Gerry, Mr. Pike, Clive Phillipps-Wolley and others thought there was an opening for a railway to the mines, and put up the money for this survey, but the mines had petered out and nothing came of it. They returned in September.[4]

Then, to everyone's surprise, Gerry got married to an American girl he had met in the States. Bess was such a good sort from the start. We were amused at some of her little American ways, and she with our English Customs. I always remember the first meal we had with them. She went round the table helping everyone to butter.

Mabel had returned from England that spring, I think; and Janet and I had gone to Victoria to meet her at the old wharf at the foot of Bastion Street.

* * * * * * * * *

People nearly went crazy trying to figure out when the new century began. Was it January 1st or December 31st, 1900? They argued and argued; some with more or less heat. *Punch* had a most amusing picture, a cartoon by Bernard Partridge hitting off the situation: a dishevelled-looking man in a dressing gown, having been up all night tearing his hair, and surrounded by endless sheets of paper covered with figures.

Nineteen hundred saw the start of the Boer War in South Africa, in which the Boers gave us quite a trouncing at first. Martin Grainger went, but we did not know him then. His interesting experiences would fill a book. Harold Payne went, too.[5]

At last our wedding day was fixed for July 7, 1900. Canon Paddon of Victoria, who went to Mayne Island every other Sunday to hold a service, consented to marry us at Harold Payne's place on Saturna.[6]   It was impossible for us to have a public wedding and function, even if we had wanted to, distances being so great.   So it was a case of having no one but the immediate family, and risk hurting the feeling of others, which we were sorry to do.   There was a wharf in Bedwell Harbour now, so Leonard and Em, the children, Mabel, Janet and I all went to Saturna on the steamer. Lil kindly pressed a bouquet of flowers from her garden into my hand at the last moment.

Gerry Payne's wedding photograph of Winifred and Ralph Grey

We had rigged the children out in new frocks for the occasion, and Mabel and I had white washing "reach-me-down" suits from Victoria, as none of us wanted to go in for a lot of expense. We had even cut out an engagement ring, and I had mother's wedding ring enlarged, as she had a tiny hand. Gerry Payne met us at Saturna wharf and took the whole party round to Harold's bay in the plunger, and stayed on as the only outside witness to the ceremony.

Afterwards, Gerry took a photograph of us all on the steps, and then most nobly took the Kloshie people home. Ralph and I rowed the Canon, Mabel and Janet up to Robson's Bay, as the latter were going to stay with our new acquaintances, Minnie, Elfie and Willie Williams on Gossip Island [near] the Pass.

Ralph had cut hay the day before, and it needed turning. So, prosaic as it may seem, we spent the afternoon of our wedding day making hay. In fact, we were "making hay while the sun shone." It was grilling hot, and I took off some of the mass of undergarments girls were still cumbered with so that I could work in greater comfort. That job done, we got supper in the little, old, half-finished shack in the big bay, sitting out on the bank afterwards to enjoy the sunset, very happy.

The old-timers at the Pass gave us a banquet in our honour. It was held in the public hall, and there were about a dozen, with their wives, and some bachelors. A "spread" was always a great occasion, and everyone did full justice to the excellent cooking of dear old Mrs. Robson and Mrs. Bennett. At the end they sang "For he's a jolly good fellow," to which Ralph had to make a suitable reply; and I got up and bowed to the company, thanking them for their kindness.[7]

Ralph had a Japanese [assistant] named Yamaoka helping him to clear the flat, and we spent several weeks chopping and piling alders near our chosen future house site, ready to fire when the fall rains came. Later, we fenced a good piece of land and planted fruit trees. Yamaoka slept in old Flannigan's tiny shack on the bank. (Ralph and his friend George Rutherford had bought Samuel Island from Flannigan, and a year or two later he bought Mr. Rutherford's share, when he went to settle in South Africa.)

Harold Payne had very kindly said we could have the use of his house on Saturna while he was away at the South African War and ours was being built. So we moved over [to Saturna] in the fall, which was very comfortable. We pulled over to Samuel early every morning; I took the boat back, did the housework and cooking, packed up a lunch for all of us, and then spent the rest of the day on Samuel, clearing and making fires with Ralph till five, when we returned to Harold's place for supper. At one time we had forty-six log piles all burning at once round our house site. When our house was finished, we moved [back to Samuel] having found water quite close to the back door when Ralph prospected for a well. Of course, we had no plumbing or water laid on.

We often used to walk along to Canoe Pass in the evening, as it was a lovely spot. Once we had a most unique sight. A killer whale had somehow lost its way and been drawn into the bay, through the narrow pass, on the ebb tide. It was thrashing about, rattled to death to find itself in such enclosed waters. We were sitting right on the last tip of rock, when it suddenly found the tide had turned. With one mighty heave, it shot through the pass on the flood tide, so close we could almost have touched it—its huge dorsal fin, glassy eye, with the white streak round it, glistening in the last rays of the setting sun. He was a happy killer to find himself in the Gulf once more.

Yamaoka was always interested in my cooking, and wanted to learn. Watching me making a pudding one day he pointed at the mixture in the bowl, saying, "He, what you put him in?": (That, what do you put in it?) Telling us of two men being wrecked, he explained, "My friend, no kill. My no friend, kill (drowned)."

Yamaoka came very near being "kill" himself. Sailing over to North Pender, he was capsized in a sudden squall off Cape Horn, Mayne Island. He clung to the keel, wet through, while the upturned boat was slowly blown the two and one half miles across Navy Channel, over to the shore of North Pender, where she was beached. The Colstons, having spied something unusual, ran down to the beach and hauled the half-dead and frozen Yamaoka up to their house and put him to bed. Old Mrs. Coulston, ever resourceful, wrapped the hot stove rings in thick newspaper and laid them round him.

Incidents of this sort happened at not infrequent intervals. All we Islanders had our eyes peeled, and could see small boats or anything unusual two or three miles away, and had to be ready for any emergency.

Life was not without its troubles, difficulties and sickness, of course, but it is nicer to forget those as far as possible, and record the happier things.

One thing which had a very happy climax, was the fact that Martin Grainger returned from the South African War in the fall of 1901 and came to British Columbia. He and his friend, Lyndhurst Giblin, went north to the mines. In the winter of 1903-04 they joined a logging outfit on Wallace Point, Pender Island, and it was there that we first met them. Walter Spalding (son of Colonel Henry Spalding of Ore Place) had come out as a farm pupil to Arthur, and was now greasing skids in this camp.[8]

Leonard rowed us over one day when we were at the Kloshie to have a look at what was going on. It was lunch time, and there was Martin, crouching over an open fire, frying unlimited eggs, which he proceeded to eat from the pan balanced on his knees. It was a comic sight. Later, he went up Knight Inlet, about which he wrote his book, *Woodsmen of the West*, which is really a classic. Unfortunately, it's out of print, though people are still asking for it, and glad to get a second-hand copy.[9]

Mabel insisted on taking over Janet's expenses now, and decided to send her to Miss Wilson's well-known school, "The Cliffs," at Duncan, as she was just fourteen. There she made friends with Judith Phillipps-Wolley, and brought her home for the holidays occasionally. We got to know the whole family, as they rented Mr. Pike's house on Saturna one summer. (Mr. Phillipps-Wolley wrote that good book, *The Chickamin Stone*, about the gold rush.)[10]

[In the fall] Mabel got another letter from Auntie Emma, asking her again to go home and nurse her. And once more we parted with her. Our darling old Auntie was seriously ill this time. There was no hope of her recovery, so Mabel stayed on to the end which was not till the following July 1902.

Money had been subscribed for building a church at the Pass, and Canon Paddon was anxious to have the font made of a natural, water-worn rock. He had energetically pulled miles and miles in a little old skiff along the shores of the Islands, searching for a suitable piece. One night, soon after we were married, he came to our tent and said he had found what he wanted on the Gulf side of Saturna, near East Point. Would Ralph go with him the next morning at 4:30 a.m. and help him get it at high tide? He camped on our beach; we made an early breakfast, and off they went, picking up a larger skiff at Gerry's, and Evan Hooson at the quarry to help. They were gone hours, but came back at last with a fine, natural font of sandstone, which had taken a lot of manoevering to get into the skiff on skids. Many of the island children have been christened from the font, Evelyn among them. (Some years later the parsonage was burnt down, Mrs. Paddon and Theo barely escaping with their lives. They lost all their worldly possessions, but saved the church.)

In the early fall, Ralph's first cousin, George Butler, of Northumberland, came to stay one day and night with us, by breaking his journey between Victoria and Vancouver. George was the eldest son of Ralph's aunt, Josephine Butler, internationally known as one

154

of the original and most energetic workers in the cause of "fallen women."[11] There was not time to do more than show him around Samuel Island and Canoe Pass, after fetching him from the wharf at Saturna. We very regretfully had to get him to Mayne Island, to catch the boat for Vancouver the following day. It meant pulling up to Robson's Bay and then, to George's astonishment, Ralph shouldered his heavy portmanteau and carried it the three miles across the island to the Pass. It was a herculean feat, but he was comparatively young, nearly forty, and very strong.

* * * * * * * *

I had a very kind letter from Mrs. Ryle, saying she was expecting her "last" baby in March 1902. I replied that I had got ahead of her this time, as my first was coming in January. It was sad and disappointing to think Mabel would be in England for the event, but we had to face it. Before Mabel left for England she and Ralph had gone to Victoria to try and find someone who would take me in when the baby was to be born. Neither St. Joseph's nor the Jubilee Hospital would handle maternity cases, and there were no nursing homes. As a very special concession, I believe Kitty Payne had arrived at the Jubilee in 1901, because Bess knew the superintendent, and could pay for a private room, so it could be kept a secret.

The best Mabel and Ralph could find, after much hunting, was a woman on North Park Street, a Mrs. MacNeil, who had taken a few cases before—or said she had. One dollar a day till the baby came, and $10 a week for two weeks afterwards, including everything.[12]

On Christmas Day 1901, Ralph rowed me down to Saturna wharf, where we had a long wait, walking up the flat to pass the time of unpleasant parting. The steamer went to Sidney now, connected with Victoria by train, and there I took a hack to the house. I had a sittingroom, where Mrs. MacNeil served my meals (not too elaborate) on a tray, and a bedroom.

It transpired that the MacNeils kept a livery stable attached to the house at the back. Mrs. MacNeil and her girl Florrie and [son] did most of the work connected with it, because the husband was generally drunk. Fortunately, it was winter, so flies were not bad, but we did not bother or know much about flies in those days. I knew no one but Canon Paddon, and shall always remember with gratitude his kindness in coming every day to take me for a walk. I made baby clothes out of some old surplices that had been given me; and Mrs. Paddon, who came once to see me, said she was sure the baby would be a "little parson" on that account.

Time dragged on. Three solid weeks I waited, looking forward to a bi-weekly letter from Ralph, and writing to him and Mabel. At last the appointed time seemed near, 6:30 a.m., January 15, 1902. Mrs. MacNeil drove me out for a walk during the morning. Said it would "do me good." Fences came in handy. At 10 p.m. Dr. O.M. Jones came.[13] Case rooms were unknown. He was a kindly man in general, but it was women's work to have babies. No fancy fixings for a poor wretch, any more than for a cow, till he was obliged at 9:30 a.m. January 16, because I fell asleep ("nearly in Jesus" as the saying goes) with no baby yet. Then he got busy. Time passed. I heard a baby crying somewhere. It couldn't be mine, because I hadn't borned it. Yes, it was mine—a little girl, Constance.

It was Thursday, so I could not let Ralph know till Saturday, but nothing seemed to matter for a time. By prearrangement, Mabel was to hear through Charlie Knox-Shaw's cable address, which message I had previously written out, and only had to fill in the

Dilston castle, BCARS photo from Grey collection, AddMSS 604

The interior of the Grey home, Samuel Island. BCARS 95455

name, "Noxious, London. Constance. Well." If a boy, he would have been Dilston, after Ralph's old home in Northumberland.

I managed to write a little note to Ralph on Friday, but by some bad mischance my letter did not come out of the mail bag on Saturday. Nearly frantic, Ralph started to pull down to Sidney for news, but fortuntely put in to Bedwell Harbour on his way, where he heard, because I had sent Em a line. So he returned to Samuel. Next mail day my lost letter came out of the bag. And he had good cause for annoyance. Some weeks before, when he went for the mail, he had been handed a book, with the covering torn, disclosing the title "Our Baby," which had caused amusement among the bachelors, and embarrassment to poor R.G. It was from Mrs. Ryle.

Dr. Jones came once more to see me during the time I was there. They didn't overdo things then, and I didn't expect any more. Perhaps a little more attention and enquiry into the treatment accorded me might have made things easier, but then he only charged $25.00. Mrs. MacNeil and Florrie went indiscriminately between me and the horses, without washing. The second day they put a basin of water beside me and said I could wash myself now. I *couldn't*! Mrs. MacNeil looked at me, puzzled. Was I shamming? She told me the woman she nursed before got up on the 4th day and seemed to expect me to. Florrie brought my meals, and always forgot either a knife or salt, or something. She was a pleasant girl, and one day said, "There! I can't never bring nobody nothing to eat without I forget something."

When the baby was a week old Mrs. MacNeil said I could get up and wash the diapers now. She put some water in a galvanized tub and left me. *It was impossible.* She consented to do them three days more, and then made a final stand. I begged her to go and buy me another dozen, which she did, rather than wash the others. All this was not as bad then as it would be now. I am just stating facts. I was used to roughing it, but there is a limit to human endurance. In the end, I had to stay three weeks, the last one finding my feet and doing for the baby (six weeks altogether).

The train left Victoria at 7 a.m. [on] a cold, dark morning in February. I paid Mrs. MacNeil to help me out to Sidney, and then took the boat to Saturna. The folks gave me such a warm welcome, though I was hardly able to walk along the wharf, carrying the baby. Ralph rowed us home so happily, and troubles were forgotten. The good ship Argo felt honored to carry our precious load. Piled up in the boat was a second-hand rattan pram with hood, which Miss Deveraux of Victoria had bought at an auction for me. It was in good condition for $3.00. As she refused to take any payment for her trouble and one or two little commissions, I gave her half a ton of coal instead. (Miss Deveraux was one of Victoria's "characters," known by sight to almost everyone for a rather unique reason. The Paddons had brought her to this country as governess to their large family, but she was now a collector of bad debts, having created the job for herself. When firms or private individuals defaulted on their payments, Miss Deveraux first made a polite request for settlement. If that failed, she camped on their doorsteps or just outside the office, in full view of everyone, till the delinquent came through from sheer shame or embarrassment. She had been known to go day after day to the same place, taking a camp stool and lunch. It was most effective.)

It took me some time to recover, and Ralph was just *too good* to me. He even washed the baby's napkins, which is the limit of self-sacrifice. At three months old [Constance] grabbed my work basket off a chair near where she was lying, and upset the contents over her face—thimble, pins, bodkin, etc. At about four months she managed to roll off a large rug outside and swallowed a wild oat seed. That caused trouble. Her throat swelled and I was up all night with her coughing and choking. At daybreak we rowed down to Boot Bay to get help from Bess, who had had hospital training. Everyone had a shot at trying to extricate the seed, now embedded in scarlet inflammation. At last Ralph took the forceps, and while Bess and I held the baby, he valiantly succeeded in yanking it out. She was always into something—till one day Gerry said, "Isn't she a bird!," an expression which meant something exceptional. From then on we called her Bird or Birdie till she was about eight or nine.

To our great joy, Mabel came back in July. She was laden with all sorts of presents and clothes: the Chippendale mirror from Mrs. Ryle, carvers from Charlie and Ellie, besides other useful things. She herself gave us our house linen, a goodly supply of everything, which outlasted anything we could have bought in this country.

Auntie Emma had left Mabel and me some money when she died, most of which we invested. Mabel kept out enough to build a nice little house not far from ours, which she called "The Loggia," because of the large, square verandah. We each contributed $500 for Leonard to buy lumber for a new house, and gave him and Em a new piano. Mabel also bought a piano. Ralph and I added two bedrooms and a little bathroom (without running water), and a verandah to our house, and had the whole thing painted.[14]

Mabel and I often pulled down to Saturna for the mail, or into Boot Bay to see Bess, with Birdie in her clothes basket bed on the stern seat, and our Irish terrier, Rikki-tikki-tavi faithfully watching over her. Sometimes we rowed or sailed down to the Kloshie on a Sunday. It was six miles, so we couldn't do it often. York was the baby [there] now; a dear, little tow-headed boy, six months older than Birdie. The Jubilee had taken Em in (she also knew the superintendent) because it was to be an eight months baby, as she had lost several by waiting the full time.

It happened that the Duke and Duchess of York (the future King George V and Queen Mary) were on a state tour of the province, and while in Victoria they visited the Jubilee. Hearing there was a tiny baby, and thinking fondly of her own children in England, the Duchess asked to see it, so the baby was produced and she held him in her arms. Being excited, the nurses failed to show her the mother, taking all the attention themselves, which was rather tough on Em. Anyway, when it came to choosing a name, she and Leonard decided on William York, and York he was called for several years.[15]

Bess was expecting another baby, and one day Mabel had a hurry-up call, by boat, to go to her assistance, as she had left it too late to go to Victoria. Bess had a sort of nurse in the house, but the baby was coming and they wanted help. It was a new experience for Mabel, but she was quite equal to the occasion. Everything was normal, and so Dolly arrived.

And then, about ten months later, it was my turn again—March 1904. Mabel and Birdie came with me this time, which was very nice; but I hated leaving Ralph to "batch it" alone. The trip to Victoria was an eye opener for Birdie, because she had never seen a train or a horse and buggy, or a street car. She only knew one little boy in pants, Tommy, the youngest Taylor at the quarry. When we reached Victoria from Sidney she was already wide-eyed with astonishment, and there on the platform was another little boy about the size of Tommy. Pointing a surprised and excited finger at him, she said, "Two Tommy Taylor!"

We had nice rooms hear the Parliament Buildings, where again I waited, but it was very different having Mabel and Birdie to keep me company. Birdie was subject to very excitable spells, sleeplessness and occasionally a sudden rise in temperature, ever since she first started cutting teeth, so we decided the excitement of town was too much for her, and Mabel took her home after about a week.

I will skim over the next two weeks. At any rate there was not a stable attached to the house. Dr. Jones arrived too late to be of assistance, and Mrs.___was not very experienced (neither was her daughter of eighteen), but we survive these things, and another darling little baby girl was the reward. At two weeks old I had to wean her, and go into the Jubilee Hospital for an operation for haemorrhoids. I paid Mrs._____to take Evelyn up to Saturna, where Mabel was waiting to receive her, and she continued on the round trip back to Sidney and Victoria the same day.

The treatment of post operative cases was rather primitive, and I had a bad relapse, which necessitated my being in hospital over three weeks. When I went home at last I should not have known my own little baby, she had grown and thrived so under Mabel's good care. Mabel said Birdie used to run out on the bank and watch for the boat to bring me home, every day, but when she saw me she was a wee bit shy at first, though it did not
ast long.

I don't know where we should have been without Mabel during these and subsequent troublous times. Birdie was a constant care and anxiety. I could never go to the wharf or any of the picnics that summer, or have anyone to the place, if I could help it. She had what we called "brain storms," sometimes lying awake for hours at night, quite good, but just unable to sleep. We sang all the old nursery rhymes, in a gentle monotone, lower and lower, till we thought she was asleep and then—up she popped again when we tried to creep away. Evelyn was just the reverse; the picture of health and contented babyhood, which was such a comfort.

Constance Grey

Janet and Constance

The Grey Home, Samuel Island

The Mayne Island lockup served as headquarters for Arthur Drummond, police constable, and as a court house for Ralph Grey, justice of the peace.

The Mayne Island Agricultural Hall. Property for the lockup and the hall were donated by Warburton Pike.

Ralph Grey with Malcolm Shaw, and Kipling and Thrush, the oxen.

The rock for the font, St. Mary Magdalene Church, Mayne Island, was transported from East Point, Saturna Island, by Ralph Grey and Canon W.F.L. Paddon in July, 1900. Mabel Foster photo

Ralph Grey served on the board that helped establish St. Mary Magdalene Church in 1898. Warburton Pike donated the property

CHAPTER FIFTEEN

Life on Samuel Island 1903 - 1909

Our days were very full. Up at 6 a.m., Ralph to do chores and land clearing (he was logging the little valley now), and I busy with the children, washing, ironing, housework and cooking till 12 noon. Ralph and Nakkie had made us a rough trail to the Loggia, round the waterfront and back by the barn. Mabel and I called this "the round trip" as we pushed the pram round and round it for exercise.[1]

Sewing all the evening, making my own and the children's clothes, I evolved a most useful garment for Birdie. It consisted of a short tunic, with waist belt and knickers to match, which most people frowned on as not suitable for a little girl. I made six sets of these one winter, ready for the coming summer, not to mention endless frocks, hats, bonnets and bodices. I also made Ralph some shirts, and by picking to pieces an old pair of cloth breeches for a pattern, I made him a new pair out of a tweed skirt of Mabel's, which will give you some idea of how voluminous our skirts were then. The joke was, no one knew the breeches were home made, and we didn't let on. It was all happy work.

We were almost too busy to have pets at this stage, though we began with "am," a motherless lamb, when Birdie was about eighteen months old. It followed us about everywhere like a dog, as I had brought it up on a bottle. The children each had a rabbit later on, and we kept large, wired-in and roofed enclosures of them to help out the larder.

The children and I stayed with Katie Dyne several times. She was fond of children, but had none of her own, sad to say. She gave Birdie and Evelyn a baby donkey, the foul of her "Loulou," which we named Alice. The children called her "Allie, p'tty girl." When it grew old enough, it pulled a little hay cart and was quite useful, hauling wood and bark for the fires.

There were two things that were fatal to forget: the boat, and the chickens. Every now and then, long after we were in bed, one of us would say, "Did you pull the boat up?," or "Did we forget to shut up the chickens?" Then there was no peace till we made sure. The boat might have been dashed to pieces, or the chickens killed by mink or raccoons.

* * * * * * * * *

The great event of that summer, July 1904, was the arrival of Ethel Spalding for a good, long visit. I went to Victoria to meet her and, oh, it was a thrill. Seven years since we had seen each other, and she had never seen Ralph, of course. She was ready for anything—picnics, fishing, camping or beachcombing.

One of Ethel's first experiences of island life was a slashing fire, which spread uncomfortably near the Loggia. Fanned by a wind, it crept nearer and nearer while we lashed it with wet sacks till we were nearly roasted and choked with smoke, taking it in turns to lie down for a few moments rest. Ethel was so anxious to be helpful, and offered to run to the well for a bucket of water. "That was one thing she *could* do!" Simple, just to drop a bucket into a well and haul up the water! But, no. She was [stymied]. That bucket refused to tip for her. I shall always remember how vexed she was with herself, but of course it was not her fault. She lacked the knack which comes with practice.

Mabel was so good in looking after the children, with the help of a girl from Victoria, so that I could go about with Ethel, and Ralph took as much time off as he possibly could. We took Ethel up to the Pass and she, Ralph and I went to dear old Fiddler's Cove, where we made a little camp.

Of course Ethel spent some time at the Kloshie, and with Arthur and [family], and then returned to us for the last week. The only thing that marred her visit, from my point of view, was the fact that Birdie was so excitable and shockingly sleepless, with these "brain storms." We decided to stay a few days at Ganges Harbour, Salt Spring Island, taking Birdie with us, to a doctor there. He told me to send for him (no phones then) *any time*, day or night, if she had a "spell," and he would come to her. The second night she was taken ill again and Ethel most nobly went off, alone, in pitch darkness, along a strange road, about a mile to the doctor. It was really heroic. She knocked and called, and finally he came down and, giving her a thermometer, told her to take the child's temperature. And with that, he let her walk back alone. I was angry!

As Birdie was a little better the next day, we went home and Ethel, her holiday over, took the boat to Victoria, and so back to England. It was a sad parting. I have never seen my "twin" again, and never shall, now.

* * * * * * * * * *

Then we decided to try Kamloops for Birdie. I had to leave my chubby, smiling little Evelyn to Mabel's good care once more. Ralph went with us and stayed two days. We went to a boarding house in Kamloops, a horrible "cheapskate" place. The daughter who served the meals "quacked" in a raucous voice through the buttery hatch, "Once again on the beef mince," or "Twice on the apple sauce." We couldn't stand that, so when Ralph left, Birdie and I went to Mrs. Roadley, a well-known woman, where we were very comfortable. She had diabetes and died not long afterwards because there was no insulin in those days.[2]

I took Birdie to Dr. Vereertbrugghen, a very clever Belgian locally known as Dr. Venburgher, or Dr. Bergenhahgen. He said, after an examination, "She is a child of nairvoos parents" (she was like a piece of quicksilver), and to me, rather puzzled, "You have the voice particulair," meaning, I hope, that at any rate I did not "quack."[3]

The change of air worked wonders. We took quite long walks on the hills, or over the swing bridge across the Thompson River. One day, to take a shortcut home, we started to cross the trestle bridge through a rock cut. To my horror, I suddenly heard the whistle of a freight train as it entered the cut, so grabbing Birdie under my arm, I raced over the remaining open ties and made one wild leap to the safety of the embankment as the train rounded the curve, almost upon us. It was a near shave. (That dangerous place, used by many, has since been done away with.)

And so our six weeks stay came to an end. I think it undoubtedly saved Birdie's life, because it built up her strength to withstand the devastating illness she had that winter of 1904-5.

At last, when nearly three, meningitis developed, and the high temperature brought on pneumonia. Twice, Ralph had to pull the twelve miles to Salt Spring Island to fetch Dr. Baker.[4] The first time he stayed all night, not expecting she could possibly pull through. When Conty finally recovered she was like a little shadow, and could not stand. I could hold her, sitting on my hand, at arm's length. I am sure she would not have pulled through if we had not had the help of Mabel's training and instinct for nursing. I used to say to myself that other people have to lose their children, so I must face it if need be. Then, I would go and get a kind smile from Evelyn, kicking in her clothes basket bed. It was such a help.

* * * * * * * * *

In February 1905 a large scowload of the very finest finishing lumber was washed onto Anniversary Island in the Gulf (so named because Ralph and I spent the first anniversary of our wedding there, and it was then adopted by all).[5] We all went out to collect what we could, make it into rafts, and tow it home. We took the children, and I rolled Evelyn (eleven months old) up in Ralph's coat and put her down to sleep while we worked. Other people came with boats, wanting in on such a good haul. There was plenty for all. Presently, Jim Robson came up to us, looking quite white and shaky. He said he had seen an old coat by a rock, and was just going to give it a cultus kick, when he noticed a baby's hand. He was really shocked, because he had children of his own.

Evelyn had another close call that summer. We were bathing at the Loggia, Mabel and I sitting on the bank, Birdie and Evelyn paddling at low water. Evelyn fell down, gulped some water, picked herself up, fell again away from shore, and though I raced down the beach the first time she fell, and had my eye on her all the time, she was limp and gasping when I picked her up. I would not have thought it possible, and it taught me a lesson. Each child had to learn to swim at five years and then I felt more comfortable.

Curiously enough, Birdie never had an accident, beyond raising bumps on her head falling around when she first started to walk. The children and I went along the beach towards Canoe Pass sometimes, and once I slipped and my foot got caught in a crevice in the rocks. Twist and turn as I would, it was stuck and would not come out. Ralph and Mabel were away. We had a prearranged signal with Ruth Payne to fire a rifle several times in succession if either of us was in trouble. But the rifle was at the house, and Birdie too small to send for it. After about half an hour of contortions I eventually pulled my leg out. It was quite bruised.

Ralph worked a yoke of oxen, which we named "Kipling" and "Thrush," or "Kimping-Dush" by Birdie. He was hard as nails, physically, with bulging muscles. One day he came home in the middle of the morning, rather crumpled up. The cart, drawn by Kimping-Dush, had gone right over his body, but he finished the load of hay and was back at work two days later.

Malcolm Shaw, son of Charlie's brother Frank, of St. Leonard's, came to us to learn farming, but I think probably the people at home had no idea what farming meant in this country. It was really occupation they wanted for him. He learnt how to handle an axe and a cross-cut saw; to milk the cow and yoke the oxen; and make himself generally useful in the house. But the whole thing was rather like trying to fit a square peg into a round hole. He was a boy with a lot of character, and really not suited to the life, though he was often good fun. Eventually, Malcolm married, returned to London, where he became an expert interior decorator. Rather a strange contrast from shouting "Gee!" and "Haw!" at Kimping-Dush the oxen.

* * * * * * * * * *

Ours was the most conspicuous house round about, so we often got strangers, wind bound. One day, our French windows being open, a very brisk lady suddenly stepped in and announced, "I'm Mrs. Miller!" in a cheerful tone, as if we should be sure to know. She wanted to leave some tracts or something. Another time it was Mr._____, a wealthy man from Pasadena, wind bound for two days. He came and ate with us, and discoursed on the delights of the nectar from clams. We had never connected the word "nectar" with clams before, being under the impression it was food for the gods.

Occasionally, a drummer came, selling the latest in churns or washboards. And he always happened to have "just one left," which he could let us have at a reduced price. When these gentry got into a community like North Pender, they had to hurry from house to house before the folks discovered they had each been offered "the last one."

[Infrequently,] Siwashes came in their canoes, and one would come up to the house, offering fish for sale. "Mika tikeh salmon? Tenas chickamin." (You like salmon? Little money.) We generally bought a whole salmon for twenty five cents, and if we added an old blouse, it was "Hyas kloshe" (very good). Once, an old klootchman came, asking, "Nesika tikeh olillee sal-lal." (We would like to pick salal berries.) "Nawitka," (yes) I told them. "Halo chickamin," they added as an afterthought (no money). "Kloshe," I said.

A travelling band of them camped near Canoe Pass and left a smouldering fire, which spread. Fires could be so disastrous, and this one crept up the bank and threatened our slashing. Ralph and I spent almost all that night getting it under control, and I had to run home at intervals to see that the children were all right, as they were alone.

I was working out at the back, near the feed room, one day when I was aware of someone quite close; and when I looked up, an unshaven man said, "I'm Jack the Ripper! Where's the boss?"

"Oh, he's around, somewhere," I answered, casually, not to let him think I might be scared. As a matter of fact, I was alone on the island, because Ralph had gone to North Pender to ship a boatload of lambs, but I wasn't going to tell him that. We had heard of him as being rather a tough character, who lived alone on Tumbo Island, near East Point. He hung around for a bit, and then went off.

A few days later, it was blowing hard, when we saw a stranger pulling madly up the channel past Samuel in a tiny skiff, as if all the demons in Hell were after him. What could be the matter? News often took some time to get around, 'though it was wonderful how it *did* travel. This time a city constable and Mr. [Ego] put into our bay two days later and wanted to know what we knew about Jack. I told him what had happened. It transpired what a wayfarer had put in to Tumbo for a night, quite harmlessly, but Jack had ordered him off or he'd shoot. The other fellow, in self protection, had shot first and, not knowing whether it was fatal or not, had "lit out" for the Pass to tell what he had done. At Tumbo they found poor Jack propped up on his bunk—dead—with an open Bible on his knees and a guttered candle beside him. It was a sad ending for a lonely fellow, who was probably the victim of nerves. The other man was acquitted as there was no witness.[6]

[Nakumura replaced Yamaoka as the Grey's farm helper.] Nakamura brought his tiny wife to the island, and she was going to wash and scrub for us at—ten cents an hour! It sounds terrible now, but she was quite content, and we thought it was enough—then. She even pulled down to Boot Bay, to scrub for Bess at that rate.

All the Japanese round about went up the [Fraser] River for the salmon fishing season in the summer, and when they came back some of them always brought us a huge fish or a carved table or stool. Once Nakki (as Birdie called him later) brought us a lot of beetles, as a great delicacy. We kind of shied off them, and asked him to demonstrate how they were eaten. He tore off the wings, and then crunched this dry, black insect with gusto! We thanked him and said we would try them, but I don't think one of us had the courage.

The Japanese were very generous, but perhaps it was because Ralph was generous to them in allowing them to cut cordwood and poles (to sell up the River) on the north end of Samuel.

We had a variety of hired help when most needed in the summer, because the Japanese were away, and I often had to help Ralph round up or shear sheep, hold lambs while he took their tails off, and all sorts of things.

One girl from Victoria could serve afternoon tea or chat to my friends if they came, but when it came to the "daily round, the common task," she fell rather short. Her family had this new delicatessen habit (which we despised), so she could not cook and would not learn. She did not last long.

Another girl was just out from London, and had no idea of country life in British Columbia or anywhere else, but was perfectly happy in her ignorance. She was so surprised to see the tides. At very low water one day she remarked, with finality, "Well, I suppose the water's all gone off in another direction," which solved the whole problem! She was right, in a sense, but not in the way she meant it. She thought the islands were loose on the top of the water, and wondered why ours did not float away. I tried again and again to get her to take the children "the round trip," but with no avail. She always brought them back in ten or fifteen minutes, saying they had been for a good walk. But I discovered that she never went beyond the Loggia "for fear of meeting lions!" She only stayed ten days.[7] The little Paynes had a good English governess, but we could not afford that.

In the spring of 1909 we had a girl from Manchester to help. She arrived in a hat decorated with a large, black wing, and the children promptly christened her Crow, and Crow she good-naturedly remained. She only knew city life, so liked taking the children for walks, and sometimes they disgraced themselves and me by throwing pellets of dry sheep manure at her. She liked going out in the boat, too, but was smart enough not to learn to row. When we went to the wharf, she thought the bachelors were fair game, and tried to make eyes at them, but they would have none of such tactics.

* * * * * * * * *

About this time something happened which was to revolutionize island life in the future. Gerry Payne bought a small launch with a gasoline engine in it. I shall never forget our puzzled excitement when Ralph and I heard a new noise on the water, coming nearer and nearer. Putt-putt-putt-putt. What could it be? We ran down to the bank and there were Gerry, Bess and Kitty in a chunky little boat, decked in at each end, chugging along, without oars or sail. The first and original "puffer." When launches first began coming around the Islands, everyone looked at their rowboats with a critical eye, hoping or trying to convert them, by installing an engine with rudder and tiller.[8]

169

Gerry was boyish in his love of surprises. One day in 1909 we were puzzled to hear orchestral music coming across the water. How could it be? What did it mean? Presently, Gerry's little puffer came into view, and the music certainly seemed to be coming from that direction. When he landed he was grinning from ear to ear. He had a portable gramophone, with a large horn on board, and was serenading us. It was the first gramophone we had seen outside of England as far as I can remember.

Wind and tide played a large part in our lives on the islands. All our comings and goings were ordered by them to a great extent, except in an emergency. Ralph had a tide book, issued by the government, which he always consulted before we planned any trip. Mabel and I never sailed alone; the gusts of wind and sudden squalls in those enclosed waters were too treacherous. But the meaning of "Look out for the boom, she's going to jibe!" even the children had to learn very early in their lives—or get a crack on the head! "Take the tiller, while I shorten the sail," Ralph would say, or "Hold the sheet a minute." In the days of our great ignorance, Mabel and I thought the sheet was the sail! Ye gods![9]

We had to go to the Pass sometimes, for one thing or another, [but] Ralph and I lived outside the inevitable bickerings of a small community. We listened to the tales of woe and ill-usage from each side, and kept on friendly terms with all by holding our tongues and not repeating what we had heard. [We] were invited to be the guests of honour when Mary Bennett married [Sweeny Colston.] The lunch was the great attraction. I sat next to one good lady who helped herself to anything and everything that came her way. It was marvellous to see. Almost anyone could "gate crash" at these functions.[10]

Another time, later, leaving Birdie with Mabel, Ralph and I walked over to the Pass, where we met Mrs. Maude, quite upset. Her Ruth had come home from England, and was now a fashionable young lady, not at all suited to island life, she told us. Sure enough, along came Ruth, tall, good-looking, vivacious, swishing skirts and large picture hat, with a very English manner, which might be interpreted as "Hawhaw." She certainly was a contrast to the rest of the islanders. It was a case of the old popular song: "Oh! Flo, what a change in Flo!/When she left the village she was shy./But alas and alack! She's come back/With a naughty little twinkle in her eye!"

But she was an exceedingly nice girl beneath this rather flashy exterior, which soon wore off. Even Harold Payne came out of his shell enough to marry her, and she made an excellent wife and mother, and a delightful neighbour for us. But, alas, too many babies coming too fast were her undoing, and she died when the fourth was born, aged only twenty-eight. It was a tragedy. She left four motherless children: Audrey, Reg, Dora and Margaret, the last two little more than babies in arms.[11]

There were infrequent visits to the Kloshie, to the Spaldings (by way of Little Bay and walk up to their place), to Point Comfort Hotel to stay with the Maudes, and more frequent afternoons with Bess and her children, and [with] Ruth Payne who our children called "Utie," and we copied them. And then, of course, these friends and relatives all came to us sometimes.

Parson Payne had fixed up an old log shack in Winter Cove as a church, with altar, tall candles and lectern—all correct—and sometimes he held a little service there for the local people, chiefly his own family, but anyone was welcome. The congregation was largely children, some of them babies in arms, but they were wonderfully good. We quite enjoyed going. Often, there would be a picnic afterwards.[12]

We generally made a trip to Victoria about every six months—one or another of us—for the dentist or what not, sometimes taking one of the children. In that way we made friends there.

Ralph went down to Victoria [in September 1906] for a few days because Lord Grey, Governor General of Canada, was coming to the capital. Ralph attended the reception, and had a talk with him afterwards, and then, by invitation, went to see him at Government House. Ralph also met Ramsay MacDonald and his wife Margaret several times. He had a leading position in the Labour Party, but had not yet been Prime Minister.

We had a short visit from Ralph's Aunt Emmie, who was visiting relations in Washington State. She was astonished that Birdie could handle a heavy pair of oars, and row her round the bay. We had bought another, smaller boat, the "Kittiwake," because Ralph was so fond of sailing, but she was only fit for a sailor to handle. The gold old Argo was still our family friend; and Mabel had a boat of her own, the Ocean Greyhound.

Another visitor was Ralph's old friend, Colonel Perrin, from Melbourne, Australia, who used to be so good, and his family so hospitable to Ralph when he was a cadet on the old sailing ship *Miltiades*. He just came between two steamer days, and then Ralph pulled him down to Saturna to catch the *Iroquois*. But no *Iroquois* arrived. There were no island phones then, so no one knew what had happened. At last, at 5 p.m., Ralph started to pull Colonel Perrin down to Sidney, because he had to catch his boat for Melbourne. They put into Bedwell on the way, but still no *Iroquois*, so on they went, arriving just after the *Iroquois* docked. Ralph slept the night in an old boat, rolled up in canvas, and then pulled the eighteen miles home. Quite a trip![13]

In browsing through Ralph's old diary, we are astonished at the enormous distances we pulled, and the number of people who dropped in for a meal or stayed the night as a matter of course. There are names we had quite forgotten—people who stayed a day or two and then passed out of our lives.

Once Mabel and I, with Birdie, had been to Sidney to fetch Janet and Judith Wolley home for the holidays. At Judith's earnest request we put into her home on Piers Island for the night, which we felt was quite an imposition. The next day we pulled on home.

One really herculean feat is worth recording. Mabel wanted the piano tuner from Victoria. I think there was only one, Herr Peters, a German. He came up on the steamer and we fetched him from the [Saturna] wharf. He enjoyed the island, and after tuning the piano we put him up for the night at our house.[14] First thing the next morning, Mabel and Janet rowed him down to tune the Kloshie piano, and then started off to take him to Sidney, another twelve miles. He could not row himself, and was quite a hefty fellow in the stern of the Greyhound. By the time they reached Hill Island it was quite dark; they ran into a nasty tide rip, and could not go on, so tried to put into Ian Mair's bay, calling for help. He came down with a lantern; they hauled up the boat, and he put them up, all three, for the night. Quite a tax on a bachelor's resources. The next morning they continued to Sidney, and then had the twelve miles back to the Koshie, where they spent the night, and finally the six miles back to Samuel the next day. Thirty-six miles in all!

One day I went down early to Boot Bay in the Argo and brought back Bess, the four children, Kitty, Dolly, John and baby Geraldine, their nurse (a dear, old, real English nanny), and Valley Taylor to spend the day. Then Fred and Jim Robson turned up to lunch, and in the afternoon Pascal de Noi Walker, his wife and little boy came to tea. So with Jess and Ada Saunders thrown in for good measure, we must have been quite a crowd. Thirteen extra people and our four selves.[15]

In reading this one might wonder how we fed these crowds that descended on us, often unexpectedly. Well, it didn't seem difficult. We had lots of eggs, rabbits and chickens. Sometimes we had butchered a sheep or calf, and occasionally a pig; or Ralph

might have been fortunate in getting a deer. I made all our bread—good brown brea.
from whole wheat flour—immense "cut and come again" cakes baked in milk pans, pies
and puddings. All the vegetables came from the garden. Then we had lots of butter,
which Ralph made, and cream.

Sometimes we had a raspberry party, in season. We picked perhaps fifteen
pounds of raspberries on meat platters, and served them with thick Jersey cream in soup
plates, and they went over "big" as the saying goes now.

Ruth Payne was a wonderful cook. She gave a lunch party for about twenty from
the surrounding islands one day, and did practically all the cooking herself. And Bess did
just about the same when we went on fishing expeditions with them.

* * * * * * * * *

We heard from Ralph's father occasionally. He was getting to be an old man
now. It seemed fitting that Ralph should go and see him before he passed on, so it was
decided he should go that winter, 1906-07, arriving in time to spend Christmas with his
father in Dublin, and then visit some of our people in London, returning in time for the
calving of our cow Flo, in February. Nakamura was to help Mabel and me with the
chores.

It happened that we had a particularly hard winter. If we slopped a little water
on the kitchen floor when carrying buckets from the well, it froze at once. The cattle well,
over near the old orchard, froze continually and had to be broken with a crowbar, and the
chickens and rabbits were in an equally bad plight.

We watched eagerly every mail for Ralph's letters, which were full of home news.
He nearly froze in some of the London houses, in spite of putting on every available stitch
of clothing. And then, just before he was due home, Flo calved. It was deluging with
rain, and had been for days, so that all low-lying ground was a lake. Nakki came hurrying
over to tell us, "Cow, she have small one."

Leaving the children with Kormi, Mabel and I put on gumboots, raincoats and
hats, and followed Nakki to the barn. There was the newborn calf, lying in a pool of
water, with Flo dripping wet beside it. We got the barrow, and somehow managed to
haul it into the barn. The ground was soggy and this dead weight of live calf kept swaying
from side to side. Twice it slipped out into the mire again, and had to be heaved back. I
must say, Nakki wasn't much use, and Mabel and I were convulsed with laughter at such
an absurd situation. We bedded it down with nice, dry hay and Flo licked it dry. From
then on, she had to be milked twice a day, of course.

[In March] Birdie and I went to Victoria to meet Ralph, and were so happy to
see him standing well out, waving. After admiring his new coat, telling him about the
children, and hearing news of his journey, I sprang it on him that Flo had calved. These
domestic events loomed quite large in our lives.

* * * * * * * * *

In June 1907 Mabel went to England again. We had several letters from her,
telling us all the news of the family. And then one night I had a very vivid dream that she
was in trouble and wanted me. We had always been so close to each other in mind and

body, often thinking of the same things, even if we were apart, that I felt sure some part of me went to her that night. She was calling me and I saw her in bed, crying.

I woke with a horrible feeling of foreboding, and told Ralph I was sure we should not get our weekly letter, as usual. Not to be caught napping this time, I wrote it all down at once, as this was the third of my sort of telepathic dreams which came true. Mail day came. No letter from Mabel. Some time later, about ten days or so, I got a letter saying that she had not been at all well, and one night had lain awake wanting me so much. It tallied with the night of my dream.

In October she wrote much more happily, saying she was engaged to Martin Grainger. He had cabled her. So like him, even now. We were so glad for her happiness. Martin came up to Samuel and had a long talk with us. He was going to England to join Mabel and bring her back later. He proposed to settle in Esquimalt, and try to find mathematical coaching work, because there was nothing profitable on the islands for him to do. He was a Cambridge University mathematical tripos man.

* * * * * * * * *

On January 11, 1908, it was blowing hard, with a sharp frost. About 10:00 a.m. Kormi arrived, very agitated and shaking with terror and cold. She had never been able to learn more than a few words of English, and evidently "sunny day" and "nice baby" did not fit this occasion. She pointed a trembling finger out to sea: "Nakamura, boat, maybe die!"

We got the telescope and went out on the bank. Yes, there was an overturned boat drifting away up the Channel. Ralph went over to Harold Payne and found that Nakamura, Kormi and another Japanese had capsized in their big fishing boat. The latter two had managed to get into their little skiff and pull to Harold's place, arriving at 5:30 a.m., but Nakamura, refusing to leave his boat, was clinging to the underside. Harold and the Parson put out in their launch and rescued him near the coast of North Pender after five hours in that freezing water. Nakamura was nearly all in. Meantime, Ralph sailed Kormi over to them, the launch towed them all back, and Ralph rowed them round to their shack. We got brandy, and put Nakki to bed with hot water bottles and blankets, and he recovered in a day or two. They were a hardy lot, those Japanese.

* * * * * * * * *

At long last, on June 3, 1908, Mabel came back to Samuel. She had been away nearly a year. On the 23rd, Martin arrived from Sidney on the launch *Blanche*, and after some deliberations they decided to go on to the Pass and get married, then and there. After a little "dolling up," we all got on board the launch and continued the journey. The children were very thrilled. Canon Paddon was hunted up, married them right away in the little church, and we all returned to Samuel.

On June 27th Mabel and Martin left for Esquimalt, and rented the little cottage on Lyall Street from Mrs. Potts, who lived next door.

Life had been a bit strenuous, and in October 1908 I had to take to my bed with some kind of breakdown. Fortunately, Mabel and Martin had been up shortly before and taken Birdie back with them, but as we had no help, Ralph looked after Evelyn, the meals and chores, which was no easy job. The news soon got round, and our good neighbours came over with food and help. Then I went for a few days to Mabel, leaving Ralph and Evelyn, a most pathetic and desolate couple. Martin and Mabel suggested a trip to Honolulu, taking Birdie for company, and leaving Evie with Mabel. And so it was arranged, to make a long story short.

On December 4, 1908, Mabel and Walter Spalding saw us off from the outer wharf, Victoria. I must confess my heart sank into my boots at leaving Ralph and Evelyn. Mabel was newly married and had Martin to keep her company now, and when I saw the size (or lack of it) of the S.S. *Moana*, I couldn't believe we were going out into the Paciic in her!

I was genuinely scared, and my fears were justified. We had an awful trip! She was just an old tub, condemned for that service twenty years before, but still on the route. Every seam opened up and I saw water running down the walls of our cabin as I lay on my bunk, too sick to move. Birdie was all right in a day or two, and made great friends with the stewardess and other passengers. All the clothes in my valise were soaked through. The captain didn't leave the bridge for three days.

The storm abated as we neared the island of Oahu, and I shall never forget the thrill of looking out of our porthole to see the sun rising on Diamond Head. It was like arriving at the moon: strange, broken craters, and jagged mountains.

I had not the remotest notion what to do when we reached Honolulu, and was still feeling very groggy, but two sugar planters took pity on us, phoned round to various boarding houses, and finally secured rooms for us with a Mrs. Gray on King Street. As if that were not enough for total strangers, they hired a hack and drove us and our baggage out there, refusing to let me pay.[16] That is American hospitality and generosity. I was overwhelmed with gratitude. We never saw them again, because they went off to the island of Hawaii, 214 miles away.

Honolulu is too well-known now to bear description, but it was Paradise to Birdie and me, who had never seen a palm tree or any tropical vegetation. It was not the up-to-date tourist resort that it is now. The District of Kaimuki had not been opened up, and the Leahi Home (which we were to know so well twenty years later) was not built.[17] We bathed at Waikiki, and hunted shells, which were still to be found. Mrs. Gray was very hospitable. She called us Mrs. Gray A. and Mrs. Grey E. with a good nasal twang. She had two boys, Ralph and Ernest, who took Birdie and me on some fine hikes. Once we went to the Punch-bowl, and another time a bigger expedition up Mount Tantalus, where they told us we could find snail shells on the leaves of trees. We spent another day out at Pearl Harbor, now a fortified base.

People told us we must not leave without seeing the famous Pali. But how to get there? Someone suggested the mail carrier and his cart. He consented to take us on his mail route (I forget what I paid). It was the least amount of cart that would hold together: several spokes out of each of the two wheels gone, a shaft broken and mended, and barely room for the driver and myself, with Birdie squeezed between us. It was a wonderful drive to the Pali, between converging volcanic hills, till we reached the precipice itself, a sheer drop of 1,000 feet. King Kamehameha is supposed to have driven his enemies over it.

Then came the thrill: driving in this old rattletrap down a very winding, narrow trail, with nothing whatever to keep the cart from going over the edge. The man made this trip every day of his life, so just let the reins hang loose, and didn't drive at all. The horse just went. Anyway, we arrived at the bottom whole; the man put us off at a lovely sandy beach some miles further on, and then continued on himself, picking us up again on the way back. We found some cowry shells we had not seen before, and saw plantations of [sugar cane].

Mrs. Gray took a party of her visitors out to a pineapple plantation, and we had fresh pineapple juice to drink, and peanut butter sandwiches for the first time. I bought some guava jelly and fresh pineapples to bring home, hoping to get them through the Customs (which I did).

Well, we had just the inside of a month there, and then caught the next boat home. When we left, friends and even strangers had draped us each with five or six of the traditional leis of real or paper flowers. Birdie was quite swallowed up in them. As the boat pulled away from the wharf, the Hawaiian band and the chorus sang "Aloha Oe," as they always do.

What a contrast! I could have made the home journey home in the Argo; it was dead calm. A flying fish flew right into the porthole of one of the passengers. We wished it had chosen ours. As we neared the Straits of Juan de Fuca, we ran into a blizzard of snow, and arrived to find Victoria under a white blanket. It was rather dismal after leaving that wonderful land of sunshine and flowers.

By some mistake no one was there to meet us, so I got the things through the Customs—we were the only passengers for Victoria—and took the streetcar out to Esquimalt. Evie flung herself on me, and in spite of Mabel's kindness, I had to promise never to leave her again. And then it was home to Ralph, January 16, 1909, Birdie's seventh birthday.

* * * * * * * * *

Ralph was so keen on getting the island in good shape that it was hard to drag him away for a day's fishing with the Paynes at East Point, or even a picnic on Sunday. He was not very interested in the actual fishing, but liked meeting the other men. He was always working for the future, but something told me the future held something different—that we could not live on Samuel forever. The children had to be educated, and there was no school. It seemed as if it would be better to raise pigs or something to bring in some ready money, but perhaps I was mistaken.

Copies of the *Illustrated London News* came our way sometimes. I made a large scrapbook of the most interesting things, and the children used to pore over this by the hour. There was a picture of little Olaf of Norway, now the Crown Prince, grown up and married; a tragic picture of the Czarevitch of Russia, not out of baby clothes; Niagara Falls frozen over; the Carlesbad Caverns, and endless things of general interest. The first flight of Wilber and Orville Wright in their queer sort of box plane was a great thrill. Birdie was always very keen on being told what was going on in the world. Already she had quite a fund of general knowledge. (In fact, when the children went to St. Margaret's School in Victoria they knew far more of world events than the town children.)

Martin and Mabel Grainger, Arthur Spalding, Elizabeth and Bea Spalding, Eric Burton and Henry Spalding, South Pender Island. BCARS 52262

1030 Wychbury Avenue, Esquimalt

Camping out, Esquimalt, while new home is being built.

CHAPTER SIXTEEN

Good-bye to Sam

At high water the tide came in over the flat at the old bay, and then slowly drained out again through an outlet. The children had grand times here. Each had a log; one, the "Lusitania," the other, the "Mauretania," which they poled in and out of this sort of culvert. There were collisons and sinkings, little knowing the future fate of the real *Lusitania*. They were happy days! But they were drawing to a close. Change was "hovering" in the air again. Sickness had taken its toll; Mabel was gone for good; but above all, the children needed to go to school.

The Islands had quite a boom. Piers Island and Prevost sold for quite large sums, and Samuel was far more attractive than either, though further from civilization. In fact, it was the only small island left. Ralph and I figured we might make it into a subdivision for summer cottages. So, after having failed to sell it whole, though a real estate firm ran a full-page ad and pictures without result, we got surveyors up from Victoria.

We went all over the south end with them, making suitable subdivisions. Mabel bought hers, with the Loggia, and we kept a piece for ourselves, with the house. Then when the surveyors tried to file the plan they were told by the Department of Lands that we must have roads connecting with each lot. So we had to begin all over again. This ran into a considerable amount of money, and by the time the second survey was completed and filed, the bottom had fallen out of the boom, and we never sold a lot. Such is Lady Luck! Other islands had sold for quite fabulous sums, $75,000 and so on; so we had had wild dreams of future wealth and comfort, but it was not to be, so why worry!

I see by an entry in Ralph's old diary for October 1909 that I was ill again, high blood pressure I know now. And that was followed by an epidemic of flu on the islands. The Paynes had it, then the children and myself, followed by Crow, with Ralph doing the cooking and waiting on us. Then he got a touch of it and I got up to help. It was a bad brand this time. In November I went to recuperate with Mabel in Esquimalt, leaving the children with Ralph and Crow.

The Hudson's Bay Company had just put the Macauley Point Subdivision on the market, in acre lots. We looked at them with interest, and after writing to Ralph about it and sending him a plan, we all decided to invest. Martin and Mabel chose a corner acre, facing on Lampson Street, and we (after Ralph had been down to see it) chose one next to theirs, fronting on the then ungraded Charles Street. As there was a Saint Charles Street the other side of town, there would be continual confusion in mail, so at the request of Mr. and Mrs. Mathews, also of Lampson Street, it was changed to Wychbury Avenue, and our number was 1030. Later, Ralph and I bought another acre adjoining, which we used as pasture for Flo, with a cow shed and feed room in one corner. These so-called acres were really one and one tenth, so we had two and one fifth, with a lovely group of fir trees. We built a ten-roomed house, with large verandah and sleeping porch for the children. Martin and Mabel built a pretty house on their lot, too, which had lots of trees.

I went home on a Wednesday, which was the long trip, when the boat put into Ganges and Mayne Island. There was a very strong ebb tide as the *Iroquois* was about to enter the Pass, so she hugged the south point to try and get a little eddy. It was fortunate for all on board that she did.

Suddenly, we heard the *Princess Victoria* "toot" and the next instant she came flashing out of the Pass on the rushing tide, far too close to shore for safety, as her Master must have known the *Iroquois* was due to go in. Our Purser, Munro, rushed to the rail with an ashen face. In that second, he could almost have touched the *Victoria,* she was so close. All knees were shaking as the *Iroquois* pitched, rolled and bucked in the swell created by the *Victoria*, and our Captain had hard work to keep his boat off the rocks.

It was this Captain Sears who, in the spring of 1911, took the *Iroquois* out from Sidney to her doom in a storm. She was top heavy and capsized. Our friends Miss Edith and Miss Isobel Fenwick were drowned, and Miss [Margaret] Barton nearly so. The Purser and most of the passengers lost their lives. Mabel and I knew Miss Barton slightly then, and Mabel had her at Ore Cottage till she recovered. So our long friendship with her began.[1]

Early in December 1909 we invited all the Payne families up, with a bran pie for the children (the bran kindly donated by Flo), which I put in a large box with strings attached to the presents. Then we had the usual big tea, and away they went. Then the Harold Paynes gave a Christmas tree which was a great success. No presents were ever expensive. The children were always content with simple games and toys.

Martin and Mabel came up to spend the last island Christmas Day with us and there was great mixing of plum puddings, with coins and one or two little trinkets. It was surprising how these things found their way into the children's helpings.

In January 1910 Evie and I spent a few days with Mrs. Paddon and Theo [at Mayne]. Ralph came up to fetch us, and we walked back to Robson's Bay by way of Fred Robson's farm, because Ralph wanted to see him on some matter. We found him and his nephew Jim Robson quite upset. They had roped Fred's good bull to dehorn it. It had given a lot of trouble and when the job was finished they found they had strangled the poor brute during its struggles. This delayed us a good deal, and when we got down to the Bay it was already quite dark and the boat was high and dry in the mud, though we had moored her out. Hunting skids, we launched her as quickly as possible.

By the time we got to the entrance of the Bay, it was blowing great guns up the channel, against a strong ebb tide. Ralph had the greatest difficulty to keep us from being swept onto the rocks of Lizard Island. We found it was impossible to make the channel, so Ralph said he would try and cut across and get to the north shore of Samuel. We shipped water continuously because the *Kittiwake* was like a cockleshell in this [storm]. I had to try and bail with one hand, with my right arm clasped tightly round Evelyn, as it seemed momentarily as if we must be upset. Evelyn never made a murmur. We had a terrible crossing, but somehow Ralph managed to nose the boat into the rocks and jump out with the painter.

I dragged Evelyn and myself up the bluff, while Ralph took the boat round to the north end bay and hauled her up, and then rejoined us. Then we had to get along the top of the bluff, in pitch blackness, stumbling over logs, falled limbs and rocks till we reached the other bay. There we were stuck! We had no boat to cross our big bay; it was absolutely impossible to get Evie round it, and I was just about "all in," So she and I sat down to wait, while Ralph stumbled away into the darkness to get the tiny skiff at Nakki's place. I tried to get Evelyn to sleep on my knee, but she was "all right mummy," and as good as gold.

About one and one half hours later at last I heard a welcome sound; the splash of oars and a tiny black speck nearing the shore. We scrambled down the bank and squeezed into the skiff. Then on landing we still had to walk across the flat, and so home at last. Poor Birdie, wide awake, was white with anxiety as she flung herself into my arms, sobbing. She thought we were drowned. She had sensed the danger when she saw it blowing and we did not come. But Crow was quite unruffled and complacent, wondering what all the fuss was about.

We had left Robson's Bay at five and got home at 7:45. Two hours and three quarters for a trip that would normally take us half an hour. It was the worst experience we ever had in connection with boats during our ten years of married life on the island (and Birdie's illness was the worst in connection with sickness).

When Ralph and I finally decided to leave the island in the spring of 1910, we had to get busy. One of the first things was to sell "Ally p'tty girl" and her cart, which Ralph and Nakki took down to the wharf in a scow he had built in our old bay. Then Kimping-Dush the oxen had to go. A logger bought them and came with a scow to take them away. We were all sorry to see these old friends go because it was the beginning of the breaking up of our old home.

Carl Cook and his wife, from Mayne Island, were going to rent the island, and came down several times during the spring, and finally camped in the Loggia some time before we left. Mrs. Cook had been a barber before she was married, and laughed openly at the way I cut Ralph's hair. Quite good-naturedly she said I "bit" it off.

Mrs. Cook was another of the island characters; a forth-right woman with her own opinions of people and things, which she was not afraid to express quite freely. "I never seen such a hat as Mrs. Grainger's. Why, it 'aint no shape at all!" Of Ralph's quiet, and sometimes apparently depressed moods, she said to me, "My, aint Mr. Grey down! I never seen anyone so down-hearted! I don't like sulky people. I always tell Carl I can't live with nobody pouting." But perhaps her choicest was when she announced, "Me and Carl cascarated that ram on the north end."

Before we left, Mrs. Cook was kind enough to tell me she "liked mangling (mingling) with people of her own kind." It was a great compliment, and I took it as such, though I could not aspire to her outspoken originality.

We left them the use of the good ship Argo, our old friend and standby for nearly thirteen years. She was still in fine shape, having had good care, and when the Cooks left some years later, she served the Arthur Drummonds faithfully. For all I know, she may still be roaming the island waters, in spirit if not in flesh.

The Mayne Island folk, our old friends, gave a dance for us in the hall at the Pass, with refreshments, which touched us very deeply. There were the old-time square dances (which were a great help to me, as I was no dancer), with a fiddler and one of the young fellows to call the figures. We were all very gay, but to Ralph and me there was a feeling of sadness, too. It marked the end of our social life with these good people, who were always so simple and cordial. It was probably our last trip up Robson's Bay, and the three mile walk, with the long hill down to the Pass, which we knew so well. I expect Ralph made a little speech, but I have forgotten. [2]

Of course, there was a lot of sorting and packing to be done. I gave my baby clothes to a woman at Saturna wharf who seemed to be adding to the population quite fast, without means of clothing the additions.

The "Lusitania" and "Mauretania" had to be left tied at their moorings—with the idea that they might remain there indefinitely.

180

We gave Nakamura and Kormi permission to stay on in the old shack. They showed great sorrow at our leaving, but I regret to say we were hardly out of sight with our belongings before they came around, helping themselves to tools, shovels, kegs of nails and anything they could lay their hands on. This in spite of the fact that Ralph had been most generous in giving them a fair share of what we were leaving behind. The Cooks were powerless, supposing we had given them leave to take the things. We had intended the Cooks to have everything we had not already given to Nakki. Such a possibility as their stealing never entered our minds, and we were quite shocked when we heard of it months later.

We all went to a farewell lunch with the Gerry Paynes, and also to the Harold Paynes. Then Crow had to be shipped off by steamer. She was a good girl, and very obliging, and put up with a good deal from the children with good nature. She wrote to us several times, and the last we heard she had married a school inspector and was very happy, so that was satisfactory.

Well, the final day came: May 4, 1910. We rented Gerry Payne's small tug, *Nora*, with a scow and her crew, Mr. Burnett and Andy Georgeson. By about eleven o'clock, having got Flo on board, hemmed in by beds, chairs, chests of drawers, bales of bankets, etc., and the *Kittiwake* securely tied on the stern of the scow, we were ready to start. The children and I took a last look round to see that nothing had been left behind, and then got on board the *Nora*. Ralph travelled with Flo on the scow to keep her company and to be ready for any emergency.

I remember with what mixed feelings I stood in the stern of the *Nora*, looking back—to the last—at the dear old island, which had been such a happy home for almost ten years, rather heavy of heart—but life still held adventure. Surveying our "Siwash" outfit—cow, boat and worldly possessions piled high on the scow—who could help but laugh! I had cooked a joint, bread, cakes, etc., for the six of us, as we had a long journey before us, and no one could tell what delays there might be. The *Nora* made slow time across Saturna Channel against a head wind, turned into Browning Harbour, through the Pender Canal, down Bedwell Harbour, and out into the Straits of Juan de Fuca with a very choppy sea.

Off Turn Point lighthouse (on Stuart Island, U.S.A.), the tide rips were so bad the men decided to put in to Hill Island for the night. The *Nora* took the children and me to Sidney, where we caught the train for Victoria, and went to Mabel in Esquimalt.

Ralph had quite a time of trying to feed, water and milk poor old Flo on the scow. The men were all up at 4:30 a.m. and finally reached Victoria Harbour about eleven o'clock. They landed the stuff at a tiny wharf, with one narrow gangplank, at the foot of Head Street, Esqimalt. It took the rest of the day to unload and bring Flo up to a little corral in the garden of "The Firs" next to us. The *Nora* departed, and Ralph had to sleep the night among the baggage. The next day we got it all up to our lot, with the help of an expressman; and the children and I joined Ralph in setting up the tents and making a good camp under our clump of fir trees, where we lived for four months.

It was a slow business getting a house built by day work; but it was done at last. The man who built the chimneys had been a master bricklayer in England, bossing about a dozen men. Then he fell on hard times and had to be content to work as an ordinary hand; and now he was his own boss again, but working alone, with no underlings to handle. He was telling us of these varying fortunes one day in his fascinating Cockney dialect, and reached the climax with this masterpiece: "After 'avin' 'ad the 'andlin' of ten or twelve men—and *then* to 'ave to be *'andled*". He broke off. Words failed. He left us to try and grasp the meaning of such utter degradation.

181

A little nuthall's sparrow built a nest in a wild rose bush, just at the entrance to one of our tents. The hen bird laid her eggs and hatched them with us constantly passing in and out, almost touching the nest.

We sold the *Kittiwake* to a man who professed to be able to handle a fast little sailboat. Ralph was so sorry to see her go, but we had no possible use for her there. We heard, not long afterwards, that the man had re-sold her. Well, we warned him!

I must skip quickly over such contretemps as being forced to bore an artesian well, which we used for two years (carrying the water into the house as we had done on the island), because the Esquimalt Water Works would not lay a water main along Wychbury Avene for one house. That meant no sewer, either, but we were accustomed to inconveniences, fortunately. It was some time before we got the electric light, also, and then we had to pay for the pole ourselves. The municipality certainly didn't encourage settlers. It was the result of some old feud with the Hudson's Bay Company, we heard.

Martin and Mabel built their house at the same time, but being on Lampson Street, could get all these connections. One day, after they had put the name of their house on the front gate, an elderly man stopped and asked the meaning of "Ore Cottage." Mabel laughed and said it was just the name of a little village in England where she had lived. Captain Bowden was delighted. He said he had been mate on Lord Brassey's yacht *Sunbeam*, which frequently anchored off Hastings. He knew Ore well, and knew of Ore Place. Now, he was retired and living with his wife just a block down Lampson Street. Mabel and I had often seen the *Sunbeam*. Talk of coincidences.

We called our place "Glendale" after the district in Cheviotdale, Northumberland, the home of the Greys. I should like to enlarge on our life there: the children's secret gardens in the clump of wild rose bushes, the ceremony of planting a fir tree to mark Ralph's fiftieth birthday, and all the good friends we made, but there must be a limit.

We were expecting a very interesting visitor in 1910, in the person of Halley's Comet, which only comes our way about every seventy-six years, so we were very lucky to be alive for this transient. The children were very keen about it and we often spoke of it months beforehand. It was rather hazy, unfortunately, when it came but we did see the "trailing skirts" faintly.

Miss Jess Saunders taught Conty, Evelyn, Randle Mathews and Frances Price in Martin's little coach house, as it was called; in reality the outside room in the garden where he was going to do his mathematical coaching. The children had grand times with Randle, roaming over Macauley Point or scrambling through the surrounding woods, looking for birds' nests and climbing every available tree. The woods were full of ladyslippers and wild lilies then, and we all took long walks, exploring the countryside.

After the summer holidays, Conty went to St. Margaret's School on Cook Street. Evelyn went, too, when she was a little older.

—And so we all plunged into this new life, with a fresh supply of energy and interest; and not one of us regrets those years spent on the Islands.

Winifred and Ralph, with their daughters Constance and Evelyn, lived on Wychbury Avenue, Esquimalt, until 1920. Ralph and Martin Grainger assisted Margaret Barton with the administrative work of St. Margaret's School for a brief period before gaining employment with the provincial government. Ralph worked with E.O. Scholefield, Provincial Librarian, and for the Forest Branch, Department of Lands. He later served with the 6th Field Company, Canadian Engineers, in Victoria, from 1916 to 1918.

Because of his logging experiences on the West Coast, Martin was asked to join the Royal Commission on Forestry as Secretary in 1910. He then helped to organize the Forest Branch, and became the second Chief Forester for the province, following H.R. MacMillan in 1915.

Winifred and Mabel lived near one another for the rest of their lives. When Martin established his own lumber business, with headquarters in Vancouver, after his resignation as Chief Forester in 1920, the Grey family moved to the mainland also. Mabel and Martin did not have any children, and they doted on Evelyn and Constance. The girls spent memorable summer holidays at the Grainger's cabin near Princeton. Evelyn made several horseback journeys with Martin and a guide, from Princeton to Hope, over the Allison Pass.

Mabel and Martin visited England on a number of occasions but Winifred never returned to see her family. She kept in close touch with many of the Spalding cousins, however. Ethel was especially helpful when Winifred began her memoirs, providing the original letters written by Amelia and Margaret Higgs.

Like his forebearers, Ralph Grey was an ardent socialist. When the Stanley Park Club, a branch of the Co-operative Commonwealth Federation, was formed in the 1930's, he and Evelyn were early members. Winifred was interested in politics, although not as keen as her husband and daughter.

High blood pressure plagued Winifred throughout her lifetime, and she experienced several heart attacks, one while at Esquimalt. But she lived to the good age of seventy-nine, dying on June 15, 1951. Ralph predeceased her in 1943.

Janet Wilde married later in life after a career as a legal stenographer. She died in 1976, at the age of ninety.

Winifred and Mabel sold Blue shortly after Mabel moved to the Loggia on Samuel Island, ca. 1904, but Samuel did not change hands until the 1920's. Winifred's daughter Evelyn recalls that Mabel broke the sad news to her while they were walking down a street in Vancouver. The shock was too much; she burst into tears.

* * * * * * * * *

Despite modern transportation links, South Pender and Samuel Islands are still considered semi-remote in the southern Gulf Islands chain. South Pender is accessible by B.C. ferries to North Pender Island, and then one must drive ten miles to reach Gowland Point. Samuel Island is privately owned and visitors are discouraged.

The road to Blue winds through the large farm originally cleared by Arthur Spalding. Arthur and Lilias remained on the farm all their lives, and it is now well-cared for by their descendants. Deer still graze in the swamp year round, and crops of lambs dot the fields every spring.

The shortcut path that Mabel and Winifred used between Arthur's and Leonard's homesteads remains popular, but a modern highway winds around the base of the hill, hugs the cliffs above Bedwell Harbour, then makes a long run out to Gowland Point and "Blue Tarpon Bay." Sitting on the grassy bank above the beach, on a quiet summer morning, you may easily imagine waking to find hummingbirds hovering over the patchwork flowers on your coverlet, skinnydipping in the sparkling cove, or gathering cedar kindling for the breakfast fire in petticoats.

Blue was demolished in the 1950's, but some of the lumber was reused in Evelyn's house, located nearby on Leonard's former property.

On the brief ferry ride to Saturna you pass Samuel Island, still undeveloped, and still owned entirely by one family. None of the buildings erected by Ralph and Winifred remains.—Only the clearing and a few gnarled fruit trees bear testimony to their hard work and immigrant dreams of prosperity.

Winifred and Ralph, Constance and Evelyn, ca. 1935

RECOLLECTIONS OF SHIRE HALL IN THE FIFTIES

BY FLORENCE UNDERHILL
(nee Holmes) Mabel's godmother and niece of Grannie Spalding

Hendon was a village, and always spoken of as such in the fifties. There was no railway, but I think an omnibus went twice a day to Hampstead, where one could get another to Oxford Street. "Old John" was for years a conductor. He was a celebrity. The shops were few, and were kept by simple country folk. There was no gas, and the lamps, few and far between, were lighted by a man with a ladder. Everyone used a lantern after dark. The old people still talked of "garroters" and "foot pads," and considered it unsafe for young people to walk over Golders Green after dark. The field walks 'round Hendon were many and very pretty. In the spring they were full of cowslips and primroses. Occasionally, we came across a snake. Poor, dear little Ellie trod on one in the garden. She and I shared the same horror of them. Dotted about Hendon were many fine, old houses and gardens. I am afraid many of them have been pulled down and the gardens built over.

Now I must try and describe Shire Hall. I always understood the house was built before Victorian times. When the Father bought it he pulled down the whole of the front of the house, leaving, on the garden side at the back, three charming rooms: the drawing room with folding doors into the library, and the dining room. These rooms opened onto a balcony with steps down onto a broad terrace. The new rooms facing the drive were a breakfast room and, across the hall, a room called the parlour. Beyond this room was another piece of the old house, an entrance into the garden and an old room called the anteroom which had huge cupboards and a small door into the dining room. The hall was spacious and in the winter an open fire gave it a great look of comfort. Two arches divided the hall from the staircase, which may or may not have been the original one. A swing door on the first landing led down a flight of steps to a gallery onto which all the servants' bedrooms opened; and a bathroom which did duty for the whole household. Once a week was considered sufficient for a bath.

Now I must try and give an idea of the garden. A beautiful lawn, with two fine old elm trees, in which there was a rookery, faced the old side of the house. The lawn was divided from the field beyond by a sunk fence. Beyond the field was the Brent, a never-ending interest to Alfred and me. The bullrushes, water lillies, moor fowls, sometimes a kingfisher, and, in their season, large forgetmenots and dragon flies, were all objects of interest. The stone steps at one end of the terrace led down to the "woody walk" as it was called. Here Alfred and I had a primrose and cowslip bank. I remember hearing that all the fine trees in this walk were cut down a few years after we left. Half way down was a beautiful old oak, which was always "home" in games of hide and seek. On the opposite side of the river was a large field called the Park Field on account of the beautiful trees.

I must not forget to describe "Sunset Cottage." This was a large garden room, built in rustic style, which would seat comfortably forty people for tea. It was used for all kinds of occasions: Tea for Mothers, Sunday school treats, parties for workers from London, and for ourselves a playroom on wet days. Alfred and I often swept it out, and sometimes cleaned the windows when we had permission to have water. Behind the cottage were our gardens, an aviary, an old ice house, and two large kitchen gardens enclosed with old brick walls. The vines were said to be very old.

The large conservatory, which the Father had built onto the house, might be described as a winter garden. It was so long that it rather dwarfed the house. It was always full of flowers, some of the plants and young trees (one of which nearly touched the roof) were sent over by the Mother's brother, Howard Reed, from Australia. A fernery, and a pool, with a little fountain in which were goldfish, was a nice, cool place where one could sit on hot days. I once heard that the whole place, after the house had been standing empty some years, was taken down and put up in some public gardens near London.

The stables and old farm yard we were very fond of. To see the cows milked, look for eggs, let out the dogs (never allowed in the house), and to talk to old Howse, the farm man, were in the summer among our pleasures. The Lodge was a mystery house to Alfred and me, and we were afraid to go past it alone, for the gate keeper had an imbecile sister living with her. We thought she was mad, and might some day rush out upon us.

When I first went to live at Shire Hall I was five. As we drove up to the front door, I saw a little boy standing on the steps in a green poplin frock with little white checks. The frock was low at the neck and had an embroidered tucker. This little boy was Alfred, nearly the same age as myself. I had a black frock with crepe tucks and a little crepe bonnet. I envied Alfred's pretty frock, which we always called his "window frock" because of the little white squares.

OLD HENDON

Memories of the Fifties
by Espie Capper

Seventy-five years ago, Hendon, as I remember it, was a very small and unimportant village with a few good houses in their own grounds, mostly situated in Brent Street. There were no lights in the street; colza oil lamps were carried by the residents who went out after dark. In course of time a little row of shops was built, an innovation which seemed to excite and disturb the quiet of the village, but before long was welcomed as a convenience. Govus, the draper, displayed things in his window that turned the heads of the village maids. "I wish I might wear such beautiful things," sighed our under nursemaid; for it was customary in those days to forbid to domestic servants, as a condition of their employment, the wearing of flowers or feathers, or white petticoats and other alluring finery.

It was a great hay-making district, and a multitude of Irish labourers came over to cut the grass. They brought their own scythes, but the rest of their luggage was of no account; it was all carried in a big cotton handerkerchief. Their confidence in their employers must have been great, for, had these been hard or inconsiderate, they must have suffered badly. Often the summers were wet and cold, and these Irish immigrants had nowhere to lay their heads but the open barns and sheds allotted to them. One season my parents and two ladies who lived close by arranged to feed a certain number, the two ladies supplying breakfast and tea, and we the more substantial midday meal and shelter.

The same ladies set up a small, exclusive school for "young gentlewomen." It flourished and grew, and in later years was removed to more spacious premises, built for them by my uncle, who had a large house in Hendon, through the grounds of which ran the River Brent. He also built a little Congregational chapel in the village, and another one in a hamlet called The Hyde. Till then the only place of worship was the beautiful old Parish Church, in which there is still a magnificent Norman font.

There was no local paper before 1875, and no organized entertainments of any kind; merely occasional magic-lantern displays conducted by my father, and enlivened by the ballads which his little daughters sang to illustrate such pictures as "The spider and the fly." Altogether social life was very simple and unexacting. Christmas excitement for the village was found in the various entertainments provided by my uncle and his family, who lived at Shire Hall—previously called Brent Lodge. The residents and their dependents all seemed to be remembered and entertained in one way or another, and not infrequently a christening took place in the house before the more festive family engagements, so that we children supposed Christmas and christening to be one and the same thing.

In the fifties the little hamlet of Golders Green lay in open country, Temple Fortune Lane and Kidderpore Hall being the best remembered names. But to us children the most important building was a large white house in a beautiful garden, notorious from the tradition that a previous tenant had kept a dead body secreted on the roof. It was an arresting story, for we all knew that dead bodies ought to be under the ground in Hendon Churchyard. Beyond Golders Green was Hampstead, then little more than a village, with many small shops in the High Street. An omnibus came out from London Bridge as far as the heath, and Hendon children coming from school for the holidays were met at Jack Straw's Castle by other vehicles.

About 1860 (I leave the exact date to the astronomers), a wonderful comet appeared, which, according to the village intelligence, portended terrible disaster. Children were taken out nightly to see it, and warned by their nurses that the world would come to an end before long. So strongly was this opinion held that it ruined the career of at least one household. The grocer's son, who had married and started a thriving little business as an ironmonger, was so convinced of the imminence of the millennium that he sold off all his stock at a loss, put up his shutters, and awaited the inevitable day, of which he gave us an appalling account. We watched for a time, wearied our nurses with asking, "Will it be today?" and then, as children will, grew tired and forgot.

* * * * * * * * *

*From *The Times*, October 7, 1932.

[Winifred made two notations on the original newspaper clipping.
The first reads: "Note: Temple Fortune Lane is still there in 1939. Miss M. Barton bought a house there for her mother and sister Fanny, and still owns it."
The second reads: "1940. This house has been destroyed by a bomb."]

NOTES

INTRODUCTION

1   For the purposes of this book, I am defining upper middle class by income and household staff. Patricia Branca argues in *Silent Sisterhood* (London: Croom Helm Ltd., 1975), that the middle class household could afford a maid-of-all work only. Both the Howard Spalding and Thomas Higgs households employed a maid or cook, and a nursemaid (1871 Census). Branca questions J. A. Bank's statement in *Prosperity and Parenthood* (London: Routledge & Paul, 1965) that the average middle class household contained, at the very least, a cook, parlour-maid,and nurse or housemaid. To support this size of staff she contends that a family would need an annual income of £400-500 , which she claims is upper middle class (p. 54). Branca gives an income of £100-300 annually for middle class families.

Estimates on the exact number of upper middle class are difficult to obtain, but Peter Laslett suggests that even by 1909 only 280,000 households out of 7,000,000 in England and Wales, or 4%, earned £700 or more annually. See Laslett, *The World We Have Lost* (London: Methuen and Company Limited, 1965), p. 214.

When Thomas Spalding died in 1888 he left an estate valued at more than £89,000. His wife Elizabeth was to receive £100 monthly to manage Ore Place until it was sold. Although Samuel Higgs left an estate valued at only £6,000, it is presumed that he had already transferred his complex business to his son Thomas. (Extract of wills index, and wills of Thomas Spalding and Samuel Higgs, Somerset House, London.) The fact that Higgs maintained a weaving concern is indicative of his business acumen, for by the 1860's most of the weaving industry in Suffolk had collapsed. The contract for navy bunting was one of the few available. See Nigel Heard,*Wool,East Anglia's Golden Fleece* (Lavenham, Suffolk: Terence Dalton Limited, 1970), p. 159; and Barbara Kerr, *The Dispossessed* (London: John Baker, 1974), p. 50.

2   *White's Directory* for 1844; *Post Office Directory* 1858; and*White's Directory* 1874; Michael Hills, Town Archivist, Sudbury, Suffolk, to editor August 11, 1983.

3   Information on Spalding family obtained from will of Thomas Spalding.

4   British Parliamentary Papers. *Papers Relating to Emigration, 1894-1899*. Vol. 28, p. 20 and p. 22.

5   For example, see Flora Thompson, *Lark Rise* (London: The Folio Society, 1979), for a description of life as a poor village family; Gwen Raverat, *Period Piece* (London: Faber and Faber Ltd. 1952) for a description of a Cambridge childhood; Winifred Peck, *A Little Learning* (London: Faber and Faber Ltd., 1952), and *Home for the Holidays* (London: Faber and Faber Ltd., 1955) for a description of a rector's family; M. Vivian Hughes, *A London Girl of the Eighties* (London: Oxford University Press, 1936), and Violet R. Markham, *Return Passage* (London: Oxford University Press, 1953) for two other upper middle class descriptions.

6   See Francois Crouzet, *The Victorian Economy* (London: Methuen & Co. Ltd., 1982), pp. 12-13, and pp. 290-291.

7   Michael Hills to editor, December 8, 1983. Samuel Higgs was not averse to expressing his opinion of the established church. See Kerr, *The Dispossessed,* pp. 51-52.

Information on Thomas Spalding's philanthropy supplied by George Musgrave, Heathfield, Sussex, to editor, October 31, 1963.

8   Rev. B.G. Thorogood, General Secretary, Congregational Church Federation, London, to editor, November 1983.

9   Recorded by Winifred in her memoirs, copied from letters supplied by Ethel Spalding, Grey Family Papers, Add. MS 604, British Columbia Archives and Records Service.

10   G.M. Trevelyan, *Illustrated English Social History*, Vol. 4 (Middlesex, England: Pelican Books, 1964), p. 158.

11   See footnote 4, Chapter Seven, for other accounts of boarding school education.

12   Jessie M. Saxby, *West Nor'West* (London: James Nisbet & Co. 1890). Printed with permission of the publisher from *Flannel Shirt and Liberty: British Emigrant Gentlewomen in the Canadian West, 1880-1914,* edited by Susan Jackel (Vancouver: UBC Press 1982). All rights reserved by the Publisher.

13   See D.V. Glass, *Population Policies and Movements in Europe* (London: Frank Cass & Co. Ltd., 1967), pp. 17-18.

14   Beatrice J. Freeman, ed., *A Gulf Islands Patchwork* (Victoria: Gulf Islands Branch, B.C. Historical Association, 1974).

15   Ibid., p. 62.

16   George Frederick Strong (1897-1957), MD, DSc(Hon.), LLD, FACP, FRCP (London) FRCP(c), Hon. FRACP, was often called "Dr. B.C. Medicine" for his efforts and achievements in medicine and social welfare. Strong received his M.D. in 1921 from the University of Minnesota, and completed post graduate work at the Vancouver General Hospital. He served at VVGH from 1926 to 1951, becoming chief of the Department of Medicine in 1946. He then went to the University of British Columbia, where he was clinical professor of medicine from 1951 to 1957. He played a key role in the formation of the Faculty of Medicine at U.B.C., and in launching the B.C. Cancer Foundation, the Western Society for Rehabilitation, and the B.C. Medical Research Institute. In 1957 the Western Rehabilitation Centre, which he helped establish in 1949, was renamed the G.F. Strong Rehabilitation Centre in his honour. (Vertical File, BCARS.)

17   Other authors included Thomas Spalding's brothers, Henry and Samuel, and Samuel Higg's son Arthur Hibble Higgs. In addition, Elizabeth Spalding's nephew, Talbot Reed, was a well-known author of boys' stories.

       Ethel Spalding attended Cambridge Training College, then Sommerville College, Oxford, 1896-1900. She lectured at Goldsmith's College, University of London, from 1905-1921, and was Principal of Bingley Training College from 1921-1932. She died in 1957.

CHAPTER ONE

1   Charlotte Pechey, widow of Dr. Richard Pechey, conducted Mrs. Pechey's Boarding School for Young Ladies on Marsh Street (now High Street), Walthamstow, from 1854 to 1871. There were several other girls' schools on the same street. Mrs. Pechey previously conducted a school at Bishop Stortford, Hertfordshire. (*Kelley's Essex Directories* for 1855 and 1859, *Walthamstow Directory* for 1861; Lyn Arlotte Local Studies Librarian, London Borough of Waltham Forest, to editor, June 11, 1983.)

       Maria Higg's two younger sisters, Margaret (Marnie), and Elizabeth (Lizzie) also attended Mrs. Pechey's school.

2   For a description of Shire Hall, Hendon, see Appendix I.

3   There were a number of Scrutton families in the brokerage and East India trade. See *Three Victorian Telephone Directories 1884-1884* (Devon: David & Charles (Publishers) Ltd., reprint, 1970), p. 50.

4   Maria's father, Samuel Higgs, listed his occupation as a Dissenting minister at the time of his marriage to Maria Hibble on August 3, 1839, at the Old Meeting House, Parish of All Saints, Sudbury, Suffolk. (First Civil Marriage Register for Sudbury, Archives, Town of Sudbury, Suffolk; Michael R. Hills, Town Archivist, Sudbury, to editor, December 8, 1983.

5   A fourth brother, William Higgs, was born in 1848, and died the same year. See William Miller Higgs, *A History of the Higges or Higgs Family of South Stoke, Oxon., and Thatcham, Berks, and Their Descendants* (Longon: Adlard & Son, Ltd., 1933), pp. 312-313, and 369-370.

6   Unfortunately, Maria's diary was not in Eve's collection of family papers.

7   Thomas Spalding Sr. (1762-1819) began the wholesale stationery business in 1789 with two partners, Thomas Hodgson and Henry Routh, and a capital of £1800. The three men had been stationers on the Strand, and Hodgson owned paper mills at Arborfield in Berks., and Horton in Bucks. Spalding soon became sole owner of the business, relocating to 147 Drury Lane, London. Under the management of his sons Thomas and Henry, and, later, his grandson John Howard Spalding, the company expanded in the late 19th century to 145-147 Drury Lane, and 34 Cannon

Street, London, E.C. They also operated a paper mill at Horton Kirby, Kent. An attempt to develop an outlet in Australia ended in bankruptcy in 1889 (see footnote 1, chapter eight). See Spalding & Hodge Limited, *Printing Papers: A Handbook for the Use of Publishers and Printers* (London: Wm. Clowes and Sons Ltd., 1905, reprint 1915), pp. 1-6; Charles A Rivington, Hon. Librarian, The Worshipful Company of Stationers & Newspaper Makers, London, to editor, May 9 and 28, 1983; Mrs. K.M. Stanley, Parish Council of Horton Kirby and South Darenth, Dartford, Kent, to editor, June 16, 1983; and Remembrances of Espie Capper, copied into Winifred's memoirs, Grey Family Papers, Add MS 604, BCARS.

The Swedish firm of Inveresk Paper Merchants acquired Spalding & Hodge in the 1960's. (Mr. A.L. Hawker, Administrative Assistant, G-P Inveresk Corporation, to editor, December 7, 1983.

8   Andrew Reed Sr. was active in bringing about the union of the Congregational Churches in England and Wales in the 1830's. In 1834 he visited the United States and Canada with James Matheson in order to encourage international communication, and in 1837 he took part in the formation of the Colonial Missionary Society. He is noted for founding five national charities: The London Orphan Asylum, the Infant Orphan Asylum, the Asylum for Fatherless Children, the Asylum for Idiots, and the Hospital for Incurables. See Albert Peel, *These Hundred Years* (London: Congregational Union of England and Wales, 1931), passim., and R. Tudor Jones, *Congregationalism in England* (London: Independent Press Ltd., 1962) passim. Further informtion provided by Fred Keay, Honorary Research Secretary, United Reformed Church History Society to editor, October 3, 1983. An illustration of the Asylum for Idiots, Earslwood, may be found in George Meason, *The Official Illustrated Guide to the South-Eastern Railway and its Branches* (London: E & W Books (Publishers) Ltd., 1970, reprint of 1858 edition.) This asylum not only cared for its patients, but attempted to prepare them "as far as possible, for the duties and enjoyments of life," pp. 180-181.

For a recent assessment of Reed as "an ambitious nonconformist clergyman" see R.J. Helmstadter, "The Reverend Andrew Reed (1787-1862): evangelical pastor as entrepreneur", *Religion and Irreligion in Victorian Society*, R.W. Davis and R.J:. Helmstadter, ed.(London: Routledge, 1992), pp. 7-28.

Sir Charles Reed was also chairman of the London School Board. See Peel, *These Hundred Years*, pp. 202-203.

9   Thomas Spalding purchased Ore Place from Sir Howard Elphinstone, D.C.L., F.R.S., (1804-1893). Elphinstone, the only son of Maj-Gen. Sir Howard Elphinstone, Bart., was a magistrate and Dept.-Lieut. for the County of Sussex, and represented the borough of Hastings from 1835 to 1837. He sat for Lewes from 1841 to 1847, when he accepted the Chiltern Hundred. He succeeded his father as 2nd Bart. on April 28, 1846. Elphinstone Road, formerly named Ore Lane, forms one side of the Ore Place estate. See *Who's Who of British Members of Parliament*, Vol. I (Sussex: Harvester Press Limited, 1976), p. 127; Sheila Pratt, Honorary Secretary, St. Helen's Park Preservation Society Ltd., Hastings, to editor July 15, 1983, and March 1984; Pamela Haines, Local Studies Librarian, Hastings Central Library, Hastings, to editor, June 1 and July 26, 1983.

10   Espie Capper, daughter of Henry Spalding, and Amelia's first cousin, wrote that Amelia had suffered two bouts of pneumonia while the family lived at Hendon. It is possible that Thomas Spalding moved his family to Ore Place, near St. Leonards, because of Amelia's poor health. Doctors recommended the sea air of Hastings as good for pulmonary complaints. See J.D. Parry, *The Coast of Sussex* (London: E & W Books (Publishers) Ltd., 1970, reprint of Brighton: Wright & Sons, 1833). Dr. Archibald R. Shaw, the Spalding's family physician may also have moved from Hendon to St. Leonards at the same time. (Memories of Espie Capper, Grey Family Papers, Add. MS 604, BCARS.)

Although only a young girl of eight or nine, Espie Capper was aware of her cousin Amelia's high spirits. She wrote, "The strictness of the home was an atmosphere she (Amelia) could not thrive in, and any excuse for leaving it was eagerly seized. I remember my mother speaking with great sympathy for Mimi, as she was then called, and later on my mother once went to stay with her in her new married home, and returned full of anxiety for her." Ibid.

Sarah Ann "Spanny" Molton (nee Foreman), beloved cook for three generations of the Higgs family, recalled Amelia as pretty and high-spirited. "Always for horses she was. When they had a new gig at The Moat, she would have it out—the horse was so lively. She whipped him up, and he tore round the corner of the street, and took the paint off. You should have heard what yer Grandfather (Higgs) said!" (Mabel Grainger to Winifred following a visit with Spanny in 1938, when the faithful servant was ninety-two years old. Copied into Winifred's memoirs.)

11   Rev. Andrew Reed Jr. married Amelia and Thomas Higgs at St. Leonards Congregational Church on August 15, 1866. Amelia wore a traditional, formal white gown and lace veil held by a chaplet of orange blossoms. Her six bridesmaids, Maria Higgs, Annie Spalding, Ellie Spalding, Annie Scrutton, Florence Holmes, and a Miss Worseley, wore white dresses with wreaths of blue convolvulus (morning glory). (Copied into Winifred's memoirs from an undated newspaper account provided by Margaret Higgs.)

12   Samuel Higgs (1816-1884) served as mayor of Sudbury from 1861 to 1869, 1864 excepted. He later acted as justice of the peace at Great Cornard, one mile southeast of Sudbury, where he farmed one hundred acres. The family home "The Moat" was so named because it is an ancient moated farmhouse, built ca. 1560. Michael Hills to editor, August 11, 1983; Mrs. Leslie McQuhae to editor, November 21, 1983; 1871 Census, Great Cornard Parish, entry 198, R.G. 10/17/16, P.R.O. "The Moat," also known as Wrong's Farm, is noted in *The Victoria History of the County of Suffolk*, Vol. 1 (London: University of London Institute of Historical Research, reprint Wm. Dawson & Sons Ltd., 1975), p. 610.

Samuel Higgs may have acquired the bunting manufacturing company through his marriage to Maria Hibble. In *White's Directory* for 1844, Thomas Hibble is listed as a bunting manufacturer, and Hibble and Higgs as maltsters. But in the *Post Office Directory* for 1858 Hibble and Higgs are listed as wool merchants, bunting manufacturers, maltsters, and agents for the Blood Manure Company.

Thomas Higgs worked for his father's company. (Letter from Amelia to sister-in-law Marnie, June 11, 1870, describes her husband as "up to his eyes in wool-gathering," copied by Winifred into her memoirs.)

13   Amelia's excellent portrait was probably copied from an illustration "Boulogne fisherfolk" in the *London Illustrated News*,

CHAPTER TWO

1   Amelia's allowance was generous enough to permit her to hire three servants, including a nurse when the children were very young. Their wages would probably have amounted to 400-500 pounds annually. See Joseph Ambrose Banks, *Prosperity and Parenthood* (London: Routledge & Paul, 1965), p. 76.

2   Unc—Thomas Alfred Spalding (1850-19)—resided with his sister Amelia and her children while studying law. He was called to the Bar by Middle Temple on November 17, 1874, and was a member of Convocation, University College, in 1875. In 1879 he served as private secretary to E.N. Buxton, Esq., Chairman of the London School Board. (E. McNeill, Librarian, The Honourable Society of the Middle Temple London, to editor, December 7, 1983; and Glenn Dymond, The Honourable Society of Gray's Inn, to editor, November 4, 1983.)

3   "Pothooks and hangers" is a Victorian way of describing printing letters of the alphabet. Also mentioned in Flora Thompson, *Lark Rise* (London: The Folio Society, 1979), p. 180.

Alfred Spalding was a member of the New Shakspere Society, and wrote *Elizabethan Demonology* (London: Chatto and Windsor, 1880; reprint ed., London: The Folcroft Press, 1970), among many other books.

The tragic scene is from "The Life and Death of King John," Act IV, scene 1.

4   "Old Grumpy" was presumably a crotchity handyman living in the neighbourhood.

5   *Hookeybeak the Raven and Other Tales with Pictures* (London: Routledge, 1877).

6   *Sancho, A Tale of a Bad Bird* (London: T. Nelson & Sons, 1920). *Sancho* was one of a series of children's books that Thomas Alfred Spalding wrote or edited for T. Nelson & Sons.

7   The Asquith family had been members of St. Leonards Congregational Church since its formation. Herbert Asquith taught Sunday School there, and the murals on the wall of the lecture

hall are believed to have been commissioned by the Asquith family. George Musgrave, *History of St. Leonards Congregational Church*, pamphlet series, 1981.

8   Howard Spalding belonged to the Swendenborg religion, and wrote seven books on the subject. For example, *The Kingdom of Heaven as Seen by Swedenborg* (London: J.M. Dent & Sons Limited, 1916).

9   Ore Place was build efficiently, with servants' quarters and dining rooms placed close to work areas. See Jill Franklin, "Troops of Servants: Labour and Planning in the Country House 1840-1914," *Victorian Studies VXIX, 12, 211-239.*

Ventnor is a resort area on the southeast coast of the Isle of Wight that Elizabeth Spalding visited.

10   The Elementary Education Act of 1879 enabled school boards to enforce school attendance for young children. Day schools for the poorer segment of the population grew rapidly, but the upper middle class families such as the Spaldings continued to employ governesses for their children.

CHAPTER THREE

1   See Winifred's Family Tree, p. xiii.

2   Thomas Alfred Spalding's chambers were at 6 Pump Court, Temple, London, EC. (Law Lists, 1875; Glenn Dymon to editor, November 4, 1983.)

3   Leonard attended Uppingham for two terms only, May to December, 1883. (Bryan Matthews, Uppingham School, Rutland, to editor, November 25, 1983.) Under the administration of Rev. Edward Thring, Uppingham was considered a technologically advanced school for its time. The boys learned practical skills such as metal work and electronics. See P.H. Gosdon, *How They Were Taught* (Oxford: Basil Blackwell, 1969), p. 122-126.

In his study of upper class emigrants, Patrick Dunae stated that among the young men attempting ranching on the Canadian Prairies, there were more Uppingham alumnae per capita than any other public school. See *Gentlemen Emigrants* (Vancouver: Douglas & McIntyre, 1981), p. 99.

4   Ralph's father, Charles Grey of Dilston, Northumberland (1825-1916), trained as an engineer/surveyor at Durham University, receiving his M.A. in 1849. In 1881 he was appointed court valuer for the Irish Land Commission. He retired to a farm at Enniscorthy in 1895, and in 1905 moved to Dublin. (Grey Family Papers, Add. MS 604, BCARS.)

Ralph Geoffrey Grey was born December 18, 1861, at Dilston. He trained for the merchant marine on the training ship HMS *Conway* from January 1875 to February 1877, then made four annual voyages to Australia on the clipper ships *Miltiades* and *Jerusalem.* He assisted his father in land valuation duties from 1881-1882, and worked on a farm from 1882-1883 before emigrating to British Columbia. (Eve Grey Smith Papers, South Pender Island.)

5   Winifred's memoirs compare favourably with those of Allan Jobson who lived in Anerley two decades later, and whose forebearers also came from Suffolk. See Allan Jobson, *The Creeping Hours of Time* (London: Robert Hale, 1977), pp. 24-65.

6   One may not assume that ingestion of these medications precipitated Amelia's terminal illness (cancer of the tongue). Consultation with Dr. Margaret Campbell, Victoria.

7   For a description of the elaborate ornamentation in Victorian homes, see Ralph Dutton, *The Victorian Home* (London: B.T. Batsford Ltd., 1954). Hand-painted tiles in dull colours were popular. Ibid., pp. 148-149.

8   Erected for the Great Exhibition in London in 1851, the Crystal Palace was dismantled and reassembled at Anerley [Sydenham] in 1854. The prehistoric monsters of concrete were located near the south entrance by the Great Lake. See Patrick Beaver, *The Crystal Palace* (Longon: Hugh Evelyn Limited, 1970), p. 136. A boy's response to the Palace displays can be found in W. Macqueen-Pope, *Twenty Shillings in the Pound* (New York: Hutchinson & Co. Ltd., pp. 354-360).

9   Blondin did not perform on wires stretched between the two 284 foot water towers, which were landmarks on the Crystal Palace grounds, but from smaller towers. (Beaver, *The Crystal Palace*, p. 113.)

10   For a critical response to the Plouquet Collection, see Beaver, *The Crystal Palace*, p. 54.

11   Brock's fireworks, with the famous set pieces, commenced in 1865. Most of the famous naval battles were recreated, including the Battle of Trafalgar, which was 820 feet across, and the Battle of Jutland, which was the last of the displays that had been produced over a seventy year span. (Beaver, *The Crystal Palace*, pp. 113, 119 and 132.)

12   Bicycles and tricycles were just coming into their own, and were extremely poplar by the mid-1890's. Winifred and Mabel apparently did not participate in the new craze.

13   The Handel Festivals, with chorus and orchestra of 4,000, commenced at the Crystal Palace in 1859. Beaver, *The Crystal Palace*, p. 119.

14   Kingsley's description of the grim life of a child chimney-sweeper in *Water Babies* was partly responsible for the passage of the Chimney-Sweepers Act in 1864, which was followed by a more effective Act in 1875, sponsored by Lord Shaftsbury.
      The growing publication of books for children, which could be enjoyed by adults also, was evidence of the increasing sympathy for children. Social historian G.M. Trevelyan has described this change of attitude as "one of the chief contributions made by the Victorian English to real civilization." See *Illustrated English Social History*, IV (Middlesex: Penguin Books, 1964), p. 158.

15   *Lays of Ancient Rome* was a "standard" in the home of Winifred Peck, too. See Winifred Peck, *A Little Learning* (London: Faber and Faber, 1952), p. 23.

16   Annie Besant worked in free thought and radical movements, and was attracted to the mysticism of Mme Helena Petrovna Blavatsky. Winifred's memoirs may not be correct here, for Besant and Blavatsky apparently did not meet until 1889, six years after Amelia's death. See Elizabeth Longford, *Eminent Victorian Women* (London: Weidenfeld and Nicolson, 1981), pp. 147-149.

17   Amelia was relaxed about her children's playing habits. Spanny Molton remembered that Amelia never became concerned if they got dirty: "One time I sez to yer dear mother, 'Look at them children a-messing up their nice dresses,' and she sez, 'Oh, Ann, there's worse things in life than spoiling clothes.—I don't mind.'" (Correspondence from Mabel to Winifred, 1939, copied into memoirs, Add. MS 604, BCARS.)

18   For the importance of summer vacations at the seaside during the late Victorian era, see J.A.R. Pimlott, *The Englishman's Holiday, A Social History*,(Hassocks, Eng.: Harvester Press, 1976); and John K. Walton, *The English Seaside Resort* (New York: St. Martin's Press, 1983).

19   After a Christmas pantomime, people staggered from the Drury Lane Theatre "in a state of pleasant shell-shock." See Brian Dobbs, *Drury Lane* (London: Cassell & Company Ltd., 1972), p. 166.

20   See the *London Times*, February 18, 1882, p. 7.

21   Maria Spalding died March 8, 1881. Cause of death was given as "parturition 15 days, peritonitis 6 days, exhaustion." (Copy of death certificate, General Register Office, London, DX 307252, June 29, 1984.)

22   Thomas (Tommy) Spalding died in June 1881. (Pamela Haines, Hastings Central Library, to editor.)

23   The cause of Amelia's death is given as cancer of the tongue by family physician Archibald R. Shaw, on the death certificate. Copy of certificate, DX 307251, General Register Office, London, June 29, 1984.

24   The young nurse's name was Jane Bowen. She had also nursed Espie Capper's husband during his terminal illness. (Remembrances by Espie Capper, Grey Family Papers, BCARS.)

25   Penshurst Place, a large estate dating from Norman Times, was open to the public. See J. Radford Thomson, *Pelton's Illustrated Guide to Tunbridge Wells* (Wakefield: S.R. Publishers Ltd., 1970, reprint), pp. 138-148.

CHAPTER FOUR

1   Andrew Reed involved his children in his philanthropic work. While pastor at Wycliffe Chapel, Stepney, he took his children with him on Saturdays to help lay out the grounds of the London Orphan Asylum at Clapton. (Fred Keay to editor, October 3, 1983.)

2   In 1882 Thomas Spalding shifted his allegiance from St. Leonards Congregational Church to the new Mount Pleasant Church, which was located closer to Ore Place. (See Musgrave, *History of St. Leonards-on-Sea.*)

3   The number of sevants was typical for a household the size of the Spalding's. To care for Thomas, Elizabeth, Ellen, Arthur, Thomas, Carina Reed and Florence Holmes, there were nine servants, not including the gardeners, in 1881. (1881 Census, file 1341242, PRO, London.)

4   David and Georgina Dowdney had seven children in 1881: Alfred, Raymond, Charles, Herbert, Edith, Irene and Kathleen. Ibid.

5   Philanthropy was an important way in which upper middle class women could influence society and utilize their business acumen. See F.K. Prochaska, *Women and Philanthropy in Nineteenth Century England* (Oxford: Clarendon Press, 1980).

6   George Frederick Arthur Belcher (1875-1947) published his drawings in *The Tatler, Punch* and *Graphic* .

7   Krakatoa volcano erupted August 26 and 27, 1883, and the dust remained in the atmosphere for three years, causing outstanding sunrises and sunsets because the particles refracted the sunlight.

8   Timothy H. Coles was a retired East Indian merchant. In 1881 he and his wife Amelia had three children: Amy, Millicent and Geoffrey (who was ten years old). (1881 Census, file 1341242, PRO, London.)

9   Ellen Pankhurst. (Ibid.)

10   In 1844 William Long Esq. "owned most of the soil" at Saxmundham, Suffolk, which had a population of 1,097. The 200-acre estate and Hurts Hall were located south of the town. See *White's 1844 Suffolk Directory*, p. 171.

CHAPTER FIVE

1   Under Grannie's administration, children's teas were not as sumptious as those served by other relatives. Espie Capper recalled that even when the Spaldings lived at Hendon the children's food was spartan. Grey Family Papers, Add MS 604, BCARS.

2   At least two of Dr. Archibald R. Shaw's sons became medical doctors. Charles Thomas (1854-1939), who preferred the surname Knox-Shaw, initially practiced at St. Leonards, and then became consulting surgeon and opthalmic surgeon to the London Homeopathic Hospital, Buchanan Hospital, and to the Hastings Homeopathic Dispensary. See *Who Was Who*, Vol. 3 (London: Adam & Charles Black 1920), p. 766.

Lauristen Elgie Shaw (1858-1923), MD, FRCP, was a consultant physician to Guy's Hospital.

3   Private schools were a secondary industry on the south coast of England after 1850. Directories for the 1880's and 1890's listed 125 private schools at Brighton, 70 at Hastings, 67 at Eastbourne, and 50 at Bournemouth. See John K. Walton, *The English Seaside Resort*, (New York: St. Martin's Press, 1983), p. 97.

4   Fairlight Glen was located two miles east of Hastings. Passage of the Bank Holiday Acts in 1871 and 1875, which gave workers a day off in August, combined with higher wages and cheap railway fares, facilitated the influx of "'Arrys and 'Arriets." As a consequence, the upper middle class were forced to go farther afield for their excursions. See Winifred Peck, *Home for the Holidays* (London: Faber and Faber Ltd., 1955), p. 19; and Walton, *The English Seaside Resort*, pp. 194-195.

5   Within a twenty-mile radius of Hastings there is a fine collection of ancient castles and ruins. Bodiam has been described as the "last great medieval fortress in England." Built ca. 1385 for

Richard II, it never saw action and is therefore well-preserved. It was presented to the National Trust by Lord Curzon in 1925.

Herstmonceaux Castle was built in the fifteenth century. It features polygonal towers rather than the circular towers of Bodiam Castle. See Fred Wilkinson, *The Castles of England* (London: George Philip, 1973), pp. 37-38, and 92; and Philip Warner, *A Guide to Castles in Britain* (London: New England Library, 1976), p. 52.

6   Edison's phonograph and the telephone transmitter were introduced about the same time in England, ca. 1878. See Matthew Josephson, *Edison, A Biography* (London: Eyre & Spottiswode, 1961), p. 166.

7   By this time there were numerous illustrated magazines publishing lithographs and photographs of places around the world, but either the Spaldings did not subscribe to them, or the magazines were not made available to the children. *The Illustrated London News* is a prime example.

8   John Hall Gladstone, Ph.D, D.SC, FRS, was a Fullerian Professor of Chemistry, Royal Institution, 1874-77, and a member of the London School Board from 1873-1894. Among his publications was *Life of Michael Faraday* (1872), see *Who Was Who*, Vol. 1, p. 277. It is believed that the Gladstone family were connected to the Spalding family through Eliza Halton, Thomas Spaldings' first wife.

9   Aunt Amelia was probably great aunt Amelia, wife of John Scarr Edwards of Danesfield, Honor Oak, and mother of Winifred and Mabel's beloved Aunt Emma.

10   Winifred was unaware that this "nonsense song" held a definite meaning, much like her favourite nursery rhymes. It is a parody of the great improvements in agriculture that were occurring in Great Britain at that time.

11   For an account of the working conditions at Bryant and May Matchworks see Lowell J. Satre, "After the Match Girls' Strike: Bryant and May in the 1890's," *Victorian Studies* V. 26, no.

12   This company owned three factories, which employed 2000 workers, of whom 1200 to 1500 were girls and women. Girls were hired at ages 13 and 14. A grim reality was the children's susceptibility to phosphorus, called "phossy jaw."

CHAPTER SIX

1   Kent College for Girls began as a small Methodist school with fifteen boarders and twenty day girls. The advertisement in a trades directory for 1887 shows that the teachers had advanced training. Miss de la Mare had an LLA (Honours); Miss Voisin had an intermediate BA with 1st class French Honours; Miss LeSueur had received a Cambridge Higher Honour Certificate; and "90% of Miss Attwater's pupils obtained Honour and Pass certificates from the Royal Academy and Trinity College." Pupils were prepared for Oxford, Cambridge, local and other examinations. The school offered: "spacious premises, lofty school and classrooms, dining hall, music rooms, hot and cold baths." It was hot water heated, and "thoroughly ventilated."

Miss de la Mare left Kent College in 1895, but the school continued to operate until 1939. The building is presently known as Carlile Lodge. (B.C. Harte, Assistant Divisional Librarian, Central Library, Kent, to editor.)

Because of the large number of schools at Folkestone at the turn of the century, "crocodiles of children taking exercise became a characteristic sight on the Lees." Walton, *The English Seaside Resort*, p. 97.

2   For an excellent discussion of the class structure in girls' private schools, see Joyce Senders Pedersen, "The Reform of Women's Secondary and Higher Education: Institutional Change and Social Values in Mid and Late Victorian England," *History of Education Quarterly*, Vol. 19, no. 1 (1979), pp. 61-91.

3   Josef Hofman first appeared in public as a pianist at the age of six. When he attempted to perform in the United States in 1887-1888, the Society for the Prevention of Cruelty to Children successfully cancelled his concerts.

4   Thomas Spalding died on June 28, 1887, aged eighty-one. In his obituary he was described as a "hard-working and munificent-hearted Congregationalist—an active member of the Hastings School Board. Originator and main supporter of British Schools at St. Leonards—Christian, philanthropist, politician, citizen and man, his life will live on in his good works for many a year." (Pamela Haines, Local Studies Librarian, Hastings Central Library to editor.)

5   Elizabeth Spalding died October 18, 1888.

6   The sale of Ore Place to the Jesuits is indicative of the rise of Roman Catholicism in Great Britain during the latter half of the 19th Century. Cardinal Vaughan, Archbishop of Westminster, noted in 1887 that the number of priests had increased from 468 in 1837 to 2,686 in 1887. See John Standen, *The End of an Era* (London: Faber and Faber, 1968), p. 72.

The Society of African Missions Fathers, Manchester, leased Ore Place to the British Army prior to World War II for record storage. The estate has now been subdivided and the entire building, including the original Spalding mansion, demolished. Bramhall Cottage and St. Helen's Ponds, shown in Winifred's map, are still there, however. (Shiela Pratt, St. Helen's Park Preservation Society Ltd., Hastings, to editor; M.E. Berkeley to editor, and Rev. M.J. Walsh to editor.)

CHAPTER SEVEN

1   Captain Richard Angel helped with the design of the *Torrens*, and was the chief owner with A.L. Elder & Co. The ship was designed especially as a passenger ship; during its career it was described as one of the most successful, fastest, and favourite clipper ships travelling to Adelaide, Australia. See Basil Lubbock, *The Romance of the Clipper Ships* (New York: The Macmillan Company, 1939), pp. 157-162. Further information obtained with the assistance of Mrs. Kay Chapman, National Maritime Museum, London.

2   Angel retired in 1890, and Leonard probably sailed with his successor, a Captain Cope. On October 29, 1890, the *Torrens* lost a foremast and main topmast in 60N., 270W., and put in to Pernambuco, Brazil, to refit. Bad luck continued to plague the ship; it caught fire before being remasted. Fortunately, the damage was slight and the *Torrens* reached Adelaide 179 days out, compared to her usual run of 74 days. Ibid.

3   Thomas Spalding left an estate valued at £89,868.12.8. Winifred and Mabel were each bequeathed £2,000, which was to earn interest at 5% per year. The money was held in trust by Thomas Alfred Spalding and Talbot Baines Reed. (Will of Thomas Spalding, No. 727, Somerset House, London.)

4   Girton College was originally established at Hitchin, Hertfordshire, by Emily Davis in October 1869, and later moved to Cambridge. Examinations were administered on the same level as those given to male students. Jemima Clough planned Newnham College, also located at Cambridge, where examinations were especially designed for women. See Duncan Crow, *The Victorian Woman* (London: George Allen & Unwin Ltd., 1971), pp. 184-185.

Winifred's opinion of second class boarding schools compares favourably with that of Winifred Peck's, who attended several boarding schools in Eastbourne. See Peck, *A Little Learning,* p. 71.

Edith Holden, born the same year as Winifred, into a middle-class Nonconformist family in Birmingham, attended the Birmingham Art School. For her career (which Winifred might have enjoyed if she had attended the Royal College of Art, South Kensington), see Ina Taylor, *The Edwardian Lady* (New York: Holt, Rinehard and Winston, 1980), and Edith Holden, *The Country Diary of an Edwardian Lady* (London: Michael Joseph, 1977).

5   Advertisements in *The Times* in 1890 listed a number of girls' boarding schools at Blackheath.

6   We are unable to trace these lines to Longfellow.

7   Swedish gymnastic classes had been introduced into England by Madam Bergmen in the 1880's. She was appointed physical training expert to the London School Board, and Swedish

gymnastics soon became part of the curriculum in most girls' schools. See Josephine Kamm, *Hope Deferred* (London: Methuen & Co. Ltd., 1986), p. 217.

CHAPTER EIGHT

1   Spalding & Hodge Ltd. declared bankruptcy in March 1889. The business had over-expanded, having two outlets in London, on Drury Lane and on Cannon Street, a mill at Horton Kirby, and an outlet in Australia. A loss of £21,000 was registered with the Australian business. Joint liabilities were returned at £217,313, with assets of £157,725. The extra branches were disposed of, and the business concentrated on Drury Lane. Spalding & Hodge were then registered as a private company in May 1892, with share capital of £120,000. They continued to operate the Horton Kirby mill. Howard Spalding was chairman of Spalding & Hodge Ltd., at the time of the bankruptcy. See *The Times*, April 16, May 8 and June 5, 1889, and the *Paper Trade Review*, April 26, 1889, and May 28, 1892. Charles A. Rivington, Honorary Librarian, the Worshipful Company of Stationers & Newspaper Makers, London, greatly assisted me with the research of this bankruptcy.

     Historian G.M. Trevelyan has noted that many patriarchal family firms collapsed in the late 1800's, which let to greater efficiency. See *Illustrated English Social History*, Vol. 4, pp. 210-211.

2   Alfred Russel Wallace wrote a number of books on natural selection and zoogeography.

3   In later life Em would remember arriving at Miners Bay, Mayne Island, on the steamer in the middle of the night. She and Thomas climbed down the ship's ladder into the huge arms of Tom Collinson, the local postmaster, who had rowed out to meet the ship hoving to in Miners Bay. (The captain did not use the Miners Bay wharf after dark.) Em and Thomas would have stayed at William Robson's Mayne Island House hotel overnight, travelling to their new home in Leonard's boat the next day. See *Saanich Peninsula and Gulf Islands Review*, December 2, 1953, pp. 1 and 7, hereafter cited as *Sidney Review*.

4   There was a mania for collecting all manner of flora and fauna during this period, spurred on by the publishing of such books as *The History of British Butterflies* by Francis Morris. See Barbara Kerr, *The Dispossessed* (London: John Baker, 1974), p. 135, and John K. Walton, *The English Seaside Resort*, pp. 166-167.

5   Walton-on-the-Naze was a favorite summer resort for Victorians, because the railway line made it easily accessible to London and interior points. See J.A.R. Pimlott, *The Englishman's Holiday: A Social History* (Sussex: The Harvester Press 1976), p. 179; and John K. Walton, *The English Seaside Resort* (New York: St. Martin's Press, 1983), p. 58 and pp. 121-122.

6   Sir Robert Ball wrote a number of easily read books on astronomy, including *The Story of the Heavens*, *Star-Land* and *Time and Tide*.

7   Barnet was formerly within the county of Hertfordshire. It became a London borough in 1965. King John gave the right to hold a market and three-day horse fair there in 1199. See Arthur Mee, *London North of the Thames* (London: Hodder and Stoughton, 1972), p. 23.

8   The first Aerated Bread teashop opened in 1880 in London. Alan Bott, in *Our Mothers*, states that for the average woman, the Aerated Bread Company teashops were her "her first experience in restaurant life." See *Our Mothers* (London: Benjamin Blom, 1932), p. 12.

     Anthony Hern has pointed out that tea shops didn't proliferate "until a sizeable proportion of the working population found itself unable to get home for a midday meal." See *The Seaside Holiday* (London: The Cresset Press, 1967), p. 79.

9   Carina, Mabel and Winifred may have been partially inspired to pay for the slum children's summer holiday by publicity given to the Children's Country Holiday Fund, which was set up in the 1880's to enable poor London children to visit the country. See Pimlott, *Englishman's Holiday*, p. 157. But obviously the three young women had been influenced by Elizabeth Spalding's good works, and the general tenor of the times. For the latter see Prochska, *Women and Philanthropy in Nineteenth-Century England*, and G. Kitson Clark, *The Making of Victorian England* (London: Methuen & Co. Ltd., 1965).

10   The Venereable Bede was a noted Anglo-Saxon scholar. Ordained as a priest in 703, he devoted his life to teaching and writing. Pope Leo XIII created him a Doctor of the Church. His writings were characterized by piety and gentleness.

11   Catherine Ryle eventually gave birth to ten children: five sons and five daughters.

12   Bishop John Charles Ryle served as the First Bishop of Liverpool from 1880 to 1900. His son Herbert was Honorary Chaplain to the Queen 1898-1901, Bishop of Winchester 1903-1911, and Dean of Westminster 1911-1925. He was also President of Queen's College, Cambridge, 1896-1901, and a prolific author. (E.G.W. Bill, Librarian, Lambeth Palace Library, London.)

13   It is assumed from this statement that Winifred remained with the Ryles as an unpaid governess.

14   Alma Tadema and his wife lived in Regent's Park. His prosperity as an artist was reflected in the luxurious Roman-Oriental furnishings of his home. See Ralph Dutton, *The Victorian Home* (London: B.T. Batsford Ltd., 1954), pp. 163-164.

CHAPTER NINE

1   At the turn of the century, Miners Bay (commonly known as "The Pass"), Mayne Island, was the community center for the outer Gulf Islands, comprised of Galiano, Mayne, North and South Pender, Saturna, and numerous smaller islands. Because the provincial government built a public wharf at Miners Bay in 1878, a small village developed there that included a post office (1880), school (1883), stores and hotels, a police lockup (1896), an Anglican Church (1898), and community hall (1900). Although most of the islands acquired these facilities by 1900, Mayne continued to be the focus of social activities for the outer Gulf Islands until World War II. Victoria Day (May 24th) and New Year's Eve celebrations were inter-island events traditionally celebrated at Mayne. See Beatrice J. Freeman, ed., A Gulf Islands Patchwork (Victoria: Gulf Islands Branch, B.C.H.A.), passim.; and Marie Elliott, Mayne Island and the Outer Gulf Islands, A History (Victoria: Gulf Islands Press, 1984), pp. 13-79.
Ann Robson and Alice Bennett had arrived with their husbands and families on Mayne Island before 1880, and soon became well-known as midwives. Many expectant mothers on the Islands journeyed to Mayne for delivery, but the safe arrival of a baby was always a risk. Elizabeth Grimmer gave birth to a son in a rowboat, enroute from North Pender to Alice Bennett's, and Em Higgs gave birth to four stillborn infants. Interview with Geraldine Goldsmith, Victoria.

2   In Chinook jargon Kloshe meant good, nice, or well. Illahee meant earth or the ground. Winifred records a jargon that rapidly died out after 1900. See John Gill, Gill's Dictionary of the Chinook Jargon (Portland: The J.K. Gill Company, 1909). Dr. Barbara Harris, Linguistics Department, University of Victoria, kindly offered further advice.
Between 1870 and 1910 Canada welcomed a large number of educated young men from England who received quarterly allowances from their families but, nevertheless, were expected to be enterprising in their adopted country. The "remittance men" who settled on the Gulf Islands formed a small enclave on South Pender, Saturna and Samuel. They chose the more remote islands because most of the best agricultural land, easily accessible to "the Pass", had been pre-empted and developed in the 1870's, a decade before their arrival.
In addition to the common bonds of heritage and education, these young men shared interests in boating, agriculture, hunting, and living an unconventional life. At the time that Winifred and Mabel Higgs arrived for a visit to the Gulf Islands in 1896, the group consisted of Ralph Grey on Samuel; Warburton Pike, Gerald and Harold Payne, Walter (Black) and Bert (Red) Drummond on Saturna; their brother Arthur Drummond on Mayne, where he was stationed as a police constable; and on South Pender Island: Leonard Higgs, his step-uncle Arthur Spalding, Gerald Anslie, Charlie Long, Arthur Stanford and Gerald Richardson. Warburton Pike and Harold Payne had visited parts of the United States before settling down in the Gulf Islands. Leonard had worked on a ranch near Good Thunder, Minnesota, prior to joining Arthur Spalding.

3   There were a number of societies that sponsored women travelling to the colonies. Efforts to bring young women to British Columbia had begun in the early 1860's when the Columbia Mission Society associated with the Church of England, and the London Female Middle-Class Emigration Society recruited young women for two "bride ships," the Robert Lowe and the Tynemouth, sailing to Victoria, British Columbia. By 1890, other female emigration societies had taken their places. See Jackie Lay, "To Columbia on the Tynemouth: The Emigration of Single Women and Girls in 1862," In Her Own Right, ed. by Barbara Latham and Cathy Kess (Victoria: Camosun College, 1980), pp. 19-41; Colonial Correspondence CO 305/20, 1863, Public Records Office, mf.: A. James Hammerton, Emigrant Gentlewomen (Longon: Croom Helm Ltd., 1979); Susan Jackel, ed., A Flannel Shirt and Liberty (Vancouver: U.B.C. Press, 1982), and F. Musgrove, The Migratory Elite (London: Heinemann, 1963).

4   Marie Lloyd made "Oh, Mrs. Porter!" a popular song in the British music halls of the 1880's.

5   The primitive conditions experienced by Winifred and Mabel on the S.S. Vancouver were the exception rather than the rule by 1896. See Stanley C. Johnson, A History of Emigration from the United Kingdom to North America 1763-1912 (London: Frank Cass, 1966, reprint).

6   Winifred's fellow passenger was a little mistaken in his estimates. Lake Superior has a water surface of 31,500 square miles, whereas Great Britain, including southern Ireland, has a surface area of more than 120,000 square miles.

7   The population of Winnipeg in 1896 was 37,983. See Alan J. Artibase, Gateway City: Documents on the City of Winnipeg, 1873-1913 (Winnipeg: University of Manitoba Press, 1979), pp. 5-6 and p. 279.

8   William and Annie Isabel (nee Speck) George settled on the west half of S22, Eden Grove, in 1885. They had seven children: Dorothy, Basil, Tom, Nellie, Percy, Evelyn and Lucy. The Georges were active in the Anglican Church. Mrs. George played the organ for services in Wapella and Eden Grove. See Mingling Memories: Wapella and District (1980), pp. 143-144; and Application for Homestead Patents, nos. 147372 and 204711, File 385-44, Saskatchewan Archives Board, Regina.

9   The population of Calgary in 1891 was 3,876. See Max Foran, Calgary, An Illustrated History (Toronto: James Lorimer & Co., 1978), p. 176.

10   General Grey, former secretary to Prince Albert, urged Queen Victoria to invite a wide variety of people to afternoon tea parties in an effort to prevent the Queen from going into retirement following the death of her husband. Victoria sandwich cake, which is a simple sponge cake filled with raspberry jam or lemon curd, and topped with a water icing or dusting of icing sugar, was served at these tea parties. See Farmhouse Cookery (London: The Readers Digest Asociation, 1980), p. 290, for history and recipe. I am grateful for the further advice of Mrs. Doreen Crawley, Victoria.

11   Horse races and small rodeos were popular events on the ranches near Calgary. The British ranchers are given credit for introducing "sports of all sorts" in the 1880's. See Frederick William Ings, Before the Fences (Privately published, 1980), pp. 59-61.

12   Herbert Church, An Emigrant in the Canadian Northwest (London: Methuen & Co. Ltd., 1929). With the assistance of his father Professor Alfred John Church, he published Making a Start in Canada (London: Seely & Co., 1889). For a further description of the Church brothers see Dunae, Gentlemen Emigrants.

13   The Guichon Hotel stood at the corner of Columbia and 4th Streets, New Westminster.

14   The Canadian Pacific Navigation Company operated the R.P. Rithet in 1896. Described as "the largest and finest of all the British Columbia sternwheelers," she served the Gulf Islands during the summer months only, because marine regulations prohibited sternwheelers from crossing Georgia Strait in winter. See Norman R. Hacking and W. Kaye Lamb, The Princess Story (Vancouver: Mitchell Press Limited, 1974), p. 92.

Captain John Jaggers was well-respected by the Islanders for his willingness to accommodate special requests from passengers. Thse included "hoving to" in mid-channel to pick up residents waiting in rowboats, as Winifred relates in Chapter Thirteen.

15   Warburton Pike was possibly returning from Telegraph Creek in northern British Columbia, where he was attempting to establish a trading post with partners Harold Payne and Clive Phillipps-

Wolley. See Gwen Hayball,Warburton Pike, an Unassuming Gentleman (Privately Published, Poole, Dorset, 1994)

Pike had studied at Oxford and mining engineering at Freiberg University, Germany, before arriving in British Columbia in 1884. His family had mining interests in southwestern England. In partnership with Charles Payne, Pike purchased property on Saturna in 1884. In addition to his mining ventures, he was often away on exploration and big-game hunts, about which he wrote for the Spectator and other magazines. He published two books, The Barren Ground of Northern Canada (London: Macmillan, 1892), and Through the Sub-Arctic Forest (London: Edward Arnold, 1896). See Dunae, Gentlemen Emigrants, and Hayball, Warburton Pike.

CHAPTER TEN

1   Winifred and Mabel travelled approximately twenty-five miles by steamer from New Westminster to Saturna.

2   "Fisher" was the local nickname for John Wessel.

3   The trunk was difficult to handle because it contained sugar. (Reminiscences of Harold Payne, Sidney Review, April 5, 1950.)

4   The first Japanese arrived on the West Coast of British Columbia in the 1880's. Many of them worked for the canneries on the Fraser River and, as fishermen, soon discovered the Gulf Islands. Japanese labourers assisted many of the early farmers to clear their island homesteads. Eventually, the Japanese rented or bought farms of their own on Salt Spring and Mayne Island, where they were successful in establishing a thriving hothouse industry. At the time of the evacuation in 1942, there were very few Japanese living on any of the islands except Mayne and Salt Spring. See Elliott, Mayne Island.

5   Canon Arthur J. Beanlands of Victoria married Arthur Spalding and Lilias MacKay at Warburton Pike's ranch on November 6, 1889. Charles Longe and Lilias's father, Joseph William McKay, were their witnesses. (Central Register, Diocese of British Columbia Archives, Victoria.) Lilias's sister Agnes was engaged to Warburton Pike at that time. (Hayball, Warburton Pike.)

Joseph William McKay played an important part in the early history of British Columbia. He was the Hudson's Bay factor at Nanaimo when coal was discovered in 1852, and he built the bastion there. In 1856 he served in the first Legislative Assembly for Vancouver Island. He succeeded C.T. Donald McLean as Chief Factor at Kamloops, serving from 1860 to 1865, and in the 1870's he was Indian Superintendent at Kamloops. McKay's wife, Helen Holmes, came to Victoria from Liverpool in 1858. Helen Point, Mayne Island, is named for her.

The McKays had six children: William, Kenneth, Agnes, Lilias, Gertrude and Aline. Lilias was born in 1871 and died in 1951. Her three sisters visited the Spalding family on South Pender frequently, and eventually had a small house built on Arthur's property.

6 Oxen were more important than horses in cultivating a new farm in the Gulf Islands. The 1891 Census lists thirty-eight oxen, but only twenty-four horses on the Islands. (Census of Canada, 1891, p. 116.)

7   "Feathering" oars meant turning the oars to the horizontal as they were lifted from the water, thus reducing them to a "feather edge".

Alfred Burke of Shaw Island, living in the San Juan Islands, was eventually caught. See David Richardson, Pig War Islands (Eastsound, Washington: Orcas Publishing Co., 1971), pp. 271-273.

8   See "Sammy the Mink" by Eve Grey Smith, Patchwork, ed. by Freeman, pp. 178-180.

9   Arthur Drummond served as B.C. provincial police constable in the outer Gulf Islands from 1894 to 1898, when he was transferred to Teslin Lake and, later, to the Kootenays. With only a rowboat for transportation, he patrolled 600 square miles of marine territory, ranging from the United States border north to Porlier Pass, Galiano Island, and from Georgia Strait west to Vancouver Island (including Salt Spring Island). (Superintendent of Police correspondence, incoming, GR 55, and outgoing, GR 61, BCARS.) See also Elliott, Mayne Island, pp. 19-24.

10   James and Joan Georgeson tended the East Point lighthouse from 1889 to 1924. They had six children; a son, Andrew, married Bay Higgs.

Hardy immigrants from the Shetland Islands, several members of the Georgeson family were well-known in the Gulf Islands for their skills as lighthouse keepers. James Georgeson tended the East Point lighthouse from 1889 to 1924. His brother Henry "Scotty" Georgeson served on the Sandheads lightship in the early 1880's, and became the first keeper of the Georgina Point lighthouse [now called Active Pass Light Station], Mayne Island, in 1885. He did not retire until December, 1920, at age 86. Both Scotty and James received Imperial Long Service Medals. Jame's two sons, Peter and Harry, were also lighthouse keepers.

11   Sma-hahl-ton does not appear in any Chinook jargon dictionary. It may be a local derivative of sah-halie, which means "high". Klootchmen is Chinook jargon for Indian woman. See Gill, *Dictionary of Chinook Jargon.*

12   Mowitch is Chinook jargon for venison (deer meat).

13   See footnote 12, Chapter Nine.

14   "...and down he went, by stock and stone, sedge and ledge, bush and rush, as if he and (sic) been born a jolly little black ape, with four hands instead of two." Charles Kingsley, *The Water Babies* (New York: A.L. Burt, Publisher, 1893), p. 56.

15   Captain Horatio L. Robertson of Moresby Island had been a river pilot in China. Freeman, ed., *Patchwork*, p. 81.

CHAPTER ELEVEN

1   Winifred's reference to fleas is not clear. Sand fleas are common to most beaches in the Gulf Islands, but they do not bite, unlike animal fleas. See Herbert S. Zim and others, *Seashores* (New York: Golden Press, 1955).

2   "She-she-gar" does not appear in any Chinook jargon dictionary, and may be a local term.

3   Michael Flannigan pre-empted Samuel Island in 1880, and probably planted the orchard.

4   Many Gulf Islanders found seasonal employment fishing or working for the canneries on the lower Fraser River. Ralph Grey worked as a cannery superintendent for one season.

Billy Trueworthy was the son of William Trueworthy of Orcas Island. When his father died, Billy and his sister were taken in by William and Ann Robson, Mayne Island, where the children attended school. See Freeman, ed., *Patchwork*, p. 17.

5   These "lampshades" were the egg casings of the moon snail (*polinices lewisii*) which are found at low tide on sand flats in the Gulf Islands.

6   The fish hawks are also known as osprey. See P.A. Taverner, *Taverner's Birds of Western Canada* (Toronto: Coles Publishing Company, 1926).

7   Because of his adventures as a young immigrant from Grey County, Ontario West, during the Cariboo gold rush and the settlement period that followed, Collinson did have some interesting stories to tell that probably sounded "far-fetched" to Winifred. See Elliott, *Mayne Island,* passim.

8   Until the community hall was built about 1900, the dining room of Robson's Mayne Island Hotel was a popular place to hold parties and dances. The Point Comfort Hotel on Mayne Island also had a large room where dances were held. See Elliott, *Mayne Island,* passim.

9   Salmon and herring are much scarcer in Active Pass now, but the area still attracts a large number of sports fishermen during the fishing season.

10   W.H. Mawdsley built Point Comfort Hotel in 1893 after forming a company. One of the share holders was Charlie Long of South Pender. In 1892 Warburton Pike loaned Mawdsley $2500, and when the loan was not repaid he foreclosed in 1895. Thomas and Alice Bennett operated the hotel for Pike from 1897 until 1899. Pike sold the hotel to Eustace Maude about 1902. (Papers on mf., Land Titles Office, Ministry of Environment, Lands and Parks, Victoria). Pike also owned the Mayne Island Hotel, which he leased to the Robsons.

11   Winifred describes the original legislative buildings, known as the "Birdcages". But at this time the new parliament buildings were well under way and located on the same property.

12   See footnote 6, Chapter Ten.

13   The New England Hotel was at 116 Government Street, and the Poodledog Cafe at the southeast corner of Government and Yates Street, Victoria. Both buildings are still standing,

CHAPTER TWELVE

1   Dr. Ryle spent ten years at Barnet before moving to Brighton. He died in 1922.

2   "Who are you?" said Lucie. "Have you seen my pocket-handkins?"
The little person made a bob-curtsey—"Oh, yes, if you pleas'm, my name is Mrs. Tiggy-Winkle; oh, yes, if you please'm, I'm an excellent clear starcher!" Beatrix Potter, *The Tale of Mrs. Tiggy-Winkle* (London: Fredericke Waring & Co., Ltd., 1972?), p. 25.

3   Wincarnis was advertised as an extract of meat and malt wine. It was a popular tonic manufactured by Coleman and Co. Ltd., Norwich and London.

4   Elizabeth Spalding left Carina 2500 pounds in trust. (Will of Elizabeth Spalding.)

5   Janet was physically disabled. She had lost one leg because of tuberculosis of the bone, and wore a prosthesis.

6   Winifred does not indicate whether Laurie had to pay for their view window. Elsewhere, seats on the first and second floor of houses on the Strand were rented at ten shillings and sixpence. See John Standen, *The End of an Era* (London: Faber and Faber, 1968), p. 44.

7   Winifred's remembrance of the Diamond Jubilee procession places Queen Victoria at the beginning, but in actual fact the State Carriage was situated midway in the procession by the time it reached Guy's Hospital. H.R.H. the Princess of Wales and H.R.H. the Princess Christian of Schleswig-Holstein accompanied the Queen in her carriage. Although a deputation of officers from the Imperial Services Troops in India and an Indian Escort preceeded the State Carriage, the Indian Princes named by Winifred were not listed in the newspaper account of the Royal Procession. There was an escort of English and foreign princes, but the "crowned heads of Europe" named by Winifred are also omitted from *The Times* account. See *The Times*, June 21, 1897, p. 17.
For another eye-witness of the Jubilee procession see Macqueen-Pope, *Twenty Shillings*, pp. 300-307.

CHAPTER THIRTEEN

1   Belville, Ontario.

2   Their new home cost $500.00, including carpenters' wages, lumber and hardware. The men brought the materials to South Pender from Victoria on a barge, making the frames enroute.

3   Dixie H. Ross & Company were located at 117 Government Street, Victoria.

4   The blue tarpon were likely perch.

5   Essential items on a homestead, a maul and froe are a long-handled hammer and wedge.

6   Isabella Beeton published *The Book of Household Management* in 1861 (London). The recipes contained in the book were published separately in *The Englishwoman's Cookery Book* in 1863, which is probably the book that Mabel used. See Crow, *The Victorian Woman*, pp. 132-133.

7   Alex Scoones bought five acres of land from Fred and Joe Burrill in 1897 at Galiano. See Freeman, ed., *Patchwork*, pp. 85 and 87.

8   Ralph Grey's free miner's certificate was dated February 4, 1898. (Grey Family papers, Add. MS 604, BCARS.)

9   Herbert Church found it difficult to stay on at Hadley Ranch after the tragic loss of his brothers Dick and Teddy, June 17, 1898. After an unsuccessful attempt to farm at Comox, the

Church family settled at Big Creek, near Williams Lake. Winifred remained in close contact with the family over the years. In the 1920's her two daughters, Evelyn and Constance, spent several memorable holidays at the Big Creek ranch. Conversation with Eve Grey Smith; also Dunae, *Gentlemen Emigrants,* p. 224; and "Diary of Alfred Francis Church", typescript, EC C47, BCARS.

10   Jacob B. de Liefde, *The Beggars, or the Founders of the Dutch Republic* (London: Aylesbury, 1868).

11   Eleanor Howard's distinguished clientele included Forbes G. Vernon, Chief Commissioner of Lands and Works, who preferred to work at her boarding house rather than in the cramped quarters of the Birdcages, financier William Adolph Baillie-Grohman (who used Warburton Pike's room when he was away, and Pike's brother Marmaduke. No doubt, many of the investment schemes and adventures (such as driving sheep and cattle into the Cassiar and Klondike, and building northern railways) tried by Pike, Clive Phillipps-Wolley, and the Payne brothers, found their origins in this stimulating, "old boys" environment. See Terry Reksten, *Rattenbury* (Victoria: Sono Nis Press, 1978), pp. 118 and 195, and Hayball, *Warburton Pike,* p. 47.

Florence Eleanor Nunn married Francis Mawson Rattenbury on June 18, 1898, at Christ Church Cathedral. Ibid., p. 119.

CHAPTER FOURTEEN

1   See footnote 4, Chapter Three for Grey family history.

Ralph arrived in British Columbia between 1886 and 1889. He worked as a reporter for the *News Advertiser,* Vancouver, for a short time before pre-empting 320 acres on Samuel Island with a partner, George Rutherford, on November 5, 1889. Ralph Grey papers in possession of Eve Grey Smith estate; Register of Crown Land pre-emptions, Cowichan Land District, Legal Surveys, Ministry of Lands, Parks and Housing, Victoria.

2   The Victoria and Sidney Railway commenced operation in 1894. Reliable steamship connections with the Gulf Islands, especially after 1901, made Victoria the preferred destination for shopping, and selling of agricultural produce from the Islands. In that year a subsidiary company of V&SR, Victoria Terminal Railway and Ferry Company, placed the SS *Iroquois* on the Gulf Islands run.

3   Later in life, Winifred confided to her daughter Evelyn that she had had difficulty that night resisting Ralph's advances.

4   Warburton Pike, Clive Phillipps-Wolley and others chartered a number of transportation and mining companies at this time. The provincial government granted thousands of acres of land, and mineral, timber and water rights to these speculators, which eventually aroused the ire of opposition politicians. See Dunae, *Gentlemen Emigrants,* pp. 119-120.

5   Martin Grainger married Mabel Higgs in June 1908.

6   Canon William Francis Locke Paddon began visiting Mayne Island to hold regular church services in 1896. Ralph Grey was active in helping Paddon to establish St. Mary Magdalene Church on Mayne Island in 1898. Warburton Pike donated the land.

7   The public hall at Miners Bay was built shortly before the Grey wedding. Winifred's account of the wedding reception is the earliest record we have of the building, which is still used for dances and community functions.

8   Martin Allerdale Grainger was born in London in 1874. After completing his education at King's College, Cambridge, where he was a wrangler in the mathematical tripos, he emigrated to Canada to participate in the Klondike gold rush in 1898. He served as a private with Lord Roberts Horse in South Africa during the Boer War and won the South African Medal with six bars. He wrote articles for the *London Daily News* while in South Africa, under the byline "Life at the Front." For example, see issues for April 10 and 11, 1901.

One of Grainger's adventures during the war involved running beside his horse for a great distance, which severely injured the arches of his feet. Thereafter, he wore moccasins—even when presented to King George V in 1920 at the British Empire Forestry Conference in London.

Grainger worked for various logging companies in British Columbia after the Boer War. This experience and his educational background led to his appointment in 1910 as secretary to the Royal Commission on Forestry. Because a Canadian was preferred for the first Chief Forester of British Columbia, H.R. MacMillan was chosen, but Grainger succeeded him in 1917. (Grainger papers in possession of Eve Grey Smith estate.)

9   Grainger wrote *Woodsmen of the West* in England in 1908. He had pursued Mabel there in order to propose marriage, and to raise money for his return passage to Canada he published a book based on his logging experiences on the West Coast of British Columbia. A place name on South Pender Island, Browning Harbour, and his friend Leonard Higgs are woven into the narrative. (Mabel is said to have returned to Canada first class; Martin in steerage.) *Woodsman of the West* was subsequently reprinted by McClelland and Stewart, Toronto, in 1964.

10   Phillipps-Wolley relied on his adventures in the Cassiar when writing *The Chicamin Stone* (London: George Bell & Sons, 1900).

11   Josephine Butler campaigned for thirteen years to have the Contagious Diseases Acts repealed. The Acts were passed in 1866 and 1869 in an effort to prevent the spread of venereal disease in eleven garrison towns in England. Any woman suspected of being a prostitute could be brought before a justice of the peace by a specially established police force for questioning and hospital confinement (imprisonment if she refused) with no legal recourse. See Elizabeth Longford, *Eminent Victorian Women* (London: Weidenfeld and Nicolson, 1981), pp. 117-128; and Crow, *The Victorian Woman*, pp. 232-243.

12   Mrs. MacNeil lived at 151 Pandora Street, Victoria. Her husband was a horse and cattle dealer.

13   Dr. Owen Meredith Jones's office was at 81 Fort Street, Victoria.

14   Blue was sold. After many owners, the house was dismantled in the 1950's. Some of the house beams were used in constructing the house for Winifred's daughter Evelyn, built nearby on Leonard Higg's property.

15   The Duke and Duchess of York visited Victoria in October, 1901.

CHAPTER FIFTEEN

1   Nakamura and his wife Kormi replaced Yamaoka as Japanese helpers on Samuel.

2   Jane Smith (Mrs. Thomas) Roadley died in 1908, age 67. (John Stewart, Assistant Archivist, Kamloops Museum Assn., August 15, 1984, to editor.)

3   Dr. Joseph Vereertbrugghen practiced in Kamloops from 1903 to 1906, when he moved to South America. *Kamloops Inland Sentinel*, passim.

4   Dr. G.R. Baker was Salt Spring Island's first resident doctor from 1898 to about 1904, when he moved to Quesnel.

5   Anniversary Island is part of the Belle Chain Islands located off the northeast coast of Samuel Island (see Winifred's map, p.   ).

6   This incident occurred in October 1903. Provincial Police constable Angus Ego outdid himself in his efforts to investigate the murder. He rowed first to Tumbo to check out the death of Barnard (Marnard) Wenzel (alias "Jack the Ripper"), then rowed to Ganges to report the death to police headquarters in Victoria by telephone, then back to Mayne Island to arrange for an inquest and to construct a coffin. He had travelled 44 miles within forty-eight hours. See Elliott, *Mayne Island*, pp. 20-21.

7   The girl from London was not exactly stupid. Cougars (mountain lions) were sighted frequently by sheep farmers in the Gulf Islands, and they were known to attack small children.

8   The first boats with inboard motors were called naptha boats. Police constable Arthur Drummond tried unsuccessfully to obtain one for patrolling the Gulf Islands in 1897. (Supt. of Police correspondence GR 55 and 61, BCARS.)

9   Jibe meant a shift in sail from one side of the boat to the other. The rope held to control the sail was called the sheet.
10   See wedding photograph of Mary Bennett and Sweeny Colston in Freeman, ed., *Patchwork*, p. 166.
11   Captain (later Commander) Eustace Maude, his wife Grace, and children Ruth, Cyrene, Valerie and George, moved to Mayne Island about 1900. Maude had served on numerous ships with the Royal Navy, the last assignment being the *Victoria and Albert*,, Queen Victoria's private yacht. The Maude family had tried homesteading in Oregon and operating a store at Duncan, Vancouver Island, before moving to Mayne Island.
        Outgoing and friendly, the Maudes quickly became the leaders of the small group of English middle-class families that settled on Mayne and the other islands after 1900. They bought Point Comfort Hotel from Warburton Pike about 1901. After operating it for a decade, they converted the building into a private residence. The large rooms were the scene of many parties that lasted until dawn. See Elliott, *Mayne Island*, pp. 52-54; Derek Reimer, ed., "In the Grand Style," *The Gulf Islanders*, Vol. 5, no. 4, Sound Heritage (Victoria: Provincial Archives of British Columbia, 1876), pp. 49-50.
        Harold Payne married Ruth Maude in 1907. Ruth did not die from childbirth, but from diabetes. (Conversation with Dora Payne, daughter of Harold and Roth Payne.)
12   Rev. Hubert St. John Payne was an Anglican minister, and a brother to Harold, Charles, Gerald and Lucy Payne, and Katie Bradley-Dyne. Hubert served initially as rector of St. Mary's Church, Esquimalt, then moved to Saturna, where he converted a Japanese boathouse into a small, unconsecrated church. He shared ministerial duties in the Gulf Islands with Canon Paddon of Mayne Island and Paddon's successors, but moved back to Victoria in the 1920's.
13   Other relatives who visited Winifred and Ralph on Samuel Island were Charlie Knox Shaw in 1906 and Carina Reed in 1909.
14   Clive Phillipps-Wolley owned Piers Island for several years. He eventually settled near Duncan with his family.
15   Pascall de Noi Walker held a position with the provincial government; Jess and Ada Saunders were good friends of the Grey family, living in Victoria.
16   Mrs. Charles B. Gray operated "The Seaview" at 1054 South King Street, Honolulu. (I am grateful to Margaret Tong, Municipal Reference and Records Center, City and County of Honolulu, for her constructive criticism of Winifred's description of the Hawaiian visit. Several errors were corrected.)
17   Winifred's daughter Evelyn spent four months in the Leahi Hospital, a tuberculosis sanitarium, in the 1920's.

CHAPTER SIXTEEN

1   Margaret Barton came to Victoria from England in 1907 with Edith Fenwick. Initially, Miss Barton was a governess in Victoria and Miss Fenwick taught at Mrs. Blakelock's school on Burdett Street. Miss Fenwick eventually established a private school of her own, employing her sister Isobel and Margaret Barton. By 1910 the school on Cook Street consisted of three buildings, with an enrolment of eighty students.
        A new school had been planned, sponsored by notable parents such as Drs. Leeder and O.M. Jones, and Messrs. Ker, Wilson and Pemberton, shortly before the *Iroquois* tragedy.—The Fenwick sisters and Miss Barton were planning an Easter holiday on Salt Spring Island.—These parents provided financial assistance for Miss Barton to carry out plans for a new school, and after one year of operation at a new site, Fort and Fern Streets, she managed to repay her creditors. The building was designed by noted architect Francis Rattenbury. Its boarding school facilities catered to "the increasing number of daughters of British and American parents then domiciled in the Orient, who found Victoria convenient for schooling due to the superb CPR Empresses which plied the Pacific at that time." (Eleanor Sanderson, *The Story of the First Seventy-Five Years at Saint Margaret's*

School for Girls, Victoria, British Columbia, 1908-1983 (Victoria: St. Margaret's School, 1983, unpaginated.)

I am grateful to Miss Janet Pitchford, an Old Girl of St. Margaret's, for supplying me with additional information on the history of St. Margaret's School. For an account of the *Iroquois* sinking, see the *Colonist,* April 14, 1911, pp. 1 and 4.

2   Residents of the outer Gulf Islands held Ralph Grey in high esteem He was a justice of the peace from September 1894 until his departure for Victoria. He willingly served on the church committee for St. Mary Magdalene Church and on the Maple Leaf Association committee which operated the agricultural hall at Miners Bay, Mayne Island. In addition, he was a member of The Islands Agricultural and Fruit Growers Association.

BIBLIOGRAPHY

Primary Sources

Canada, *Census, 1891*

Church, Alfred Francis. Typescript of Diary, 1898. EG C47, BCARS.

Church, Herbert. *An Emigrant in the Canadian Northwest*. London, Methuen & Co. Ltd., 1929.

_____. *Making a Start in Canada*. London: Seely & Co., 1889.

Gill, John. *Gill's Dictionary of the Chinook Jargon*. Portland: The J.K. Gill Company, 1909.

Gladstone, Florence M. *Notting Hill in Bygone Days*. London: Anne Bingley, 1969.

Grainger, Martin Allerdale. Papers, Eve Grey Estate.

_____. *Woodsmen of the West*. Toronto: McClelland and Stewart, 1964, reprint of 1908 edition.

Great Britain, *Census, 1871 and 1881*.

Grey, C.G. "The Story of His Official Life." Privately published. Grey Family Papers, Add. MS 604, BCARS.

Higgs, William Miller. *A History of the Higges or Higgs Family of South Stoke Oxon and Thatcham, Bers. and Their Descendants*. London: Adlard & Son, Ltd., 1933.

Holden, Edith. *The Country Diary of an Edwardian Lady*. London: M. Joseph/ Webb & Bower, 1977, 1978 printing.

Hughes, M. Vivian. *A London Girl of the Eighties*. London: Oxford University Press, 1936.

Ings, Frederick William. *Before the Fences*. Calgary?: Privately published, 1980.

Jobson, Allan. *The Creeping Hours of Time*. London: Robert Hale, 1971.

Macqueen-Pope, W. *Twenty Shillings in the Pound*. New York: Hutchinson & Co. Ltd., 1948.

Markham, Violet R. *Return Passage*. London: Oxford University Press, 1953.

Peck, Winifred. *Home for the Holidays*. London: Faber and Faber Ltd., 1955.

_____. *A Little Learning*. London: Faber and Faber Ltd., 1952.

Raverat, Gwen. *Period Piece*. London: Faber and Faber Ltd., 1952.

Sanderson, Eleanor. "The Story of the First Seventy-Five Years at Saint Margaret's School for Girls, Victoria, British Columbia, 1908-1983." Pamphlet. Victoria: St. Margaret's School, 1983.

Sonnenschein, Adolf, and Nesbitt, Henry. *The New Science and Art of Arithmetic for the Use of Schools*. London: Swan Sonnenschein & Co. 1899.

Sonnenschein, Adolf. *The ABC of Arithmetic*. London: 1873.

Spalding, Ethel Howard. *England: A Social and Economic History 1760 to 1830*. London: George Philip & Sons, 1935.

Spalding, John Howard. *The Kingdom of Heaven as Seen by Swendenborg*. London: J.M. Dent & Sons Limited, 1916.

Spalding, Thomas Alfred. *Captain Bluecoat's Tales from Japan*. London: Thomas Nelson and Sons, Ltd., ?.

_____. *Elizabethan Demonology*. London: The Folcroft Press, 1970. First published London: Chatto and Windus, 1880.

_____. *Federation and Empire*. London: H. Henry & Co., 1896.

_____. *The House of Lords: A Retrospect and Forecast.* London: T.F. Unwin, 1894.

_____. *The Work of the London School Board.* London: P.S. King and Son, 1900.

Spalding & Hodge. *Printing Papers: A Handbook for the Use of Publishers and Printers.* London: Wm. Clowes and Sons Ltd., 1905. Reprinted 1915.

Subury. First Civil Marriage Register for Sudbury. In private possession, Sudbury, Suffolk.

Thompson, Flora. *Lark Rise.* London: The Folio Society, 1979. Reprint of 1939 ed. published by Oxford University Press, London.

Secondary Sources

Artibase, Alan J., ed. *Gateway City: Documents on the City of Winnipeg 1873-1913.* Winnipeg: University of Manitoba Press, 1979.

Banks, Joseph Ambrose. *Prosperity and Parenthood.* London: Routledge & Paul, 1965.

_____ and Olive. *Feminism and Family Planning in Victorian England.* New York: Schocken Books, 1964.

Barrow, Margaret. *Women: 1870-1928.* New York: Mansell Publishing, 1981.

Beaver, Patrick. *The Crystal Palace.* London: Hugh Evelyn Limited, 1970.

Bott, Alan, ed. *Our Mothers.;* London: Benjamin Blom, 1932.

Branca, Patricia. *Silent Sisterhood.* London: Croom Helm, 1975.

Brandon, Peter. *The Sussex Landscape.* London: Hodder and Stoughton, 1974.

Burnstyn, Joan N. *Victorian Education and the Ideal of Womanhood.* London: Croom Helm, 1980.

Chapman, A. Beatrice Wallis and Mary Wallis Chapman. *The Status of Women Under the English Law.* London: George Routledge & Sons, Ltd., 1909.

Crouzet, Francois. *The Victorian Economy.* London: Methuen & Co. Ltd., 1982.

Crow, Duncan. *The Victorian Woman.* London: George Allen & Unwin Ltd., 1971.

Cunnington, C. Willett. *English Women's Clothing in the Nineteenth Century.* London: Faber and Faber Ltd., 1937.

Dobbs, Brian. *Drury Lane.* London: Cassel and Copmpany Ltd., 1972.

Dunae, Patrick A. *Gentlemen Emigrants.* Vancouver: Douglas & McIntyre, 1981.

Dutton, Ralph. *The Victorian Home.* London: B.T. Batsford Ltd., 1954.

Elliott, Marie. *Mayne Island and the Outer Gulf Islands: A History.* Victoria: Gulf Islands Press, 1984.

Finlaison, A.G. and Ansel, C. *Rates of Mortality.* London?: Gregg International Publishers Limited, 1973.

Franklin, Jill. "Troops of Servants: Labour and Planning in the Country House 1840-1914." *Victorian Studies* VXIX 12:" 211-239.

Freeman, Beatrice J., ed. *A Gulf Islands Patchwork.* Victoria: Gulf Islands Branch, B.C. Historical Association, 1961.

Glass, D.V. *Population Policies and Movements in Europe.* London: F. Cass, 1967.

Glover, Judith. *The Place Names of Sussex.* London: B.T. Batsford Ltd., 1975.

Gosden, P.J. *How They Were Taught.* Oxford: Basil Blackwell, 1969.

Hacking, Norman R. and Lamb, W.Kaye. *The Princess Story.* Vancouver: Mitchell Press Limited, 1974.

Hammerton, A. James. *Emigrant Gentlewomen*. London: Croom Helm Ltd., 1979.

Hayball, Gwen. *Warburton Pike, an Unassuming Gentleman*. Poole, Dorset: Privately Published, 1994.

Heard, Nigel. *Wool: East Anglia's Golden Fleece*. Suffolk: Terence Dalton Limited, 1970.

Hern, Anthony. *The Seaside Holiday*. London: The Cresset Press, 1967.

Jackel, Susan, ed. *A Flannel Shirt and Liberty.*. Vancouver: U.B.C. Press, 1982.

Jones, R.Tudor. *Congregationalism in England*. London: Independent Press Ltd., 1962.

Josephson, Matthew. *Edison, A Biography*. London: Eyre & Spottiswode, 1961.

Kamm, Josephine. *Hope Deferred*. London: Methuen & Co. Ltd., 1965.

_____. *Indicative Past: A Hundred Years of the Girls' Public Day School Trust*. London: ?

Kerr, Barbara. *The Dispossessed*. London: John Baker, 1974.

Kingsley, Charles. *The Water Babies*. New York: A.L. Burt, Publisher, 1893.

Kitson Clark,; G. *The Making of Victorian England*. London: Methuen & Co. Ltd., 1962.

Laslett, Peter. *The World We Have Lost*. London: Methuen & Co. Ltd., 1965.

Latham, Barbara, and Kess, Kathy, eds. *In Her Own Right*. Victoria: Camosun College, 1980.

Longford, Elizabeth. *Eminent Victorian Women*. London: Weidenfeld and Nicolson, 1981.

Lubbock, Basil. *The Romance of the Clipper Ships*. New York: The Macmillan Company, 1939.

McGregor, O.R. *Divorce in England*. London: William Heinemann Ltd., 1957.

Meason, George. *The Official Illustrated Guide to the Southeastern Railway and Its Branches*. London: E & W Books (Publishers) Ltd., 1970. (Reproduction of 1858 edition.)

Mee, Arthur. *London North of the Thames*. London: Hodder and Stoughton, 1972.

_____. *Sussex*. London: Hodder and Stoughton, 1964.

Millet, Kate. *Sexual Politics*. New York: Doubleday & Company Inc., 1970.

Musgrave, Rev. George. "History of St. Leonards-on-Sea Congregational Church." Pamphlet series, 1981.

Musgrove, F. *The Migratory Elite*. London: Heinemann, 1963.

Page, William, ed. *The Victoria History of the County of Suffolk*. Vol. 1. London: University of London, Institute of Historical Research, 1975. Reprint from original edition of 1907.

Parry, J.D. *The Coast of Sussex*. London: E & W Books (Publishers) Ltd., 1970. Reproduction of original edition published by Wright & Sons, Brighton 1833.

Pedersen, Joyce Senders;. "The Reform of Women's Secondary and Higher Education: Institutional Change and Social Values in Mid and Late Victorian England," *History of Education Quarterly*, 19 (#1) 1979: 61-91.

Peel, Albert. *These Hundred Years*. London: Congregational Union of England and Wales, 1931.

Phillipps-Wolley, Clive. *The Chicamon Stone*. London: George Bell & Sons, 1900.

Pimlott, J.A.R. *The Englishman's Holiday: A Social History*. Sussex: The Harvester Press Ltd., 1976.

Potter, Beatrix. *The Tale of Mrs. Tiggy-Winkle*. London: Fredericke Waring

& Co. Ltd., 1972 (?).

Prochaska, F.K. *Women and Philanthropy in Nineteenth-Century England.* New York: Oxford UIniversity Press, 1980.

Reimer, Derek, ed. "In the Grand Style," *The Gulf Islanders.* Sound Heritage Series, no. 5. Victoria: BCARS, 1976.

Rekstein, Terry. *Rattenbury.* Victoria: Sono Nis Press, 1978.

Richardson, David. *Pig War Islands.* Eastsound, Wash.: Orcas Publishing Co. 1971.

Sandon, Eric. *Suffolk Houses.* Suffolk: Baron Publishing, 1977.

Satre, Lowell J. "After the Match Girls' Strike: Bryant and May in the 1890's." *Victorian Studies,* Vol. 26 (Autumn 1982).

Saxby, Jessie M. *West Nor'West.* London: James Nisbet & Co., 1890.

Seaman, L.C.B. *Life in Victorian London.* London: B.T. Batsford Ltd., 1973.

Stearns, Peter N., ed. *The Rise of the Modern Woman.* St. Louis, Miss.: Forum Press, 1978.

Stephen, Leslie, and Sidney Lee. *Dictionary of National Biography.* London: Oxford University Press, 1937-1938.

Taylor, Ina. *The Edwardian Lady.* New York: Holt, Rinehard and Winston, 1980.

Thomson, J. Radford. *Pelton's Illustrated Guide to Tunbridge Wells.* Wakefield: S.R;. Publishers Ltd., 1970. Reprint.

Tomlinson, Alice. "St. Margaret School: 75 Years of Service With Love." *The Islander*, May 1-2, 1983.

Turner, Barry. *Equality for Some.* London: Ward Lock Educational 1974.

Vicinus, Martha, ed. *Suffer and Be Still.* Indiana: Indiana University Press, 1972.

_____. *A Widening Sphere.* Indiana: Indiana University Press, 1977.

Walton, John K. *The English Seaside Resort: A Social History 1750-1914.* New York: St. Martin's Press, 1983.

Warner, Philip. *A Guide to Cstles in Britain.* London: New England Library, 1976.

Weinreb, Ben, and Christopher Hibbert, ed. *The London Encyclopedia.* London: Macmillan, 1983.

Wilkinson, Fred. *The Castles of England.* London: George Philip, 1973.

White, Cynthia L. *Women's Magazines 1693-1968.* London: Michael Joseph Ltd., 1970.

Zim, Herbert S. and others. *Seashores.* New York: Golden Press, 1955.

Directories

Henderson's B.C. Gazetteer and Directory for 1905. Vancouver: Henderson Publishing Co. Ltd., 1905.

Kelly's Essex Directory. 1855-1859.

Three Victorian Telephone Directories, 1884-1885. Devon: David & Charles(Publishers) Ltd., reprint, 1970.

Walthamstow Directory,. 1861.

Watkins Commercial and General London Directory. 1854.

White's Suffolk Directory. 1844. Devon: Davie & Charles (:Publishers) Ltd., reprint, 1970.

The Williams Official British Columbia Directory, 1897-98. Victoria: Williams B.C. Directory Compay Ltd., 1898.

Who's Who of British Members of Parliament. Vol. I. Sussex: Harvester Press, 1976.

Who Was Who. Vol. 1-5 (London: Adam & Charles Black 1920-19?)

Newspapers

Illustrated London News, London.

The Colonist, Victoria.

Saanich Peninsula and Gulf Islands Review (Sidney Review).

The Times, London.

INDEX